COMPASS THERAPY
Christian Psychology in Action

By

Dan Montgomery, Ph.D.

Copyright © 2009, 2018 by Dan & Kate Montgomery

Note: This book does not take the place of professional counseling or supervision. All case studies are composites that de-identify counselees. The term "counselee" used in this book is synonymous with other common designations such as "client," "patient," or for pastoral counseling, "parishioner."

To order: www.CompassTherapy.com

Compass Therapy® and Self Compass® are registered trademarks of Dan & Kate Montgomery.

Cover Design: David Gagne. Editing: Woodeene Koenig-Bricker. Photo Credit: Dave O'Dell.

Published by: Compass Works
Lulu Press

ISBN: 978-0-557-02288-5
Printed in the United States of America

Library of Congress Cataloguing-in-Publication Data
Montgomery, Dan
Compass Therapy: Christian Psychology In Action/Dan Montgomery
p.   cm.
ISBN 978-0-557-02288-5
1. Psychotherapy 2. Personality Disorders 3. Christian Psychology
4. Christian Counseling 5. Pastoral Counseling 6. Pastoral Ministry
7. Pastoral Theology 8. Chaplaincy 9. Counseling Theory

JOURNAL RESOURCES

American Journal of Psychiatry
American Journal of Psychology
American Journal of Psychotherapy
American Psychologist
American Sociological Review
Annals of the American Psychotherapy Association
Annual Review of Sociology
Applied and Preventive Applied Psychology
Archives of General Psychiatry
Archives of Suicide Research
Biological Psychiatry
Canadian Journal of Psychiatry
Clinical Child and Family Psychology Review
Clinical Psychology Review
Cognitive and Behavioral Practice
Comprehensive Psychiatry
Counseling Psychology Quarterly
Criminal Behaviour and Mental Health
Current Directions in Psychological Science
Directions in Psychiatry
Eating Disorders: Journal of Treatment and Prevention
Educational and Psychological Measurement
European Psychologist
Gerontologist
Health Education and Behavior
Imagination, Cognition and Personality
International Journal of Psycho-Analysis

Journal of Positive Psychology
Journal of Primary Psychiatry
Journal of Psychiatric Practice
Journal of Psychodynamic Counseling
Journal of Psychological Inquiry
Journal of Psychology and Psychotherapy
Journal of Psychology: Interdisciplinary and Applied
Journal of Psychosomatic Research
Journal of Psychotherapy
Journal of Psychotherapy Integration
Journal of Research in Personality
Journal of Schizophrenia Research
Journal of Social and Clinical Psychology
Journal of Theory and Psychology
Korean Journal of Clinical Psychology
Law and Human Behavior
Personal Relationships
Personality and Individual Differences
Personality and Social Psychology Bulletin
Political Psychology
Professional Psychology
Psychiatry and Clinical Neurosciences
Psychiatry Today
Psychoanalytic Quarterly
Psychological Bulletin
Psychological Reports
Psychological Science in the Public Interest
Psychology of Addictive Behaviors
Psychotherapy: Theory, Research, and Practice
Schizophrenia Bulletin
Self and Identity
Social Science & Medicine
Sociology of Health and Illness
Southern Medical Journal
The Israeli Journal of Psychiatry and Related Sciences
Trauma, Violence, and Abuse

FULLER THEOLOGICAL SEMINARY

"At the core of Compass Therapy is the divine endowment of human spirituality in each person that comes to expression through the mental, emotional and physical spheres of the self. Through diagrams and dialogue this book takes the reader directly into the counseling experience where a therapeutic alliance between the therapist and the counselee is created, releasing the innate spiritual capacity of the self to overcome negative and counter-productive personality patterns of behavior. Dan Montgomery rightly views emotional and mental health as more than merely removing pathology; rather it is the movement of the self in relation to others where identity, intimacy and community are actualized as an achievement of the holistic self.

I am not aware of any other book that succeeds as well as this one in providing both professional therapists as well as Christian counselors with a theoretical and practical model that combines psychology and theology in an integrated way. It has a profound simplicity that covers a wide range of personality disorders. Readers will say, 'Now I see why typical patterns of dysfunctional and disruptive behavior have a common root but also a specific cause.' Put it on top of your reading list!"
— *Ray S. Anderson, Senior Professor of Theology and Ministry*

HANDBOOK OF INNOVATIVE THERAPY (Wiley, 2001)

"I believe that an eclectic system of this type will eventually be the system of the future...a step in the direction we must eventually go to really become a profession based on science."
— *Raymond J. Corsini, Ph.D., Editor*

ABPP DIPLOMATE IN CLINICAL PSYCHOLOGY

"In my forty-five years of work as a psychologist, I rate Dr. Dan Montgomery in the top 1% of professionals I have known in the mental health field. Dan is a brilliant theorist in the field of counseling and therapy."
— *Everett L. Shostrom, Ph.D., Distinguished Professor of Psychology*

PSYCHOTHERAPY & NEUROPSYCHOLOGY

"As an established theory in the field of counseling and psychotherapy, Compass Therapy delivers the Self Compass and the Human Nature Compass growth tools for empowering treatment strategies. This book brings a much needed spirit of hope even for difficult clinical syndromes involving personality disorders."
— *Joseph VanDenHeuvel, Ph.D., Licensed Psychologist*

MARRIAGE AND FAMILY THERAPY

"Compass Therapy is insightful and practical, providing valuable tools for assessing strengths and weaknesses within an individual's personality. The Self Compass and Human Nature Compass promote balance and wholeness in the therapeutic journey. I highly recommend this book for experienced psychotherapists and counselors, as well as students and interns."
— *Carol D. Lee, LMFT, San Carlos, CA*

PASTORAL CARE AND COUNSELING

"Compass Therapy offers both clinical and pastoral counselors a map, guide, and center for helping clients sort out life and choose direction. Dan Montgomery has pulled together many years of study, writing, and practice with an established model of personality and interpersonal behavior. He provides a workable set of tools for the care-giving process. I am glad for the wide influence of the compass approach in counseling."
— *David Augsburger, Ph.D., Professor of Pastoral Counseling, Fuller Seminary; author, "Helping People Forgive"*

PASTORAL MINISTRY

"A must read for any counselor who practices within the realm of a spiritual background. I have known Dr. Montgomery for thirty years and have benefited from his writings and supervision. This user-friendly book is worth reading and re-reading for years to come."
— *Rev. Dr. Bernardo Monserrat, Santa Fe, NM*

CHAPLAINCY

"Compass Therapy is easy to learn and apply. Examples of how to use compass theory abound. All therapists, pastors, and chaplains who want to deepen their counseling skills will find it valuable."
— *Kenneth Swetland, D.Min., Campus Chaplain and Professor of Ministry, Gordon-Conwell Theological Seminary*

THEOLOGY

"Dan Montgomery's Christian personality theory is innovative and biblically sound."
— *Gordon D. Fee, Ph.D., Professor Emeritus of New Testament Studies, Regent College*

PRINCETON SEMINARY PASTORAL THEOLOGY

"Compass Therapy makes a very important contribution to counseling and how the Christian faith and psychology can work together to bring healing into person's lives. The case studies are excellent. Dan Montgomery uses a wide range of techniques including role-playing and imaging, which are helpful and empowering to the client."
— *Rev. Abigail R. Evans, Ph.D., Chair of Practical Theology; author, "Healing Liturgies for the Seasons of Life"*

GORDON-CONWELL CLINICAL COUNSELING

"Therapists and pastoral counselors will find this book a helpful and refreshing guide for the task of helping people find wholeness. Compass Therapy presents a dynamic paradigm for understanding the human predicament, while at the same time outlining strategies for intervention leading to growth."
— *Raymond Pendleton, Ph.D., Director of Clinical Counseling & Professor of Pastoral Psychology, Gordon-Conwell Seminary*

SANTA CLARA UNIVERSITY & STANFORD UNIVERSITY SCHOOL OF MEDICINE

"In *Compass Therapy: Christian Psychology In Action*, Dan Montgomery adds to the impressive and growing list of Compass Therapy books that well integrate Christian perspectives with psychological theory and practice in an easy to read, thoughtful, and compelling manner. The book provides Compass Theory tools for counselors, therapists, clergy, and pastoral caregivers to understand and help those who struggle with a wide range of personality, behavioral, emotional, and relational challenges."
— *Thomas G. Plante, Ph.D., ABPP, Professor of Psychology; author, "Contemporary Clinical Psychology" and "Spiritual Practices in Psychotherapy"*

TABLE OF CONTENTS

PART I:
INTRODUCING COMPASS THERAPY®

1
CONSTRUCTING THE SELF COMPASS

Welcome to the Compass Therapy approach to counseling and therapy, where the dynamic rhythms of human nature find a home. Where therapeutic strategies incorporate the mental and emotional, physical and spiritual dimensions of human existence. Where health and dysfunction converge in meaningful continuity. And where counselees (clients, patients, or parishioners) discover the connections between identity, intimacy, and community.

Please join me in examining how the Compass Model organizes counseling and personality theory into a system simple enough for counselees to grasp, yet sophisticated enough to assure therapists of progress with severe disorders. Through the lens of compass theory you'll see how the major personality disorders in the *Diagnostic and Statistical Manuel of Mental Disorders* relate to one another and to health psychology, enhancing your diagnosis-to-treatment acumen.

You'll also discern a golden thread of hope that invigorates the hard work of doing therapy. Although God was banned from much psychology and psychotherapy in the twentieth century, many therapists and counselees acknowledge and appreciate God's presence in the twenty-first century. When struggling to transform suffering into wellbeing and exchange inner chaos for fulfillment, they discover that God reaches out with a helping hand.

Compass Therapy and Christian Psychology

All theories of counseling include underlying assumptions and core beliefs about God, human nature, personality, and healthy versus unhealthy behavior. Compass Therapy holds that people are ontologically related to the transcendent, personal, and loving Creator known through the Christian faith. This does not exclude other perceptions of God or other ways of construing human values within the therapeutic setting. It simply underscores the fact that since cardinal values of Christianity include compassion, empathy for those who suffer, and motivation to heal and transform persons who have lost their way, Christian psychology offers a viable worldview from which to practice psychotherapy.

Compass Therapy weds faith and science. The facets of psychology pertinent to the healing of persons include motivation, sensation and perception, learning and memory, personality and social integration, and lifespan development: all are grounded in a God who understands and utilizes counseling and therapy as yet another means of calling people to exercise freedom rightly and benefit from the identity, intimacy, and community he has invited them to know.

From a Christian perspective, Christ embraces people in need, seeking to transform their personal crises through the power of the Holy Spirit present within the alliance of therapist and counselee (Montgomery, 2006, pp. 71-74).

It is as though the Holy Spirit says to any therapist who is open, "Come. Let us work together with your counselee. Let me inspire you with insight and direction to help tame your counselee's anxiety and heal their pain. Have courage in guiding them to give up the patterns that are defeating them: the manipulations of pleasing, placating, seducing, calculating, controlling, arguing, intimidating, avoiding, or withdrawing. Through a therapeutic bond that draws upon my wisdom, help them find a pathway that leads to flexibility, discerning love, and personal power without guile."

If your therapeutic experience is anything like mine over the past thirty years, you may have noticed that the Trinity comforts and heals beyond religious category or human constraint, and that the Holy Spirit does indeed enhance your effectiveness as a healer of the soul.

The Continuum of Personality

The theoretical power of Compass Therapy lies in locating dysfunction within a larger model of health psychology that generates both diagnostic and therapeutic capability. Even rigid personality trends and disorders are revealed as growth deficiencies for which the Compass Model provides hope and transformation.

When viewed through the compass lens, personality dysfunction exists on a continuum with healthy functioning and wellbeing (Horney, 1954; Leary, 1957; Shostrom, 1976; Carson, 1991; Satir, 1983; Pincus, 1994; Kiesler, 1996; Millon & Grossman, 2007a; Montgomery & Montgomery, 2009).

This normalcy—psychopathology continuum reveals a spectrum of organic connection ranging from normal human development through mild, moderate, and severe levels of personality and interpersonal dysfunction (Volleburgh, 2001; Krueger, 2002; Clark, 2005; Plante, 2010).

In fact, numerous studies have shown that various symptoms of abnormality are not unique to psychopathology, but are also distributed throughout normal populations (Shostrom, 1979; Torgersen et al., 2001; Watson, 2005; Cohen, 2006; Twenge et al., 2009).

The realistic hope for personality growth is central to Compass Therapy, and supported by the findings of modern neuroscience and personality research that reveal plasticity as a primary characteristic of the human brain, allowing for personality malleability and transformation throughout the lifespan, even into old age (Caspi & Roberts, 2001; Sharoots, 2003; Roberts, 2006).

5

The Self-Circle and the Spiritual Core

Rather than construing personality as an isolated set of traits or drives, compass psychology takes an *interpersonal* perspective, holding that understanding personality requires knowing the social context of how a person relates to others in daily life (Sullivan, 1953).

Contributions to the interpersonal tradition which undergird principles of compass theory include research studies by: Freedman et al., 1951; LaForge, Leary et al., 1954; LaForge & Suczek, 1955; Leary, 1955, 1957; Leary & Harvey, 1956; Shostrom, 1963, 1964, 1970, 1972; Shostrom & Knapp, 1966; Carson, 1969, 1991; Shostrom & Riley, 1968; Shostrom, Knapp, & Knapp, 1976; LaForge, 1977, 1985; Conte & Plutchik, 1981; Anchin & Kiesler, 1982; Kiesler, 1983, 1992; Freedman, 1985; Wiggins, 1985, 1995; Wiggins & Broughton, 1985; Anchin, 1987; Benjamin, 1987; Safran & Segal, 1990; Andrews, 1991; Wagner et al., 1995; Lorr, 1996; Locke, 2000; Kiesler & Auerbach, 2004; Horowitz et al., 2006; Locke & Sadler, 2007; and Gurtman, 2009.

Personality, then, is viewed as a complex set of behavioral processes that endure across time—a set of recurring interpersonal patterns that characterize a person's life. These patterns are not just psychological, but physiological and spiritual, for they encompass the whole person.

Construction of the Compass Model begins with that archetypal shape, the circle, as a representation of the self. The circle represents a person's selfhood that endures over the lifespan—the center of consciousness and free agency that provides unity and continuity throughout life's journey. Although the self may be fragmented by inner conflicts or torn by traumas, something remains uniquely identifiable about being "you."

The outer circle represents a self-boundary between each person and the world. This self-boundary is like the semipermeable membrane of a living cell, a lipid-protein layer that allows nutrients to enter and waste products to leave, but blocks toxic substances from poisoning the cell.

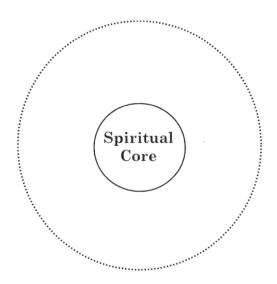

As long as the self-boundary remains sufficiently open to exchanges with the environment, persons can give and receive communication, and negotiate to meet their own or other people's needs. However, psychopathology (Axis I and II categories of the *Diagnostic and Statistical Manual of Mental Disorders*, hereafter referred to as *DSM*) can impair this ability, leaving people with self-image distortions, blocked need gratification, and frustrating relationships.

The Spiritual Core

If the outer circle stands for self-continuity throughout life, what does the inner circle labeled "spiritual core" represent? This circle symbolizes the sacred center of personality. The equivalent of a nucleus within a living cell, the spiritual core is the depth dimension of personality from which people find self-identity and develop intimacy with others and with

God, whom William James called "the Great Companion" (1890/1950, p. 316).

From the spiritual core arises the "I am" quality of personal existence, the sense that human beings are endowed with the capacity for awareness and freedom of choice. God is the transcendent "I AM" who invites the finite "i am" of every person into a relationship of communion and communication with God and others. For a fuller treatment of this topic, see *Compass Psychotheology: Where Psychology and Theology Really Meet* (Montgomery & Montgomery, 2008).

Psychospiritual maturity involves developing wisdom and loving kindness that reflect the image of God in persons. This means interacting with others in a spirit of mutuality that nurtures respect and caring, rather than manipulating people as objects according to self-interest (Montgomery, 1975). The merging of psychology and spirituality provides an understanding of human nature and supports a counselee's pursuit of a meaningful life. Indeed, spirituality is a genuine frontier for research in helping people develop increased wellbeing and fulfillment (Moss, 2002; Miller & Thoreson, 2003; Seeman et al., 2003; Crossley & Salter, 2005; Shaw et al., 2005; Anandarajah, 2008; Plante, 2009).

Therapists themselves may or may not share value structures that converge with a spiritual tradition, yet they learn how to be respectfully present to counselees of every metaphysical or religious background. Studies show that counselees appreciate this respect (Bienenfeld et al., 2007; Carmody et al., 2008; Gold, 2009; Worthington et al., 2011).

For example, for the Jewish counselee, the spiritual core may reflect the inner image of God. For the Christian counselee, the spiritual core provides a point of intersection with Christ's resurrected presence and the inner witness of the Holy Spirit that one is a child of God.

For the Buddhist counselee, this spiritual core represents a liberation from illusory cares, a unity with Being-itself in which the false versions of selfhood fall away.

For the Islamic counselee, the spiritual core involves submitting to the will of Allah, as witnessed by kneeling in prayer five times a day.

For the New Age counselee, the spiritual core involves manifesting God within—realizing that God is in all things and through all things, and that all things, including one's self, are on a journey of returning to God.

For the agnostic or atheistic counselee, the spiritual core may stand for the center of choice and responsibility through which one's essence is cultivated and one's inner truth is followed.

The spiritual core of personality exercises another crucial function, that of acting as a person's center of gravity (Horney, 1945); inner locus of control (Rogers, 1961); nuclear atom in the total psychic system (Jung, 1968); inner supreme court (Maslow, 1971); higher self (Assagioli, 2000); spiritual self (Frankl, 2006), and the "I am" center of awareness and free agency (Montgomery & Montgomery, 2009).

While the spiritual core emerges out of the interactive connections of Mind and Heart, Body and Spirit, it nevertheless transcends the very human nature it acts to integrate, and imparts integrity and autonomy despite the vicissitudes of life. However one wishes to define its source and substance, the spiritual core differentiates Homo sapiens from other mammals by bestowing a sense of responsibility for behavior, and the faith to prevail against adversity.

The spiritual core is indigenously present within individuals, whether educated or illiterate, free or imprisoned, rich or poor. Compass psychology asserts that core fear generated by unresolved inner or outer stressors can diminish the core trust that enables the spiritual core to fulfill its healthy function. For this reason, the formation of the spiritual core as the center of free agency, identity, and meaningful connection to others deserves attention in psychotherapy. Thus, the promotion of a counselee's core trust generates hope, self-efficacy, and resiliency (Stajkovic, 2006).

The Self-Circle

While the circle shows the unity of the self, and the spiritual core houses its sacred center, what accounts for the inner tensions of personality, with their diversity and complexity?

Adding two intersecting lines to the self-circle generates four quadrants that represent opposing forces within the personality. These four quadrants create categories that render intelligible both intrapsychic and interpersonal tensions.

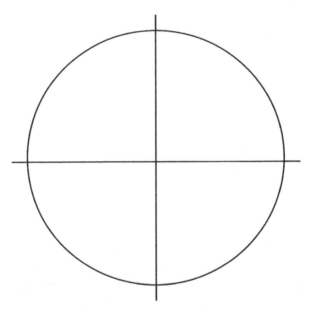

The Self-Circle

To understand personality within this framework, it is necessary to ask, "What universal polarities belong within every person's personality?" Carl Jung (1968) suggested that sensing and intuiting, thinking and feeling, belonged in the self-circle. The problem with these elements was that they described human nature more than they did described personality. Even more, the three terms of sensing, intuiting, and feeling were too similar to one another to form true polar opposites. Though Jung's concept of the self as a circle with inner polarities foreshadowed modern personality theory, a need remained for factor analysis research to reveal the universal nature of the polarities within personality.

The Self-Circle Becomes The Self Compass®

Since Jung's time personality research has empirically validated the model of the self as a circle with inner elements. Research has moved beyond Jung's model of the *mandala* (1968) to propose the *interpersonal circle* (Kiesler, 1996; Benjamin, 2006), the *actualizing model* (Shostrom, 1976; Shostrom & Montgomery, 1986), the *circumplex model* (Plutchik and Conte, 1997; Wiggins, 1995, 1979; Carson, 1969; Guttman, 1966; Schaefer, 1965), and the *circulargram* (Millon et al., 2004; Millon & Grossman, 2007).

A classic study by the Institute of Personality at Berkeley discovered through the factor analysis of five thousand cases that recurrent styles of intrapsychic and interpersonal dynamics possess two basic dimensions: affiliation and power (Leary, 1957). This is the foundation of my own term "Self Compass," an easily understood metaphor that suggests a universal latitude and longitude of the self (Montgomery, 1996; Montgomery & Montgomery, 2008).

The dimension of affiliation exists along a continuum from friendliness to hostility, from love to anger. Love implies caring, nurturance, and forgiveness. The opposite of love is assertion, which entails expressing, confronting, and challenging. In compass terms, the Love/Assertion polarity results.

The dimension of power exists along a continuum from control to being controlled, from dominance to submission. The opposite of strength is weakness, which stands for vulnerability, submissiveness, and uncertainty. Employing self-explanatory terms, compass theory frames this dimension as the Strength/Weakness polarity. Strength implies power, dominance, and control.

The Compass Model locates these two polar axes of Love and Assertion, Weakness and Strength as points within a compass-like circle representing the self (Shostrom and Montgomery, 1978, 1986, 1990; Corsini, 2001; Montgomery, 1996, 2006; Montgomery & Montgomery, 2007, 2008, 2009). The circle stands for a person's unique identity that persists throughout life. The compass points express the dynamic interplay of forces within one's personality and interpersonal relations.

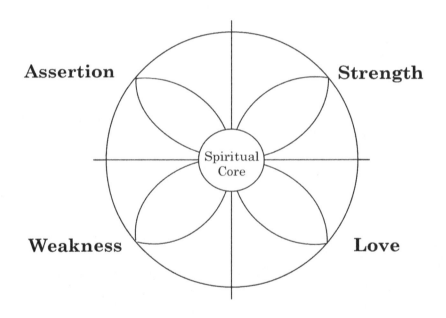

The Self Compass

Taking the first letter of each compass point yields the anagram "LAWS" which portrays the empirical principles of personality and relationships derived from the Self Compass. As Part II on personality patterns will show, these LAWS shed new light on how personality disorders are related to one another and to personality health.

The figure-eight rhythms within the Self Compass connect opposite compass points through the spiritual core. These rhythms capture the ever-varying movement possible in an individual's experience of Love and Assertion, and Weakness and Strength, as well as in a host of derivative behaviors.

Well-balanced persons develop a flexible rhythm between caring assertion and humble strength, as appropriate to unfolding life situations, yet expressed in ways unique to each individual. But these Self Compass rhythms can become stuck on one compass point to the exclusion of another, much as a physical compass gets stuck if its needle no longer swings freely between compass points. A person ends up stuck on one or more compass points, unable to access the others. The consequence is that the Self Compass no longer provides 360 degrees of creative choice.

Personality stagnates when a rigid pattern inhibits a person's ability or willingness to learn from life experiences. This immobility leads to a wide range of psychopathology. Both Compass Therapy and the Five-Factor Model of personality affirm that a lack of flexibility creates neuroticism and a closed perceptual field (Saulsman, et al., 2004; Montgomery & Montgomery, 2009).

Personality Rigidity

Without the rhythmic integration of Assertion, love generates unhealthy dependency upon others, while Assertion without the balance of Love fosters aggression at the expense of others. Strength without Weakness becomes arrogant control, whereas Weakness without the balance of Strength results in avoidant aloneness.

Personality trends and disorders constrict life in the form of *growth deficiencies* based on ineffective coping patterns. Interactions with others become stereotypically repetitive and don't allow for core-to-core sharing on an "I-Thou" basis (Buber, 1970). The predictable rigidity of psychopathology

13

dehumanizes both personality and relationships, including one's relationship with God.

Such rigidity relies on a constricted range of one or two behavioral responses that are expressed intensely and often, whether or not they are appropriate to a situation (Sullivan, 1954; Shostrom, 1979; Wacthel, 1982; Kiesler, 1996; Montgomery, 2006). This explains why rigid behaviors aggregate into well-defined trends or patterns pervasive enough to operate in all spheres of psychosocial functioning (Gude et al., 2004).

In its essence, psychopathology is not chaotic and random but specific and predictable. By knowing the location of a personality trend or pattern on the Self Compass, the therapist gains X-ray vision into its structure and function, and can logically deduce its antidote. That is, by understanding a particular pathology's rhyme and reason, you foresee how to transform its growth-resistant rigidity into a rhythm of actualizing growth (Tracey, 2005; Montgomery & Montgomery, 2008, 2009).

A Diagnosis-to-Growth Model

Compass Therapy offers therapeutic intervention by diagnosing where a person is stuck on the Self Compass and formulating goals for transforming personality deficiencies into actualizing growth. This allows therapists to counsel in a spirit of warranted optimism. Alfred Adler writes, "The construction of a goal premises the capacity for change, and a certain freedom of movement. The spiritual enrichment which results is not to be undervalued" (1927/1965, p. 44). As therapy moves forward, counselees develop increments of freedom that increase creative coping. Stagnant patterns lose their grip as counselees take experimental growth stretches into unused compass points where they have the opportunity to experience new, more gratifying outcomes.

Compass Therapy suggests that as counselees outgrow the restrictions of dysfunction, they make progress in com-

14

bining love with assertion and integrating weakness and strength, which mature into the psychospiritual virtues of caring and courage, as well as humility and self-esteem.

Just as psychopathology invades the personality with a pernicious influence in all spheres of psychological functioning (Gude et al., 2004), so actualizing growth can spread throughout a counselee's personality and relationships until a day comes when the individual graduates from therapy and continues growing on their own (Montgomery, 2006, pp. 71-74).

In summary, therapy facilitates actualizing growth that promotes personality development, expansion, aliveness, and transformation toward the integrated rhythms of compass living. By contrast, psychopathology emerges from personality fixation, constriction, stagnation, defensiveness, and repetition compulsion.

What accounts for the prevalence of these self-defeating behaviors in human beings? Within the context of Christian psychology, the presence of negative forces within human nature and individual behavior point toward a breech of communion with God. Whether framed as original sin or hardness of heart, sin pervades humankind as a separation from the image and purposes of God, creating an ever-present tension within the human condition: an existential struggle between good and evil, between wholeness and fragmentation, between seeking and doing God's will or perpetuating rigid patterns of self-will. Jean-Paul Sartre put it this way: "All human beings are guilty in principle, of self-deception, of inauthenticity, of playing a role or trying to disguise one's actual personality behind a façade" (Stumpf, 2003, p. 466).

Whether sin comes to a person through genetic transmission, childhood learning, victimization, family of origin dynamics, psychosocial stressors, or self-styled resistance to God's unfolding will, sin remains sin. Compass Therapy takes the position that we are all sinners and knowingly or unknowingly resist the health and wholeness that God desires. We all stand in need of God's grace and guidance.

Yet with the redemptive atonement that Jesus Christ provides through his life, death, and resurrection, humanity receives God's gracious provision for mercy and reconciliation. People are called to grow more whole by acknowledging their shortcomings and surrendering their rigid patterns and resistances. The Holy Spirit empowers individuals to grow in existential communion with God; a "clarification of grace" that Rollo May viewed as the meaning of salvation, whether mediated through religion or psychotherapy (1989).

The therapist can participate in this process by praying for guidance in applying the principles of health in the face of psychopathology as a means of delivering God's healing love within people's personalities and relationships, in respectful dialogue with counselees' belief systems and free choices.

The following four chapters show how the Self Compass offers a framework for empowering therapists to neutralize the restrictions of dysfunction and invite counselees to develop an enduring wholeness—all the while utilizing the therapeutic alliance as a human relationship that radiates interpersonal health.

2
EXPANDING THE SELF COMPASS

Within the LAWS of personality, no compass point is superior to another. For instance, love isn't better than assertion, and strength isn't better than weakness.

Healthy people express both tender care and diplomatic assertion. They are competent and strong, yet humbly aware of their weaknesses. In short, well-balanced individuals maintain free and rhythmic access to all four compass points of the Self Compass, and to their spiritual core (Shostrom & Montgomery, 1978). By explaining these concepts near the beginning of therapy, counseling takes on an educational dimension and motivates counselees to participate.

What are these LAWS and how do they benefit counselees as well as influence the process of therapy?

Love is the glue that connects people together by way of interest, affiliation, and gentleness. The love compass point is shorthand for the thoughts, feelings, and sensations that reflect an individual's caring. Kindness. Thoughtfulness. Consideration. Forgiveness. Goodness. Tenderness. Compassion. Fondness. Fidelity. Fellowship. Friendship. Sacrifice. These experiences are woven together in loving compassion for self and others.

Therapists do well to remember the psychology of the obvious—that counselees need to learn how to love themselves. Counselees are stimulated in self-love by internalizing the care the therapist shows for them and by talking through any other blockages they feel toward self-compassion. Once these blockages are resolved, the Love compass point is activated and counselees learn to treat themselves kindly even when things go badly. They can nurture themselves even in the face of rejection from others. For this reason, self-compassion can prove more valuable than self-esteem for dealing with negative events like anger, depression, and pain (Leary et al., 2007).

In the development of a healthy personality, psychology and spirituality agree that loving others as you love yourself makes an invaluable contribution to personal wellbeing and fulfilling relationships.

However, no one remains loving all the time, nor is it healthy to do so. While love lets you stand with-and-for others, assertion enables you to stand over-and-against others, so as not to lose yourself in pleasing them.

Assertion imparts the courage to express your point of view, challenge unfairness, and resist exploitation or manipulation. Research on "hardiness" affirms the value of existential courage and the ability to grow from stresses rather than succumb to them (Maddi, 2004; Maddi et al., 2006).

Assertion preserves individual differences and builds the adult coping skill of negotiating for one's reasonable rights or the rights of needy persons. Assertion is more constructive than aggression, which Compass Therapy defines as moving against others with suspicion and hostility.

Diplomatic assertion involves respecting others and hearing them out, even while standing up for one's point of view, taking interpersonal risks of self-disclosure, and confronting social injustice.

Since everyone experiences anger occasionally, especially when their interests rub like sandpaper against the wishes of others, compass theory suggests that assertion is best expressed in rhythm with caring. This kind of interpersonal diplomacy raises the probability of successful conflict resolution.

Most therapeutic interpretations involve a degree of confrontation in that the therapist is offering a perspective that lies beyond the counselee's current awareness. An interpretation implies that a counselee's mode of operation is not as effective or as realistic as it could be. Even mild interpretations tend to challenge a counselee's self-image. Thus interpretations are a form of assertion that need a rhythmic connection to the therapist's caring and empathy.

Weakness reflects the universal experience of uncertainty, vulnerability, and soul-searching. The Self Compass offers a novel understanding of weakness by suggesting that this compass point helps people develop humility and empathy for others. Recent research shows that contrary to dictionary definitions of humility, which often emphasize its association with self-abasement, participants reported consistently positive views of humility (Exline & Geyer, 2004). You might go so far as to say that the Weakness compass point is the foundation of personality health because it contributes to a teachable spirit. Nonetheless, the experience of weakness is usually uncomfortable, if not downright painful. Grief. Disappointment. Anxiety. Terror. Depression. Identity diffusion. Frustration. Emptiness. Guilt. Suffering. Alienation. Self-doubt. Shame. Hopelessness. Helplessness.

Therapy invites counselees to disclose their weaknesses within a warm interpersonal climate (Rogers, 1965). The psychotherapy literature reflects wide agreement that the first and foremost task of a therapist is to create an accepting and empathic context (Strupp, 1989). This encourages counselees to admit and release core fear, which then paradoxically strengthens a counselee's core trust. When counselees talk more openly about weaknesses, they are cultivating humility and acknowledging limitations (Tangney, 2000).

Strength reflects the human need for competence, confidence, and self-worth. It captures the conviction that one's existence matters. Achievement. Drive. Zest. Enthusiasm. Vision. Dedication. Competence. Discipline. Perseverance.

Dignity. One of the most reliable ways for developing durable self-worth is through an actualizing proclamation: "I am a worthwhile person with strength and weaknesses." This perspective is affirmed and reinforced throughout therapy, and gradually assimilated into a counselee's whole human nature—Mind and Heart, Body and Spirit.

Research supports the actualizing view that resilient self-esteem does not come from rigid strength that is narcissistic or compulsive, but through a learning orientation in which the counselee makes progress toward goals, while framing setbacks as opportunities for growth and the development of new strategies (Crocker et al., 2006). Indeed, rigidly high levels of self-esteem often lead to instability, whereas more moderate self-views of individuals with integrative self-structures can offer greater stability, increased resilience, and a means of coping with stress (Showers & Zeigler-Hill, 2008).

Employing The Self Compass

Incorporating the Self Compass diagram in a session is simple. The therapist can show a graphic of the Self Compass and say something like, "One of the building blocks of your therapy is this compass diagram. Notice that it's divided into four compass points that are essential to every person. The Love compass point stands for all the love and caring you've ever received or given, but its opposite, the Assertion compass point, is just as important. Loving helps you care for others; Assertion lets you express yourself and stand up for your feelings and values. Now I wonder if you might explore how the Love/Assertion polarity relates to you."

By asking counselees to locate and elaborate on their own experiences within the Self Compass, you involve them in assessing and describing their own behavior. Two things happen. First, they begin to develop an *observing self* that will help them reflect on their behavior throughout the therapy. Second, they enjoy talking about themselves in compass

20

terms by sharing significant life experiences that relate to a given compass point. This prepares for continued exploration of the relationship between their current functioning and their actualizing growth toward holistic health.

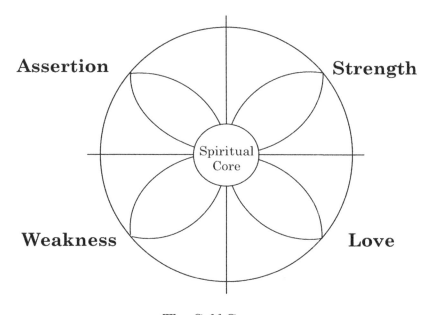

The Self Compass

Personality researchers have frequently found that this process of developing "psychological mindedness" is associated with successful treatment outcomes (McCallum and Piper, 1997). Accordingly, by introducing the Self Compass early in therapy, you invite the counselee to become a motivated collaborator in the therapeutic alliance. Substantial evidence links proactive counselee participation with beneficial outcomes in therapy (Orlinsky et al., 1994).

Once you have explored the terrain of a counselee's reflections on love and assertion, you launch the next expedition. You might say, "This second polarity represents times in life when you've felt especially weak or particularly strong. Weakness equals anxiety, vulnerability, and uncertainty.

Strength describes your experiences of confidence and adequacy. How would you say these two compass points relate to you?"

As vital information from your counselee's life history comes forth, you discern how he or she has typically handled the Weakness/Strength polarity. Is he stuck overly exaggerating weakness at the expense of strength? Has she developed a superior attitude to compensate for her fear of showing weakness?

The rapport you build and the insights you gain help form a diagnostic impression of the counselee's personality configuration. You may find out that the man who is a confident physics professor at work is a dependent depressive at home. Or the woman who has mastered yoga for relaxation goes to pieces when stressed by her hyperactive three-year-old son.

You and the counselee are working together like Sherlock Holmes and Watson, searching for relevant clues and deducing growth goals that will help to solve the mystery of self-growth that has eluded the counselee. The spirit of mutual curiosity and discovery generated by exploring the Self Compass adds momentum to motivation, self-reflection, and personality integration—key ingredients for awakening counselees to full engagement in their own change process (Weiner, 2009).

Here's a glimpse of how such dialogue can work. Let's say you've just heard Nancy's disclosure about how she sees herself and her significant relationships in terms of the Self Compass. You begin to formulate a treatment strategy with her.

Therapist: "So Nancy, it sounds like you could benefit from more assertion in order to hold your own with your husband. Is that right?"

Nancy: "Yes, he just makes so many choices about furniture, vacations, and where we eat out without getting my input. I don't think he's trying to be bossy. But I do need to let him know what I'd like more often."

Therapist: "One of our goals can be strengthening your use of the assertion compass point. Working on how to diplomatically express yourself instead of not saying anything. Now what about strength and weakness?"

Nancy: "Well, in my nursing work I feel very confident. Everyone treats me with respect. So that's okay. But where I get shaky inside is with my teenage daughter. She wants so many things! I give in too easily. I think I feel intimidated by her."

Therapist: "It's like you feel strong at work but weak in the presence of your daughter, especially when she puts pressure on you to buy her something."

Nancy: "Exactly. I've tried to set boundaries but she just keeps on until I give in."

Therapist: "Well, we can build your staying power through some role-playing and help you develop more self-confidence in her presence."

Nancy: "That would be great."

The Self Compass is a user-friendly tool that helps a therapist develop a diagnosis-to-treatment strategy, form an estimate of how many sessions may be needed, generate action techniques for intervention and growth-enhancement, monitor a counselee's progress, and determine when therapy is ready for termination. Sharing the Self Compass demystifies therapy and engages counselees as dialogue partners in the therapeutic enterprise. Counselees get excited when they know they can directly influence their own functioning.

One of the limitations of traditional therapy has been the lack of emphasis on understanding the particular personality dynamics that each counselee brings into therapy. The next chapter will give you tools for deciphering the major forms of psychopathology you are likely to run into during your career.

By adding layers to the central working model of the Self Compass, you will comprehend a vast amount of clinically sophisticated material in a way that feels intuitive and easy to recall. Most of all, you will grasp the crucial link between differentiated psychopathologies and specific strategies for guiding your counselees toward actualizing growth.

3
THE COMPASS MODEL & PSYCHOPATHOLOGY

The Self Compass not only shows counselees how to integrate the four compass points into their personality and relationships, but also reveals what happens when they are "stuck" on a compass point. Counselees intuitively grasp the metaphor of being stuck or frozen in place to explain their unconscious exaggeration or avoidance of one or more compass points.

A rigid personality trend arrests actualizing growth, stranding a counselee in a lifestyle characterized by too much dependency, too much aggression, too much withdrawal, or too much control, or a combination of these trends. Not only do these distortions effect self-functioning, they impinge upon interpersonal relationships.

If the counselee has a spiritual orientation, these trends undercut its effectiveness by seeing God as too Pollyannaish and syrupy sweet (Love compass point), too wrathful and persecutory (Assertion compass point), too aloof or emotionally absent (Weakness compass point), or too authoritarian and dictatorial (Strength compass point). For a fuller treatment of this topic, see *Christian Counseling That Really Works* (Montgomery, 2006, pp. 85-95).

Rigid behavior often begins in childhood as recurring attempts to ward off anxiety. For instance, a shy child avoids the Strength compass point by collapsing into Weakness, or an aggressive child exaggerates Assertion and avoids Love.

During therapy you can develop an intelligible explanation for the origin of fixation on a particular compass point, though in most cases the root cause involves a combination of genetic predisposition, traumatic experiences, the arresting of psychosocial development, and spiritual stagnation that disrupts normal growth and shunts an individual's concentration from flexible coping to defensive self-protection.

Compass Therapy's characterization of rigid trends as *growth deficiencies* carries with it the invitation for actualizing growth, thereby generating hope for counselees.

Using the Trends Self Compass

Anna Freud (1936/1946) described how specific defense mechanisms, which I call manipulative trends, need challenging by a therapist so that counselees can come to grips with their underlying concerns.

Likewise, Karen Horney (1994) issued fair warning that a counselee's manipulative trend is like a neurotic web that can entrap and neutralize the naïve therapist. This is not to speak pejoratively of counselees, but rather to explain why counselees both seek help and resist it.

Contemporary contributors to the literature in counseling agree that the personality style of counselees and the way they approach therapy are crucial determinants of their response to intervention (Blatt & Felson, 1993; Miller et al., 1997; Weiner, 2009; Aron, 2010).

Alfred Adler, Harry Stack Sullivan, Karen Horney, Virginia Satir, Everett Shostrom, and Aaron Beck, among other clinicians, have in their own way described the four manipulative trends of dependency, aggression, withdrawal, and compulsive control.

Locating these trends around the Self Compass brings the wherewithal to systematically challenge and therapeutically dismantle them. The Trends Self Compass that results identifies manipulative trends within the context of healthy personality.

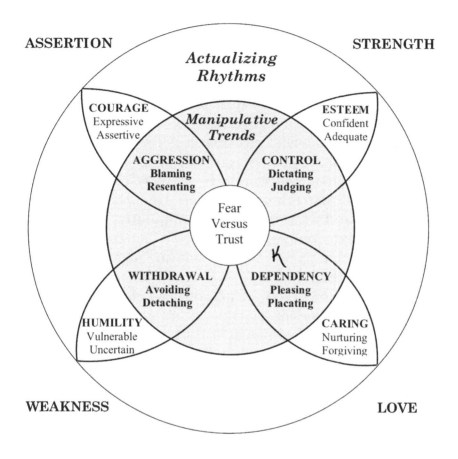

ASSERTION   *Actualizing Rhythms*   STRENGTH

COURAGE
Expressive
Assertive

Manipulative Trends

ESTEEM
Confident
Adequate

AGGRESSION
Blaming
Resenting

CONTROL
Dictating
Judging

Fear
Versus
Trust

WITHDRAWAL
Avoiding
Detaching

DEPENDENCY
Pleasing
Placating

HUMILITY
Vulnerable
Uncertain

CARING
Nurturing
Forgiving

WEAKNESS   LOVE

Trends Self Compass

Notice how the Trends Self Compass shows the familiar healthy compass points on the outer layer, describing their actualizing expression. Moving around the compass in clockwise fashion, the counselee sees that actualizing Love fosters nurturing and forgiving. Healthy Weakness expresses vulnerability and uncertainty. Diplomatic Assertion offers expressiveness and assertiveness. Humble Strength yields confidence and adequacy. You can point out that personality and relational health results when these polarities are expressed rhythmically and in balance.

27

Next, the therapist describes how the shaded circle reveals the unconscious hidden agenda that governs each trend. This circle is smaller than the actualizing circle and bordered by a thicker ring to indicate that manipulative trends contract the personality, constricting freedom by diminishing creativity. The therapist points out, too, that trust in the spiritual core is now overshadowed by core fear, the driving force that underlies the distress of manipulative living.

By now counselees will search to see how these descriptions might pertain to them and their troubles. They also want to understand what the word "manipulative" means.

"You manipulate yourself and others when you're feeling sad, but acting happy as though nothing is wrong," you might say. "Or when you hate something but say you love it." You find your own way of helping the counselee grasp that fear-driven behavior results in incongruence, where thoughts don't match feelings or body language, and where persons lose touch with what is really going on inside them.

While everyone is occasionally dependent or aggressive or withdrawn or controlling, a manipulative trend congeals into a fixated way of life that has dehumanizing repercussions (Adler, 1927/1965; Montgomery & Montgomery, 2007).

"How does this relate to the LAWS and the Self Compass?" the counselee may ask.

You take a quick trip around the compass, summarizing these universal manipulations. "If we're stuck on the Love compass point, we're too nice to everyone and become dependent. We please and placate others, and forget about ourselves. If we're stuck in Weakness, we withdraw from life to avoid situations that make us uncomfortable. We solve anxiety by detaching from people. If we overdo the Assertion compass point, we get mad a lot. We blame others for our aggression and resent them for making us angry. And if too much Strength is our issue, we try to control everything by dictating how life should be and judging people when they keep falling short. By balancing all these compass points we gain the advantage of the best that each has to offer."

The counselee nods, taking a closer look at the Self Compass. "I think I see myself in there."

"All right," you say, handing over the diagram. "Where do you see yourself and how do you suppose you got there?"

This productive direction heightens counselee awareness of how a particular trend creates interference and compass short-circuits. By talking about it, they make the trend more *ego-dystonic*, or distanced from themselves, rather than *ego-syntonic*, or merged with themselves. Gradually, counselees come to understand that a manipulative trend is not a moral fault, but a skewed way of functioning. Recognizing how they are manipulating self and others brings with it the freedom to choose otherwise.

This creative analysis of manipulative trends against the backdrop of health psychology eventually leads to outgrowing the trend—the very reason why many counseling theorists consider these trends as impersonal invasive structures that require challenging and changing (Kiesler, 1996).

For instance, Wilhelm Reich (1933/1980) observed that manipulation tenses body musculature, terming it character armor. Karen Horney (1945/1994) described manipulation as a tragic waste of human potential. Carl Rogers (1965) viewed manipulation as a struggle for authenticity between the ideal self and the real self. Joseph Wolpe (1969) described rigid trends as maladaptive behavior that could be unlearned. Eric Berne (1985) construed the self-fulfilling nature of manipulative trends as negative life scripts. Albert Ellis (1994) noted that a manipulative mindset is held in place by a set of irrational assumptions. Aaron Beck (2007) referred to manipulations as exaggerated cognitive processes.

Understanding the particular ways that core fear infuses and drives the manipulative trends (Dependent, Aggressive, Withdrawn, and Controlling) provides vital clues for com-

pass interventions that facilitate healing and promote transformation.

The Deteriorating Effects of Core Fear

It is fear of people's disapproval that drives the *dependent
trend*, where a counselee is stuck on the Love compass point.
The unconscious strategy avoids assertion and strength by
pleasing and placating others, even if this leaves one bereft
of an identity. Dependent counselees are compelled to seek
others' good opinion and to require constant reassurance.
Dependency makes individuals feel directly responsible for
anyone's unhappiness. They suffer guilt as though it's their
fault that someone else is discontent, depressed, or angry.
Fritz Perls (1989) called this the martyr complex. Karen
Horney (1950/1991) pointed out the underlying masochism
that is a hallmark of dependency.

Contrast this dependency with its polar opposite, the *aggressive trend*, where a counselee stuck on the Assertion
compass point feels neither guilt nor concern for anyone's
happiness. Rather, they make others walk on eggshells and
experience a sadistic glee in upsetting others by arguing
over trivial issues or blindsiding them with probing accusations. Chronic suspicion combined with an undercurrent of
hostility riddles the aggressive trend, coupled with fear of
intimacy (Love compass point) and fear of humiliation
(Weakness compass point). The Strength compass point is
subverted into stubborn pride.

You can see here how the exaggeration of Assertion into
the aggressive trend creates a distorted experience of other
compass points. Harry Stack Sullivan (1953) referred to this
as parataxic distortion: the tendency to distort one's perceptions of self and others through unconscious fantasies. Since
aggressive counselees don't like being thought of as ruthless
and exploitive, they project this aggressive posture onto the
world by blaming and attacking others for being ruthless
and exploitive. This is what energizes their persecution

complex. By distorting the Love and Weakness compass points, they manufacture the pseudo-intimacy of charm and the pseudo-innocence of being "victims."

In the *withdrawn trend*, counselees are stuck on the Weakness compass point, and avoid the development of healthy Strength, Assertion, and Love compass points. By pulling back from normal risks out of fear that others will ridicule their inadequacies, withdrawn counselees hide in a cave of solitude. They may feel interested in impersonal activities like reading novels, playing video games, and building collections, but when it comes to relationships they remain numb and detached.

When others express impatience with the withdrawn person's lack of energy and avoidance of responsibility, these counselees take this as confirmation of their own theory that they are indeed unworthy.

Horney (1950/1991) believed that withdrawn counselees were the hardest patients to treat because of the thick, impenetrable boundary cocooning them. This explains why the Trends Self Compass diagram shows a thicker ring of fear that separates those imprisoned in manipulative trends from the semi-permeable self-boundary of people pursuing an actualizing life.

The *controlling trend* counselee is stuck on the Strength compass point with an overriding need to appear on top of things at all times. This illusion of superiority and perfection reflects a compensatory fear of the Weakness and Love compass points. This is why it is practically impossible for a control-oriented person to admit a mistake, nurture someone, or express the need for love.

Because of this fixated need for power, controlling counselees set unrealistically high standards and constantly judge others for falling short. It is also easy for them to become workaholics, since they are so busy planning for all contingencies and conscientiously checking off "to-do" lists that they are unable to relax and play.

Controlling trend counselees resist forming a therapeutic alliance because they distrust anyone's judgment but their own. In therapy they have a consuming need to show how much they know, and by implication, how much the therapist has to learn. In other words, they have an unconscious need to show how much they don't need therapy.

Personality Patterns

A thicker ring of core fear encases personality disorders with even more inflexibility than manipulative trends.

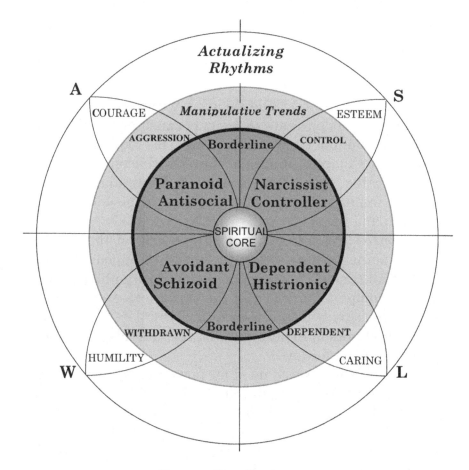

Personality Patterns

In this category of psychopathology, pervasive lifestyles sown from the root system of manipulative trends have rigidified into differentiated patterns that are highly resistant to change and growth. You can readily remember them by their location on the Self Compass.

- ✢ The *dependent* and *histrionic* patterns are located on the Love compass point, where the dependent trend intensifies into chronic pleasing and placating (dependent) or the melodramatic craving for attention (histrionic). Both patterns share intense needs for approval and affection (Millon, 2007a), as well as a fixated focus on others that blocks access to the spiritual core.

- ✢ The *paranoid* and *antisocial* patterns are stuck on the Assertion compass point, where the aggressive trend develops into edgy suspicion (paranoid) or impenitent exploitation (antisocial). These two patterns frequently "co-vary as personality mixtures" (Millon & Grossman, 2007b, p. 203), and share an undercurrent of hostility (Beck et al., 2007). They consider others as adversaries over whom they must triumph (Montgomery & Montgomery, 2008).

- ✢ The *avoidant* and *schizoid* patterns are located on the Weakness compass point, where the withdrawn trend intensifies into fearful loneliness (avoidant) or isolated detachment (schizoid). Both patterns create flat affect, a lack of motivation in personal development, and massive deficiencies in interpersonal skills (West et al., 1995).

- ✢ The *narcissistic* and *compulsive* patterns are lodged on the Strength compass point, where striving for superiority pushes the controlling trend into either the grandiose entitlement of the narcissist or the judgmental perfectionism of the compulsive (Montgomery & Montgomery, 2008). These two patterns share a common preoccupation with issues of "adequacy, power, and prestige" (Millon & Grossman, 2007a, p. 271). Both patterns are quite comfortable taking control and dictating (Beck et al., 2007). Both patterns share the demand for perfection, the narcissist seeking the glory of ambition and the compulsive enforcing the status quo (Millon et al., 2004, p. 357).

✦ The *borderline* pattern blends elements of the top and bottom halves of the Self Compass, flip-flopping in rapid swings from one extreme to its opposite (Montgomery & Montgomery, 2008). A built-in ambiguity within the pattern makes unpredictable whether the person will come across as a "top dog" (Strength and Assertion compass points) or an "underdog" (Love and Weakness compass points). Millon et al. describes this oscillating fluctuation as the "rigid fluidity" of the borderline pattern (2004, p. 505).

Personality Patterns vs. Personality Disorders

While the *DSM* term "personality disorder" captures the severity and rigidity of an inflexible personality pattern, it can have a side effect of diminishing self-esteem and creating a sense of futility about the future (Corrigan, 1998; Holmes and River, 1998). Research shows that counselees often internalize stigmatizing labels and believe they are less valued because of their disorder (Link, 1987; Link & Phelan, 2001; Corrigan & Miller, 2004). Self-stigmatizing can lead to decreased treatment participation.

Thus interventions that challenge self-stigma and facilitate empowerment are more likely to increase counselee engagement in all aspects of care (Speer et al., 2001). For this reason Compass Therapy emphasizes the big picture of a *health psychology* that encompasses a counselee's personality rigidity, providing positive directions for growth even while presenting counselees with relevant aspects of their trends or patterns. Compass theory and the Positive Psychology movement both emphasize the importance of establishing strong goals for health psychology as a means of understanding and modifying unhealthy behavior.

The nine personality patterns presented in Part II include: dependent Pleaser, histrionic Storyteller, paranoid Arguer, antisocial Rule-breaker, avoidant Worrier, schizoid Loner, narcissistic Boaster, compulsive Controller, and borderline Challenger.

These counselee-friendly labels contain both a clinical element from *DSM* and a common sense element that counselees immediately understand. Presenting them throughout therapy as patterns that the counselee is outgrowing creates a spirit of optimism. You might say, "I really like how you turned a deaf ear to the inner voice of your old compulsive Controller pattern in order to enjoy that party so much." Or, "It sounds like the dependent Storyteller pattern is making a bid to create false guilt again." Or, "I can see why you stole so many CDs from your employer; the Rule-breaker pattern makes it seem totally to your advantage to do so."

Clinical observations demonstrate the therapeutic benefit of increased self-knowledge generated by this type of skillful interpretation of counselee behavior (Levy, 1990; Meissner, 1991).

Psychosis

Counselees may move from a severe personality pattern into a psychosis, or they may enter psychosis from a genetic predisposition that is triggered in adolescence or adulthood, with or without a precipitating crisis.

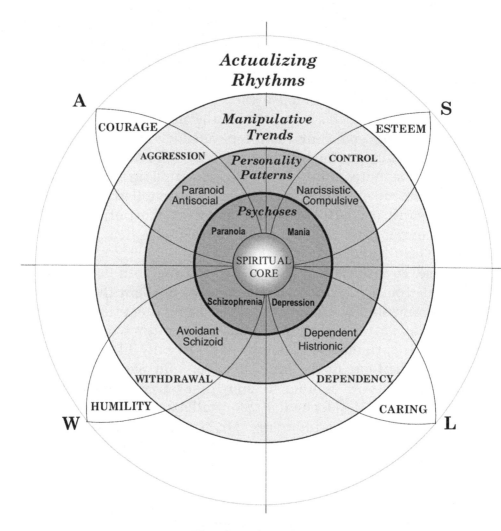

The Compass Model

The thickest ring in the Compass Model diagram indicates the severe constriction and dissociation from reality that psychosis brings. This "ring of fear" represents an episodic or chronic crisis of personality sufficiently acute that the spiritual core succumbs almost entirely to anxiety, depression, schizophrenia, bipolar mood swings, or other Axis I syndromes (Shostrom & Montgomery, 1986). Not only the core, or nucleus of the self, but one's whole human nature—Mind and Heart, Body and Spirit—are uniformly disturbed.

It is harder to predict compass point placements in psychosis. On the other hand, the therapist can often deduce a compass interpretation from the structure and function by reasoning backwards from the symptoms of the psychosis itself to the Self Compass. Noting whether the distinctive features include anxiety, depression, paranoia, violence, withdrawal, grandiosity, or obsessive-compulsive symptoms helps you find which compass points are over-functioning and which ones are under-functioning. These observations help you form a treatment strategy of growth stretches into unused compass points and better modulation of exaggerated compass points.

I once worked with a young woman who had spent three years in a psychiatric ward. Her primary diagnosis during that time was paranoid schizophrenia. The doctors had given her little hope of recovery because of the recalcitrance of the symptoms and her determination to outsmart everyone who treated her. Mary's presenting façade when she came to the university counseling center where I worked was that of a demure, well-dressed, and compliant person. I immediately recognized the dependent Pleaser pattern at work. But when she described the auditory and visual hallucinations of a demonic figure named Mary Lou, who would appear in mirrors and scream vulgar names and vicious threats at her, I recognized the presence of the paranoid Arguer and antisocial Rule-breaker patterns.

By the second month of therapy I had conveyed to Mary that her fragmented Self Compass had split into warring factions. Mary Lou represented her anger, assertion, and strength of identity, while Mary (her presenting self) constituted her love, vulnerability, and many fears.

For the next several months I took special interest in Mary Lou, the wild and aggressive dimension of her personality. I encouraged Mary to pay attention to the hallucinations so we could invite Mary Lou into a creative dialogue. This terrified her at first, but because I wasn't afraid of Mary Lou, she gradually developed curiosity instead of fear toward this alien part of herself. A turning point came in the tenth month when she spontaneously told me, "I think I get it now. Mary is the part of me that wants to please everybody because my dad is a senator and that's how he brought me up. But Mary Lou wants to give everyone the finger and say, 'Screw you! I want to be a real person!'"

I commended her for this brilliant deduction, and was even more fascinated by what she said next: "You know what? I don't think I need Mary Lou to fight the world for me anymore. I can tell people if I disagree with them, or I can agree with them if I choose. I don't need to split myself in half any longer."

Over the next two months the auditory and visual hallucinations faded away as Mary's sense of integrated identity and genuine connection to people increased. Her Strength and Weakness compass points gave her a relaxed confidence, and the integration of Love and Assertion balanced caring for others with standing up to them when needed. When Mary stopped by to visit me several years later, I felt amazed at the maturity and stability of this young woman, and was pleased that she gave me permission to tell her story in the hope that it might help others.

People catastrophically stuck on the *Love compass point* become especially vulnerable to major depression and suicidal ideation. They also are prone to develop generalized anxiety and even the kind of disorganized schizophrenia that Mary exhibited. These symptoms often arise as a consequence of an irreparable loss of a significant other upon whom they have profoundly depended. In Mary's case, the event that precipitated her psychotic break at the age of eighteen was the loss of boyfriend who, though he had se-verely abused her, was the only source of love she had ever known. Without external security, dependent-fixated indi-viduals can regress into infantile dependency, coiling into a fetal position, or histrionically pouting, giggling, and seduc-ing in attempts to capture people's attention and approval, all of which Mary had done in the psychiatric hospital.

Persons severely stuck on the *Assertion compass point* have learned to cope with threat by acting out aggressively. They can decompensate into paranoid schizophrenia, both discharging anger and projecting it onto others. Now they vent their hostility through wild rages and explosive as-saults (antisocial), or in smaller doses of being secretive, touchy, and irritable (paranoid). Because of Mary's split per-sonality, she had exhibited many of these traits as well.

Schizophrenia, particularly catatonic withdrawal, is the psychosis that arises from extreme rigidity on the *Weakness compass point*, creating a world inhabited solely by one's self. Mounting evidence suggests the identification of avoidant, schizoid, and schizotypal personality patterns as schizophrenia-spectrum disorders. In compass terms, it is the isolating effect of social anhedonia (interpersonal aver-sion) in addition to genetic factors that renders individuals vulnerable to the onset of schizophrenia (Gooding et al., 2005, 2007; Fogelson et al., 2007).

The *Strength compass point* manifests psychosis as the manic striving often linked to bipolar syndromes. In the manic phase, narcissists seek an exalted and pompous state of euphoric excitement, as though striving to recapture the glory of an earlier time in which they knew they were ad-mired and invincible.

Stormberg et al. (1998) found that bipolar patients exhibit narcissistic pattern characteristics while in the manic phase. On the other hand, compulsives are more prone to develop control-oriented symptoms like obsessive-compulsive syn-dromes that strive to manage anxiety through rituals, counting, tics, hoarding, obsessive doubting, compulsive thoughts, and insisting on cleanliness and order.

While medical compliance to pharmacological treatment contributes to a counselee's recovery from psychosis, the psychiatric patient can benefit from a compass overview of the personality pattern(s) they adopted earlier in life, and what they can do now to expand their personality toward the health psychology embedded in the Self Compass. Redemptive hope, then, provides a vision for transforming chronic suffering into the wisdom and balance of a renewed life. The psychiatric patient has as much right to this prospect as any person, and needs this hope to make forward progress.

Actualizing Health

The Self Compass offers a range of resourceful behaviors that help counselees make creative choices that gradually dismantle constricting trends and patterns.

At the actualizing level (as seen on the Compass Model diagram), counselees learn to relate with a relatively high degree of self-awareness and interpersonal discernment: the growth aim of all therapeutic strategies.

With the LAWS of personality as their guide, they learn how to express love for someone without letting that person take advantage. They selectively assert themselves if someone seeks to manipulate them, yet recover without falling back into chronic defensiveness. They discover how to form core-to-core relationships with others, while reserving the right to protect themselves against all forms of manipulation.

As the Love and Assertion compass points are informed by one another, they yield virtues of *caring* and *courage*. The synergy of Weakness with Strength results in the virtues of *humility* and *esteem* for self and others. These complementary virtues develop from within, knit together by the spiritual core—the "I am" center of awareness and choice.

Thus the Compass Model provides a working overview for transforming psychopathology in the direction of personality wholeness and effective relationships. Actualizing development takes form in a manner unique to every counselee. Gradual progress toward wholeness is the aim.

Compass theory asserts that no one is immune from some degree of personality rigidity, which is part of the human condition. Yet a counselee can make substantial gains toward psychological and spiritual maturity (Andrews, 1991). The cadenced, self-correcting polarities of the LAWS of personality form a solid basis for a resilient self-identity that allows counselees to find their core selves and develop a center that holds.

4
PERSONALITY PATTERNS & THE SPIRITUAL CORE

Guiding counselees into the territory of new insights and behavioral experiments requires examining the dark side of their personality patterns.

Playwrights and screenwriters know that a personality pattern is a set of partially unconscious assumptions that directly affect how characters perceive, think, feel, and act. A good actor must live a pattern from inside out, showing the little nuances of body language, voice tonalities, eye movements, and especially motivation that make a character come to life.

Therapists likewise must know how appealing and familiar these patterns are to those who live them, and how they offer security by seeming to ward off anxiety. And it is true that each personality pattern worked for the person at some stage of life because it represented a creative attempt to cope with personal and interpersonal anxiety. But in the long run all patterns fail, since they are too narrowly focused to remain adaptive.

Nevertheless, as long as a pattern's structure remains intact it functions as the organizing principle of perception. Most counselees will show evidence of patterned behavior, perhaps in the moderate form of a trend or the more severe form of a pattern. Compass Therapy is fundamentally action-oriented, in that it seeks to reboot the self-system by developing an actualizing perceptual field and coaching individuals to try out new compass points that gradually replace fixated patterns with a balanced and creative behavioral repertoire. The underlying assumption is that the Self Compass has been available to them since birth; it just hasn't been fully employed until now.

The Pattern as Autonomous Complex

Why are personality patterns so alluring to individuals who cling to them? I agree with Gordon Allport that a pattern exists as an autonomous complex within the personality (1937). It functions much like a tapeworm within its host, taking energy and usurping what would rightfully belong to the host, and giving nothing back but its own waste. This is the mystery of iniquity, identified even in the Bible, which troubles people from one generation to the next and defies rational explanation.

Any one of the personality patterns we are about to explore has the power to speak, think, feel, and act as though it is a living person. The truth is that these patterns are neither living nor responsive to life, yet they act with a purposeful autonomy. Often when counselees try out a creative new thought, feeling, or action, the personality pattern will assert itself as if to say, "Don't you dare change or something bad will happen!" Sullivan called this the defensive alarm mechanism of patterned behavior (1954). It is just as predictable as the patellar reflex which occurs when a doctor taps a patient's knee.

Though Freud (1938) documented the resistance levied by defense mechanisms, a personality pattern's ego-syntonic autonomy goes way beyond the theory of transference. More often than not, the pattern makes repeated bids to take over the counseling dialogue, and without vigilance a therapist and counselee can sit there powerless to intervene.

Yet from the view of Compass Therapy, the form this resistance takes provides vital information about how a coun-

44

selee thinks, feels, and acts in everyday life (Messer, 1992). For instance, the histrionic pattern leads to non-stop talking that drives a counselee to perform rather than communicate. The therapist can gesture for a "time-out" (as officials do in an athletic game) to help move through this resistance and make relevant points.

Or, in the case of the avoidant-patterned counselee, the therapist can point out the psychology of the obvious by saying gently, "It's like your unconscious came up with a solution to anxiety long ago: 'If I just sit here and say nothing, then nothing bad can ever happen.'"

By knowing in advance where patterns and their concomitant styles of resistance reside within the Self Compass, the therapist can impart new information throughout the therapy, gradually strengthening counselees' resolve to escape from the pattern by challenging their own resistance.

This process of pattern identification, and the forming of a compass conception of what life could be without the pattern, works even when there are pattern combinations involved. Just as all colors on an artist's palette originate in the primary colors of red, blue, and yellow, so all personality patterns and their combinations originate in exaggeration or avoidance of Love and Assertion, or Weakness and Strength. The LAWS of personality and relationships link together the potential for actualizing growth with manipulative trends, personality patterns, and psychoses.

For instance, someone who combines both compulsive and dependent patterns will not only compulsively set about seeking other's perfect approval, but will experience an inner conflict between controlling everyone's reactions while needing others to control them in an authoritarian way. This neurotic conflict is like prizing your new car so much that you are afraid to drive it, while at the same time offering the keys to anyone who needs a ride. In this particular case, you can see the neurotic dilemma in which the counselee's unconscious resentment of people (compulsive control) co-exists with an unceasing quest for people's approval (dependent pleasing).

When counselees learn to discriminate between the false voice of their pattern and the true voice of their spiritual core, the pattern loses its allure. The therapist's clear vision into the nature of these patterns is passed on to the counselee as though through a vaccination that gives them immunity toward the pattern.

In this manner, patterns are gradually flushed out, brought into consciousness for constructive reflection, and increasingly discarded in favor of new behavioral experiments that yield more satisfying results. Otherwise, therapy will bog down or last forever with only marginal results. No wonder therapists can burn out and not know why.

As a therapist, you know you're making progress as you illuminate these ineffective coping strategies and watch counselees replace them with signs of an integrated Self Compass. Many pseudo-problems and wild-goose chases fade away as substantial personality growth occurs.

To glimpse the change process at work, I will include compass interventions for each of the patterns in the following chapters. You can take it from there with your own repertoire of techniques. Once your unconscious has had time to absorb these strategies, your clinical intuition will take hold and your counselees will feel the difference.

Expanding Versus Contracting the Spiritual Core

Counselees can benefit from seeing a graphic symbolizing what happens to the spiritual core as they make the transition from patterned-living to actualizing growth. One of the defining traits of personality and relational health is inner-direction versus other-direction (Riesman et al., 2001). This means that in perceiving life situations, healthy persons trust their human nature and spiritual core for decision-making. They weigh alternatives, assess inner needs and environmental requirements, and make open-ended choices that they modify in light of feedback. By contrast, inflexible individuals react to situations through personal and interpersonal rigidities.

Research using the *Personal Orientation Inventory*, the first personality assessment to measure both psychopathology and actualizing health, has yielded empirical ratios regarding inner versus other-direction (Shostrom, 1976, pp. 75-78). Individuals at the *actualizing level* possess a ratio of 1/3; that is, they rely on their own core being three times more than they rely on other people. The person at the *manipulative trends* level, on the other hand, shows a ratio of 1/2, looking to others more than does the actualizing person in making life decisions. The *personality pattern* level shows a ratio of 1/1.5, indicating even greater other-directedness. The psychotic scores show a ratio of 1/1, which results in the extreme confusion of not knowing whether to trust the self or others.

The Spiritual Core diagram illustrates the inner-direction versus other-direction ratios, revealing the ever-constricting effects of fear-driven inflexibility that intensifies as one moves downward from actualizing health through progressively more rigid forms of functioning. Counselees can readily understand this by noting the thickening and contracting self-boundaries.

Yet the diagram generates hope for actualizing growth no matter where a person is stuck in the chain of behavioral rigidity. Viewed from bottom to top, there is an ever-ascending spiral of increasing trust in the spiritual core and freedom to move rhythmically through the creative range of a fully functioning Self Compass.

Here Compass Therapy agrees with modern psychoanalytic therapy that *unconscious* dimensions of behavior need working through at the levels of mind, heart, body, and spirit for lasting transformation that bears fruit in love, work, and play.

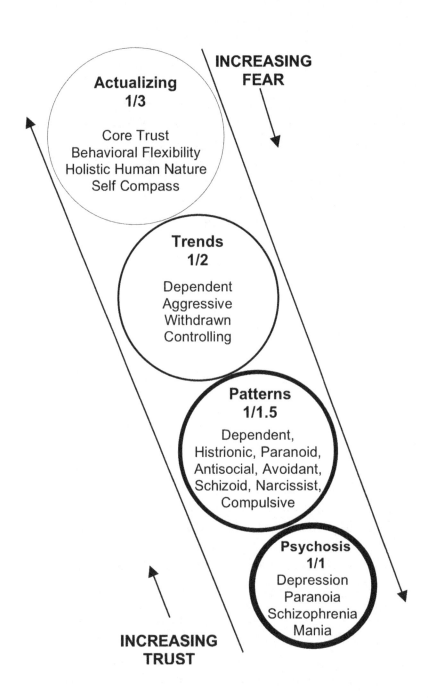

INCREASING
FEAR

**Actualizing
1/3**

Core Trust
Behavioral Flexibility
Holistic Human Nature
Self Compass

**Trends
1/2**

Dependent
Aggressive
Withdrawn
Controlling

**Patterns
1/1.5**

Dependent,
Histrionic, Paranoid,
Antisocial, Avoidant,
Schizoid, Narcissist,
Compulsive

**Psychosis
1/1**
Depression
Paranoia
Schizophrenia
Mania

**INCREASING
TRUST**

Spiritual Core

5
DEEPENING THE THERAPEUTIC CONVERSATION

As a prelude to the chapters on personality patterns, let's briefly explore some aspects of therapeutic communication that encourage the development of counselee transparency and transformation.

Communication is the heart pulse of therapy. The dialogue that develops between a therapist and counselee incorporates body language, emotional nuances, cognitive insight, and spiritual discernment—an interpersonal dynamic that evokes the whole human nature of each person. This is what makes counseling so different from other health professions like medicine, dentistry, or optometry. In counseling and psychotherapy you utilize your own personality and human nature as an interactive force in calling forth your counselee's human potential.

While some therapies set down rules of engagement that keep the therapeutic communication at a strictly clinical level, Compass Therapy suggests that it is wise to build a rhythm between clinical professionalism and personal naturalness that helps a counselee feel at home. Sullivan called this interpersonal posture that of a "participant observer" (1954, pp. 19-25).

If the counselee grew up in the town where you spent your last vacation, it's a natural point of discussion to spend a couple of minutes talking over your mutual impressions of the place. This builds rapport, develops a fellow feeling, and prepares for the next round of therapeutic exploration.

That said, how do you deliver interpretations and interventions that get down to the action of healing and transformation? And especially, how do you impart new information to counselees about any personality patterns that are arresting their human development?

Here are four principles that help keep the therapeutic conversation alive with meaning and flowing with continuity: emotional rapport, diplomatic warm-up, stroking the spinal cord, and putting the skunk on the table.

Emotional Rapport

Emotional rapport takes top priority throughout therapy. In fact, there is no effective therapy without emotional rapport; there is only talking or questioning or preaching.

Rapport involves curiosity, humor, listening, asking interested questions, exchanging ideas, and speaking in short enough sound bites that counselees can maintain their attention while feeling that you understand them. Whenever this rapport is broken for any reason, you can interrupt what you're doing and immediately begin reflecting what the counselee is feeling. Before long, trust is restored and the conversation can resume.

Carl Rogers' original research revealed the considerable role that building and maintaining rapport plays in promoting behavioral change. Rogers especially highlighted the therapist qualities of warmth, genuineness, and empathy that invite a reciprocal authenticity from the counselee (1951, 1957, 1974). Today these qualities serve just as effectively for deepening the therapeutic conversation and alliance (Patterson, 1984; Eckert et al., 1988; Lambert & Bergin, 1994; Stubbs & Bogarth, 1994).

In fact, a review of forty years of research involving hundreds of studies on process and outcome in therapy concludes that a therapist's contribution in helping counselees to achieve a favorable outcome "is made mainly through empathetic, affirmative, collaborative, and self-congruent (i.e., genuine) engagement" (Orlinski et al., 1994, pp. 270-378).

Diplomatic Warm-up

Counselees want to be trusted with the truth you perceive about them and their life situation. Yet while they value straight talk, they don't want to feel embarrassed or emotionally wounded by what you tell them. So take it easy. Stay mindful of their feelings.

Wachtel (1993) encourages communication that minimizes counselee distress. He suggests that therapists cultivate the art of gentle inquiry, so that exchanges build trust by proceeding in a spirit of exploration rather than interrogation.

In other words, when you are shifting into a phase where you are about to offer realistic but painful information, warm up the counselee and proceed kindly.

Dan: "Ellen, we've been talking a lot about how hard you're trying to make your son behave. But I'm wondering a bit why your husband seems so out of the loop. It's like you're doing the disciplining all by yourself."

Ellen: "Well, that's more or less true. But Larry is very busy at the bank just now. They've opened a new branch and he's actually saddled with two jobs."

Dan: "So you empathize with the pressure Larry is under. But I'm wondering who is empathizing for you?"

Ellen: (Looks down, her eyes momentarily tearing). "Maybe that's why I feel so alone in this. I have to enforce all these boundaries. I didn't have any brothers, so I don't know much about teenage boys."

Notice that Ellen has changed the subject. And even though she is deepening her disclosure about her feelings of loneliness and anxiety in handling her son, I need to diplomatically bring Larry into the equation so that he is not completely off the hook.

Dan: "That sounds doubly troubling. Not only are you feeling overwhelmed, but you're very uncertain about what is appropriate or not in your son's behavior."

Ellen: "That's right. I'm really floundering. But I'm determined to make Jeffrey shape up. If I can't control him, who will?"

Dan: "Now back to your husband. When was the last time you two had a date, good sex, or a heart-to-heart conversation?" (I am moving beyond emotional reflection in order to stimulate her thinking about the quality of the marriage bond. My clinical hunch is that Larry may have become so invisible to her as an absentee spouse and father that she is afraid to even broach the topic. However she responds, at least we are laying the foundation for more specific exploration in future sessions).

Ellen: (Looks me directly in the eye). "I've gotten so used to how things are at home that I don't even think about Larry and me. It was good between us until he got this job last year. I don't think we've had sex since then. We never talk about Jeffrey. He doesn't ask and I don't want to burden him."

Without knowing it, Ellen has strengthened my working hypothesis that she is stuck on the Love compass point in the dependent pattern as far as she and Larry are concerned. But on the other hand, she has become stuck on the

Strength compass point in the compulsive controlling pattern with regard to the teenage son. I jot this in my notes but do not pursue it for our time is running out. I move into summarizing to help Ellen develop emotional closure for this particular session.

Dan: "Ellen, you are a brave person to single-parent your son, and I appreciate how openly you've talked today about the strained relationship with Larry. We've got to end for now, but notice how these dynamics are played out this week, and we'll keep exploring next time."

Now Ellen's unconscious can retrieve recent memories that paint in bolder strokes the gap between her and Larry (both how it developed and where it's headed) and she will become more ready to accept what would otherwise be a startling revelation: that her son Jeffrey has replaced Larry as a surrogate spouse in her life.

Stroking the Spinal Cord

Rather than exuding an artificially aloof bearing meant to convey clinical objectivity, Compass Therapy suggests that you go ahead and be human, professional role and all. It's good clinical practice to know how deeply people need attention, support, and caring, and to provide these qualities in no uncertain terms.

Eric Berne (1984) called this offering of positive regard "stroking the spinal cord." He noted that giving a compliment or warmly commending a person literally perks them up. This positive human engagement stimulates the brain/body connection, lights up billions of neuronal synapses, registers in several locations within the brain, and strengthens the therapeutic bond.

When you can say it authentically, you might try something like, "That is a powerful insight," "I am amazed by the courage you are showing," "That is the funniest story I've heard in a long time," or "You have a fascinating life narrative."

Putting the Skunk on the Table

Administering a psychodiagnostic battery of your preferred assessment tools provides an objective measure of a counselee's personality structure and dynamics, strengthening your formulation about what's wrong and how to fix it. In my own testing, I have often included the *Millon Clinical Multiaxial Inventory* (Millon & Bloom, 2008) because it is integrated with the personality disorders found in *DSM*. The *MCMI* provides both a narrative summary and a clinical profile that you can translate into compass terms for understanding how a counselee functions within the Self Compass and the LAWS of personality and relationships.

The utmost delicacy is required in communicating to counselees the nature of their personality rigidities, since they may feel as vulnerable as a dental patient hearing the results of an examination. Yet therapists have an ethical mandate to impart this information when it contributes to understanding psychopathology or helps the counselee participate more effectively in resolving presenting problems.

Further, a good dentist knows to say, "Okay, this poke is going to sting a bit, but then you'll feel better." Patients still don't want the needle and may resent the dentist for the invasiveness of the shot. But they do want the end result of healthy teeth. So, when you are going to administer some truth serum to a counselee, and you anticipate temporary pain, you can say, "I've been pondering something that may represent new information for you...and may be a little shocking. But once we develop the overview, this insight will serve you well. Should I go ahead?"

Rare is the counselee who will stick fingers in both ears and shout, "No!" If you've developed decent rapport, something inside the counselee will say, "This is why I'm here."

Here's an example from my own practice. "Ron," I said, "we've reviewed pretty thoroughly how your parents left you to your own devices a lot, and didn't much encourage conversation or activities in your life."

"Right," said Ron, waiting for the poke. "I grew up all alone."

"Well, I'm afraid there are repercussions to that scenario that have lasted to this day."

"You mean that I don't like people?"

"Exactly. And more than that, you've built a castle around yourself and filled the moat with water and alligators so that nobody can get close to you."

Ron smiled wryly. "My first wife would agree. She'd pester me for days to talk to her and then I'd bite her head off."

"The bad news is that this will never go away on its own. The clinical name for it is the schizoid Loner pattern."

Ron sat up in his chair. "Does that mean I'm schizophrenic?"

"No. Schizophrenia is a genetic illness in which you have hallucinations and live in another reality. The schizoid personality pattern just means that you've split off your thoughts from your feelings, and this brings a hollow numbness inside. Then, to keep this loner pattern intact, you detach from people and withdraw into a shell. Does that make sense?"

Ron nodded. "That's me. I could stay on my computer for weeks if I didn't have to go to work."

"That's a very honest assessment. Would you like me to tell you more about the consequences of this pattern so you can think over whether you want to keep it or not?"

"Go ahead."

"The Loner pattern won't let love in or out, won't let you seek friendships that involve opening up, and will make you live and die a lonely man. How do you feel about that?"

"I guess I knew deep inside something like this was happening. I just got used to it and figured it was bad karma."

"Actually, Ron, a fair number of counselees I've worked with started out even more schizoid than you. They somehow found the motivation to give life a second chance. You know, trying to see other people as more than just pests to get rid of."

"Sounds hard to do. I get nervous when anybody's around. I just like to be quiet with my own thoughts."

"But isn't that just what brought you into therapy—that you're sick of thoughts rolling around like marbles inside your head?"

Ron shifted uncomfortably in his chair. "I do get sick of hearing myself think."

"Perhaps one of our goals, along with diminishing those repetitive thoughts, can be to enrich your connection to people. There's no good reason you can't learn to have feelings and express them like anybody else."

A look of relief came over Ron's face. "Okay, but I'm going to need training wheels like a little kid on his first bike."

"That's what we're here for. It's safe to learn some new things now. And you've got plenty of intelligence to help you along."

By being upfront and direct, I began shifting Ron's concentration to actualizing growth and laid a foundation for the ongoing transmission of information about his schizoid Loner pattern even as he began to outgrow it.

Now let's explore nine of the most common personality patterns, and see examples of compass interventions for each.

PART II:

PERSONALITY PATTERNS
& COMPASS INTERVENTIONS

6
DEPENDENT PLEASER PATTERN

Therapists encounter the dependent pattern frequently because people suffering from it are accustomed to seeking support and advice from others. The upper quadrants of the Self Compass are deactivated to such a degree that counselees possess little self-esteem (Strength point) or courage (Assertion compass point). An overly exaggerated Love compass point leads them to submissively seek approval by pleasing and placating, while an inflated Weakness compass point creates an undercurrent of anxiety.

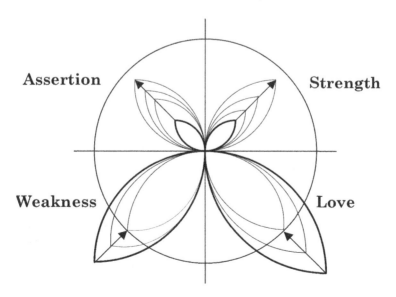

As in all personality patterns, the actualizing quality of a compass point is lost when taken to an extreme and left unbalanced by the opposite compass point. Therefore, even though dependent counselees want to give and receive love more than anything else in the world, genuine love—which requires the integration of Strength and Assertion with Love and Weakness—eludes them. The overblown Love compass point skews behavior toward self-sacrifice without self-preservation, submissiveness without assertion, and giving without receiving. Beneath their warmth and niceness lies a desperate search for acceptance and approval (Pincus & Wilson, 2001).

Rejection is feared more than aloneness, so the dependent takes no risks toward individuality or independent thought or action that might lead to alienation from sources of nurturance (Beck et al., 2007).

Unconscious forces are set in motion by these dynamics. A dependent-patterned person can be seen as cooperative and gracious by others, yet has actually undergone identity foreclosure, meaning that self-development is arrested with a childlike focus on safety and gratification, much like a fetus needs the mother to feed it and provide oxygen through the umbilical cord. Not knowing they can cut the psychological umbilical cord by developing the healthy expressions of Strength and Assertion, they fear independence instead of acquiring it (Oldham et al., 2009). Nor do they comprehend that healthy people would find them more lovable for replacing clinging vine dependency with authentic selfhood.

The over-exaggeration of the Love compass point alone leaves a counselee adrift in a sea of masochism. It's not that dependent Pleasers like pain, because they don't. It's just that they don't realize how this subservient pattern creates the fundamental reason for this distress: the pain of feeling constantly on edge about keeping people happy and the pain of needing other's approval for whatever they do (Cogswell & Alloy, 2006).

The dependent pattern exists as a pure prototype of fixation on the Love compass point, but can occur in combination with the adjacent compass points of either Strength or Weakness. When combined with the Strength compass point, counselees develop compulsive controlling features; combined with the Weakness compass point, the dependent develops avoidant depressive features. In all cases, however, the Assertion compass point is decommissioned.

The Therapeutic Impasse

The therapeutic impasse of every pattern centers on the point of greatest resistance to a more rhythmic and actualizing life. For dependent Pleasers to move beyond this impasse requires giving up the need for other's support and approval in order to develop self-support and self-approval. The success of the therapeutic alliance and treatment outcome depends upon making this transition.

In this light, the therapist does well to recognize how spouses, children, or friends often take the dependent counselee for granted and order them around. One young woman's parents lived sixty miles away, yet left a message on her answer-machine saying, "We'll be out of town for a week. Be sure and feed the dog in the morning and evening."

This demeaning treatment bewilders the love-stuck person and heaps up gunnysacks of hurt and resentment in the basement of the unconsciousness. Even so, the dependent keeps trying to put on a happy face. As one husband put it, "I just keep smiling and being a doormat."

On the other hand, the very reason for coming into therapy often involves a rupture in their dependent way of life, some fresh and painful experience of rejection or abandonment in which they feel their very existence is threatened (Massion et al., 2002).

So it is a fact of life that dependent counselees—in order to make progress in developing serenity and personal power—will receive disapproval, the withdrawal of support, and loss of protection from unhealthy persons who have thrived on their lack of identity, especially those who are themselves stuck in narcissistic or aggressive patterns.

Compass Therapy suggests helping counselees develop vision not only into their own pattern, but also into the manipulations of anyone who takes unfair advantage, imposes guilt trips, or causes undue duress.

Once dependent counselees begin to open up, they will pour out long-buried feelings of insecurity, anxiety, disappointment, and dejection (Bienvenu & Brandes, 2005). This is an excellent development because even though they feel like they are coming apart at the seams, in actuality they are becoming less of a stereotype and more of an individual self.

Therapeutic Questions for Pleaser-Patterned Counselees

The therapist can frame the characteristics that comprise the thinking, feeling, and behavior of pleaser-patterned counselees as questions, reflections, or interpretations designed to help them gradually understand and differentiate their core selves from the constraints of the pattern.

- ⬦ Are you aware of an inner need to take care of others and make them feel loved?

- ⬦ Whenever there is an argument do you automatically take a peacekeeping role?

- ⬦ When you were growing up, did you feel responsible for making your parents happy?

- ⬦ Were you discouraged from assertive behavior in the name of being a "good boy" or "good girl?"

- When faced with a decision do you usually worry about what other people will think?

- Do you feel guilty about spending time and money on yourself?

- Do you feel happy if people approve of you—and sad, guilty, and anxious if they don't?

- Do you have difficulty in understanding people's motives, especially if they take advantage of you?

- If someone compliments you, do you play it down and quickly forget it?

Pleaser Pattern

Compass Point: Love

Manipulation: Pleasing & Placating

Thoughts: Deferent to Childish

Feelings: Timid to Submissive

Actions: Accommodating to Docile

Growth Needs: Assertion & Autonomy

Origins

Those who exhibit the Pleaser pattern are likely to enjoy an idyllic first year or so of life. By receiving consistently warm care, they form an expectation that they will be nurtured and develop an implicit trust in those they live with to meet all of their needs (Benjamin, 2003).

But when the toddler begins to show a desire for autonomy, the parent does not allow it. Instead, the parent continues nurturing the toddler in babying ways. The parent discourages exploration, overly protects, and immediately relieves any frustration the toddler experiences. This continues during preschool and school age years. An example is a mother who insisted on remaining with her son every day of his first week of kindergarten.

The smothering parenting style is one of pervasive control. It does not occur to the parent that there will be any other response but compliance. "The consequence of relentless nurturance is dedicated submission" (Benjamin, 2003, p. 224). These children experience difficulty in developing a sense of competence and dignity when parents discourage their autonomy and peers tease them about their immaturity and undue sensitivity.

Pleaser dependency can also develop in the context of aggressive parenting that exaggerates anger to intimidate the child. In this case, Pleasers fear for their self-preservation and evolve a dependent-compliant response to avoid parental anger or displeasure. In other words, because the parent is stuck with aggression on the Assertion compass point, the child learns not only to decommission this compass point in their own development, but undergoes generational reversal by adopting a Love-oriented Self Compass fixated on being a good boy or good girl.

Consequently, they neglect inner interests, talents, and feelings in favor of attending to what their parent expects and demands. They are given the impression that inner direction is selfish and inconsiderate. This impoverished self-determination accounts for the feelings of depression and emptiness that Pleasers secretly harbor, despite their efforts to appear happy.

Another origin of the Pleaser pattern stems from early deprivation due to the loss of a warm and supportive mother by death or illness, or its equivalent: the emotional absence of a nurturing parent. A parent who is physically absent, suffers from depression, or is emotionally shutdown can leave the child with nagging insecurities.

Clinical Literature

The dependent pattern is widely recognized in clinical literature. Both Freud's and Abraham's concept of an "oral character" views the pattern as exhibiting many traits of infancy: total dependency, lack of assertion, a tendency to cling to others, separation anxiety, and insatiable needs for constant care, affection, and support (Freud, 1938; Abraham, 1911/1968). Fenichel (1945) aptly describes the oral dependent as a "love addict."

Horney (1945) describes the "compliant type" as a person who chronically "moves toward people" with pleasing and placating behaviors. Fromm (1947) sees the dependent pattern as creating a "receptive orientation" characterized by interpersonal naiveté and Pollyannaish gullibility. Tyrer agrees that there is a Pollyanna-like view of the world that makes them regard duplicitous motives of manipulative individuals with imperceptive childlike trust (Tyrer, Morgan, Cicchetti, 2004)

Mind

Compass Therapy concurs with Cognitive Therapy that all personality patterns exhibit automatic self-talk; that is, subliminal vocalizations that embody a counselee's thoughts and assumptions about life. Since self-talk involves mental rumination, a kind of repetitive rehashing of conscious and unconscious beliefs, the purposeful revision of self-talk has a direct impact on how counselees interpret reality, and what emotions they feel as a consequence.

The automatic self-talk of the Pleaser pattern centers on constant worry about what other people think of them. It sounds like this:

✦ I'm responsible for the happiness of others.

✦ I should never offend another person.

✦ I must keep the peace at all costs.

✦ I should take everyone's problems to heart.

✦ It is selfish to think of my own needs.

✦ If I'm nice to them, others will like me.

✦ I must keep my real feelings to myself.

Under the dictates of this pattern, a person should be able to endure anything, trust others, and like everyone. Albert Ellis summarizes Pleaser self-talk as "irrational beliefs (that) it is essential that one be loved or approved by virtually everyone...one should be dependent on others and must have someone stronger on whom to rely...one should be quite upset over other people's problems and disturbances" (1962, p. 61).

Pleasers project their inner neediness indiscriminately onto the world. They assume that others, too, need constant reassurance and rescuing. Thus, it is unthinkable to consider that others might perceive Pleaser worrywart behavior as irritating, their constant rescuing as interfering, or their smothering over-protection as insulting.

By drawing upon one's own courage and gentleness, the therapist can guide counselees caught in the dependent pattern to become aware of the negative outcomes this pattern wreaks on the personality and relationships.

The Approval Immunity Diagram

You can help neutralize some of this neediness by showing the counselee the Approval Immunity diagram.

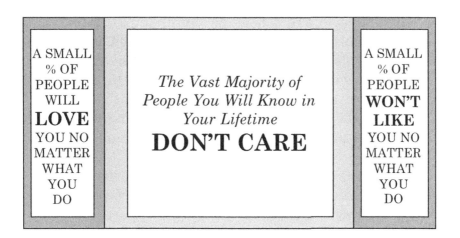

| A SMALL % OF PEOPLE WILL **LOVE** YOU NO MATTER WHAT YOU DO | *The Vast Majority of People You Will Know in Your Lifetime* **DON'T CARE** | A SMALL % OF PEOPLE **WON'T** LIKE YOU NO MATTER WHAT YOU DO |

You explain: "This diagram represents all the people you will ever meet in your lifetime. The column on the left shows that a small percentage of those people will like and love you, no matter what you do. It may be that they find you easy to be around or that their personalities are compatible with yours. It would be very hard for you to convince them not to like you. Do you know anyone like that?"

The counselee explores recollections of such persons.

Then you continue: "This column on the right represents a small percentage of people who will not like you, no matter how hard you try to change their minds. It may be they feel superior to you or simply that they are crabby to begin with. Whatever the reason, it's important not to invest any energy in them because they will only use it against you. Have you met a person like that, or encountered one as a clerk or coach or teacher?"

The counselee explores any such recollections.

You continue: "This brings us to the most important column—the one in the middle that represents most of the people you will ever meet. You need remember only one thing about them: they don't care one way or the other about you, because they are too busy paying bills, solving problems, and experiencing their own pressing agendas to think about you. These include people in school, at church, on athletic teams, in your neighborhood, at restaurants, in movies, at the mall, and wherever else you meet them. They may be cordial for a moment or look right past you, but the main thing to realize is that you are a blip in their stream of consciousness, so much so that they have no recollection of seeing you or talking to you that day. Now, what does this awareness bring up inside you?"

The counselee explores reactions to this information.

Once the main point of this diagram is processed and embraced as a growth goal, most counselees report a new level of freedom around others, a freedom to express or interact with less submissiveness.

Heart

You can build counselee trust by foretelling the most frequently experienced emotions that Pleasers are prone to feel. The Compass Model predicts that Pleasers are secretly haunted by anxiety, guilt, and doubt because dependency exaggerates both the Love and the adjacent Weakness compass points.

A side note: the Pleaser often seeks out a marriage partner or friends who are equally unbalanced top dogs stuck on the Assertion or Strength compass points. The Pleaser naïvely believes that a powerful partner will protect them from the demands of life. Though sometimes the strategy works, it often backfires because top dogs unconsciously select Pleasers precisely to lord their power over them. In extreme situations this leads to spousal abuse.

The dependent Pleaser's anxiety stems from the fear of disapproval, particularly if they think they have upset someone. Guilt constantly invades because they fear they haven't done enough. Doubt dogs their days because there is no inner center of gravity, no way of saying to one's self and other people: this is my choice (or my feeling, preference, or opinion) whether you like it or not. A relentless insecurity pervades their relationships with spouse, children, relatives, and co-workers. Even the Pleaser pattern's affability is riddled with a sense of inadequacy, the fear of not coming across just right.

An ironic consequence of the pattern makes Pleasers disown the very approval they seek from others. Someone says, "You sure are a great mother," and the dependent person replies, "Oh no, I just do what any mother does." Or the boss presents a Certificate of Achievement at a company banquet, and the dependent response is, "I haven't done anything to deserve this."

While feelings of anxiety, guilt, and doubt abound, there is one emotion the Pleaser altogether denies from consciousness: anger. Assertive feelings like anger might disrupt one's security and acceptance. Therefore, anger, annoyance, or irritation are summarily repressed, and if accidentally expressed, apologized for profusely because they threaten the very nature of one's dependency on others for support.

Body

For Pleaser counselees, there is no "there" there. The therapist does well to realize how completely body awareness and sensorimotor activity is suppressed by the lifelong habit of looking outward to others for how they should feel and act. This outer-directed "radar" readily picks up external signals but is not attuned to the person's emotional and somatic functioning. Thus, rather than feeling like "somebody," they instead feel more like a "no-body."

69

Breathing shallowly from the thorax contributes to somatic anxiety that can leave them breathless when under stress. The lack of relaxed abdominal breathing deprives the brain and body of oxygenated red blood cells. Such a devitalized state interferes with cognition and promotes panicky feelings. Hyperventilation can occur during times of tension or conflict. For this reason relaxation techniques and training in abdominal breathing are powerful therapeutic allies for helping dependent counselees transform their incessant undercurrent of uneasiness into a solid foundation of visceral and psychological serenity.

The body language of counselees stuck in the dependent pattern reveals that interpersonal contact is made largely through the top third of the body, particularly the face and arms. The pattern's ready smiles, soft-spoken voice, and friendly eyes evince appeals for love and support. Not wanting to give the impression that they are in any way critical or confronting, a confident gaze is avoided. In contrast to the torso, the legs seem limp and unsteady. This works against "standing up for one's self" or challenging unfairness in the world. A tendency for slumped posture owes in part to an underdeveloped muscular system and the inner psychological habit of leaning on others for support (Lowen, 2006).

Building Strength and Assertion

The *book-stacking technique* is effective for building body awareness and strengthening a counselee's courage to say "no" to other people's undue requests or expectations. To execute this technique, you ask the counselee to stand in front of you with arms extended and palms up. You load them up one by one with several books, saying as you do so, "This represents all the burdens people lay on you without considering how heavy they are." Once the counselee is loaded to capacity, you say, "Now while you are feeling the weight of these burdens, tell me what you are aware of."

Compliment them on any descriptions they offer, and if they miss certain obvious qualities, prompt them with, "What about your body? How does it feel right now when you've accepted all of these jobs?" Or, "Can you form a plan in your mind to say 'no' to the next person who wants to add another book?"

After waiting for another minute so that the impact of the load can sink into the psyche, you reverse the process by saying, "Okay, each time you tell me to remove a book I will. This will represent you standing up to a person and telling them that you can no longer accept assignments that belong to them."

Here you will hit a temporary therapeutic impasse, because the counselee will not want to disappoint anyone's hope or risk their ire. But keep coaching them, so they can successfully assert themselves to remove the books. "Go ahead now, and tell me to remove the first book."

If the counselee complies in a mousey voice, you stop the technique and say something like, "I noticed that you barely whispered that request for me to take a book away. If I were a manipulative person I wouldn't respond. Try putting some gusto into your voice and demand that I remove the book."

The counselee does so, and you remove the book.

"That was good assertion. Now ask again and really mean it."

The counselee does so with even more firmness and you remove another book. "Excellent," you say, "I'm really starting to believe you. Now for the last two books, try actually enjoying your assertion and feeling the relief of not having to carry these books anymore."

The counselee does so and you remove both books. The two of you laugh and sit back in your seats.

"I want to compliment you for doing a great job asserting your reasonable rights," you say. "What was it like?"

"It was hard at first, but I think I'm getting the idea that the world doesn't come apart at the seams if I say 'no.'"

"I wonder if for homework this week you might practice some diplomatic assertion when you need to? Next week we can talk over what happens."

"Yes, I'd like to. And I'm saying that because I mean it!"

Spirit

The dependent pattern creates a bottomless pit of need, lodged in a fear-filled spiritual core. This is the unforeseen consequence of living for people's love and approval, yet upon receiving it, finding that it's never enough to fill the hole within.

Interpretation of Existential Transference

At some point during therapy, the therapist can offer an interpretation aimed at facilitating a paradigm shift from fear to serenity as a foundation for living.

Here's an example of how I used this concept in a session with a forty-year-old woman who was seeing me in a church setting.

"It seems as though you are experiencing an existential transference toward key people in your life. It's like you are unconsciously asking them to play God by supplying you with assurance that you are a good and loving person. But this actually feeds anxiety because it's based on measuring yourself by their standards and leaves you constantly in doubt about your decisions and your own identity. How would you say this in your own words?"

"Well," said Barbara, "I guess I've never felt very secure about where I stand with anyone, so I try all the harder to do whatever will make them happy."

"I wonder if you might try substituting the seeking of assurance from someone to asking God directly for inner assurance. Human beings can be pretty unreliable about dispensing grace. But God is good at it. What do you think?"

"I've tried very hard to please God, but I'm sure I fall short."

"That's a humble admission, and with it you join all humanity. But if you were God and you heard Barbara say that, what would you tell her?"

"Well, I think I'd say, 'Honey, it's alright. You're plenty good enough for me and I love you very much.' But isn't that being arrogant, Dr. Montgomery?"

Since I was dealing with a Christian counselee, I said, "Christ on the Cross showed how precious you are to God. By accepting this love deep within yourself, you are actually delighting Christ's heart."

Barbara put a hand over her heart. "My goodness. I never thought of myself giving joy to God."

In Compass Therapy, existential transference means that every human being is precious to God, and that all material and relational attachments point beyond themselves toward that ultimate connection with the Divine that lies at the heart of the cosmos. People may fall in love with a house, a car, a person, a child, a career, or a goal, but none of these created things can dwell within the spiritual core like a heart-to-heart relationship with God.

The philosopher Augustine had it right when he suggested that there is a God-shaped hole within every person that only God can fill. Conversely, when grace and love flow from inner communion with God, then core trust outweighs core fear and one feels less desperate for other people's approval.

I concluded the session with Barbara by saying, "I wonder if you might consider an experiment this week in which you pray to God to grant you self-acceptance and serenity. It is peace in your spiritual core that will help relieve your anxieties and leave you more free to interact with others without needing them too much."

Research supports transpersonal and faith-based interpretations within a counselee's worldview, suggesting that religious and spiritual endeavors increase chances of recovery (Koenig, 2004; Pargament, et al., 2004; Reyes-Ortiz, 2008; Plante, 2010).

Taking a Stand Against Dependent Servitude

Another spiritual deficiency built into the dependent pattern is the loss of self-determination. Compass theory explains it this way: the dependent person's Self Compass is leveraged out on the Love compass point, cutting off the normal polarity swings from Love to Assertion or Strength. The dependent pattern thus distorts love into pleasing others at the expense of the autonomy that Assertion and Strength would bring. The spiritual travesty here—which Karen Horney (1945/1994) calls a "tragic waste of human potential"—is that someone else will choose their destiny for them.

Unfortunately, there are always one or two people like a counselee's parent, spouse, or friend, who are more than willing to accept this role of playing "God Junior" and guiding the counselee's life. Far from stepping aside as the counselee takes steps toward self-determination, they will often attack the counselee's newfound confidence and try to pull the dependent Pleaser back into their orbit.

The upshot is that counselees must develop enough of a sustained focus on self-responsibility to blast out of other people's gravitational pull and establish a life based on self-chosen terms. Only then can they find and pursue the individuated path that is God's will for them.

To provide a launch in this direction, I recommend that the therapist find a piece of music with lyrics that convey a Declaration of Independence theme in no uncertain terms. One song I use is called, "This Is My Life," recorded by Billy Joel.

To utilize this music therapy technique, you simply ask counselees to close their eyes, relax back into the chair, and respond to the music according to what it means to them.

Once you've finished playing the song, you invite them to open their eyes and share any discoveries they have made.

Secular Spiritual Values

For the non-religious counselee the discussion of spiritual values may run more along the lines of integrating the psychospiritual virtues that promote mental health and interpersonal effectiveness: *caring* for self and others (Love compass point), *courage* for challenging unfairness and manipulation (Assertion compass point), *humility* for admitting deficiencies and empathizing with other people's struggles (Weakness compass point), and *esteem* for both self and others (Strength compass point). These compass growth goals not only strengthen meaning and purpose in life, but also support inner spiritual peace.

Sample of a Growth Strategy for the Dependent Pattern

Compass Therapy partners with other theories of counseling so that therapists are encouraged to draw upon their own approaches and clinical experience, even while applying compass tools. This means that therapist creativity, as well as sensitivity to the unique needs of each counselee, work together to determine the growth strategy that a therapist selects.

I close this chapter by sharing a sample growth strategy that may prove helpful when working with dependent counselees. Subsequent chapters will end by exploring tips and techniques pertinent to those patterns.

Therapy with the dependent Pleaser usually starts well and proceeds rapidly for a few sessions, since the Pleaser wants to feel your approval. This is a good time to build rapport and lay the foundation for Strength and Assertion by commending any insights the person expresses or behavioral qualities they show that reveal the least bit of individuality.

The next step is to integrate psychodynamic insights with the kind of parenting they experienced, how they handled any brothers and sisters, and when they first noticed the onset of marked dependent behavior. Now is the time to let them talk about possible advantages of dependency, submissiveness, and non-competitiveness—what they gained from these behaviors and how the behaviors seemed to work for them at the time. This leads naturally into an exploration of the disadvantages of one-sided dependency: the opportunities they missed, the ways certain people took advantage, the lack of social visibility, the secret loneliness that came with a lack of identity, and the lack of assertion and confidence that they admired in others but lacked in themselves.

The novice therapist can get trapped in this phase of exploration and discussion by not shifting into the next phase of active coaching and skill building. In other words, while the Pleaser will comply with superficial talking therapy, sometimes giving the therapist what the therapist seems to want, they will begin to resist active strength-enhancement and assertiveness training steps.

Here lies the difference between therapy that meanders in undifferentiated directions and therapy that moves forward in providing counselees what is needed to outgrow defeating patterns.

To move into the action phase of therapy, you maintain rapport and conversational ease, but add the ingredient of behavioral experiments. Just as a coach training athletes, you teach and encourage counselees to handle current interpersonal relationships in new ways that bring gradual advances in personal presence. "What were you feeling when Judy said that to you...How could you have handled her more assertively...?" "When Ben picked you up thirty minutes late, what did you really want to say to him?" "When you wanted to change banks and the teller frowned at you, how might you have held your ground instead of capitulating?"

To outgrow habitual responses, the counselee needs new perceptions to support this risk-taking. For instance, the counselee says, "My buddy Jason wants to borrow my new car, but he's wrecked two other cars and I don't trust him. What can I say?" The therapist suggests, "This is probably one of those instances that everybody faces if they're going to become more of an individual. You just tell him the truth and then relax your body and breathing to help counter your usual anxiety. And you say in your head, 'There, I've stood up for myself and Jason can think what he wants about it. But I feel great that my car won't get wrecked!'"

By now the counselee is getting acclimated to transferring insights and growth suggestions from therapy sessions into real life. Although there will be occasional relapses, you can show patience when they occur, stop long enough to trouble-shoot them, and keep focused on complimenting the counselee for any increments of change in the directions of Assertion and Strength.

Eventually, when the counselee has become fairly adept at self-preservation and self-expression, the question will arise about how to integrate newfound strengths with the lower quadrants of Love and Weakness. After all, the counselee doesn't want to change from a clinging vine to a know-it-all arrogant bully.

So you now use cognition, emotion, physiology, and spirituality to cover the new ground of how to apologize or make amends if the counselee shows too much aggression, and how to experience forgiveness and caring for those in the counselee's life who are making behavioral adjustments to the counselee's use of the LAWS of the Self Compass.

For example, your counselee's friend Jason may make a promise that he doesn't keep. You guide your counselee to form a rhythm between Love and Assertion, first by calling Jason on his misbehavior. If Jason develops a reliable track record, then the counselee can move toward trusting again. But if Jason lies or makes another shallow promise, the counselee firms up the self-boundary by assessing whether further trust is warranted. A mature quality of love with discernment replaces the naïve gullibility of the dependent pattern.

You can tell when you are nearing completion of therapy, because there is less need for the therapist to guide sessions, and more autonomy with less distraction in the counselee's life. At this time you can move from once a week to every two or three weeks, to help the counselee make a successful separation and get on with life beyond therapy.

7
HISTRIONIC STORYTELLER PATTERN

Histrionic-patterned persons are compelled to market their wares by displaying talents and oozing charm to maintain the social spotlight (Jaspers, 1948; Fossati et al., 2003). They appear gregarious, entertaining, and larger than life in order to make people consider them special, a maneuver which masks shaky self-esteem and a hollow spiritual core (Flanagan & Blashfield, 2003). As shown in the diagram, therapists need to reinforce the Strength and Assertion compass points to balance out the Storyteller's misguided quest for Love (Schwartz, 2001; Beck et al., 2007).

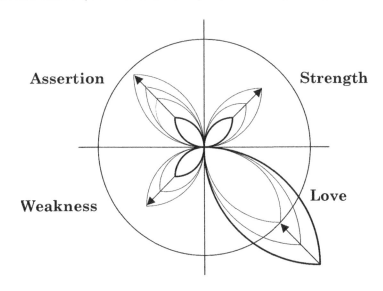

The Pattern's Interior

For histrionics, love is everything. To be the best of friends, to find a new romance, to pluck down the moon and the stars. Unlike the Pleaser pattern, which is self-effacing and non-competitive, the histrionic pattern distorts the Love compass point into an extroverted demand for reassurance that one is attractive and loveable (Millon & Davis, 1996).

Compass theory labels this the histrionic "Storyteller" pattern to highlight the distinctive feature of constant talking. So great is the need for center stage that Storytellers butt into conversations, hijack topics, make eye-catching gestures, display erratic moods, hurry or slow the cadence of speech for dramatic effect, and weave fragments of storylines into a patchwork of disjointed tales. The hearer wants to say, "Please get to the point," or "Now how does this relate to what we were talking about?" but finds this difficult because the histrionic actually engages in an extended monologue.

This stream-of-consciousness talking is often punctuated by overreacting to something that someone says which the Storyteller takes personally. These ideas-of-reference comprise beliefs that other people's statements or acts have special reference to oneself when in fact they do not. They make prototypal Storytellers prone to disrupt normal communication with bursts of envy, flirtatious innuendos, rolling of the eyes, crocodile tears, and hilarity. Especially if they feel insulted, they resort to pouting and moping. For milder histrionics, similar manipulative ploys are acted out at a lesser level of intensity, all with the aim of capturing and keeping interpersonal attention.

Histrionics invest their prime energy in the Love compass point, with little awareness of diplomatic assertion from the Assertion compass point, a stable sense of self-worth from the Strength compass point, or humility from the Weakness compass point. In fact, they avoid the Weakness compass point by reflexively exiling unpleasant thoughts or feelings to the unconscious. Without Weakness, however, histrionic Storytellers do not accept their losses nor develop a teachable spirit. Impulsive behaviors supplant introspection or constructive reflection and undercut learning from life experiences.

The histrionic pattern exists as a pure prototype of fixation on the Love compass point, yet can unconsciously incorporate features drawn from the adjacent compass points of Strength or Weakness. In the case of Strength, the counselee develops narcissistic self-glorification; but in the case of Weakness, the Storyteller develops avoidant self-recrimination with depressive features. If there are marked swings between the Love and Assertion compass points, then cyclothymic or bipolar features prevail. More typically, though, the opposite polarity of Assertion is shut down and prohibited expression.

Storyteller-Patterned People:

    ✤ Thrive on praise and perceive themselves in terms of their impact on others (Morse et al., 2002).

    ✤ Dread being alone, feeling inner emptiness most acutely when there is no audience.

    ✤ Are quickly bored, easily disappointed, and prone to change their mind with sudden arbitrariness.

    ✤ Love to attract attention by saying outlandish things, laughing loudly, or behaving seductively.

    ✤ Are usually prone to seductive and charming behaviors, but when stressed can explode into anger.

    ✤ Experience memory difficulties because of scattered thinking combined with emotional flightiness.

Origins

Storyteller-patterned persons are usually rewarded from an early age with too much attention for good looks and charm rather than competence or industry. Praise is lavished on them for being funny or cute. They come to believe they are the center of the universe and something is wrong with them if the applause stops. What sense of competence they do possess is based on manipulating others' reactions, rather than on authentic self-development. They learn how to steal the limelight and sabotage potential competitors.

A girl may model her mother's Storyteller pattern, or the father may pay particular attention to his daughter because of how captivating she is. The girl can be favored over her mother, learning to use her charm to control the father, especially if her father is aggressive toward her mother. "Daddy's little girl" is not abused sexually, but becomes the "other woman" in her parent's marriage (Benjamin, 2003). If the daughter makes the angry dad calm down by using the power of her charm, then everyone's problem is solved.

Another source of the Storyteller pattern is a never-satisfied father or mother who finds nothing pleasing in the child, nothing judged as appealing. Such children can become trapped, straining the limits of credibility to prove that they are worth loving. They devote their lives to searching for ways to elicit admiration and respect, exaggerating the facts of life to appear special.

Clinical Literature

The first psychosocial descriptions of what is now known as the histrionic personality disorder came from nineteenth century German psychiatry and described the symptoms of emotional impulsiveness (Feuchtersleben, 1847), underlying irritability, and the need to refer every life occurrence back to one's self (Griesinger, 1867).

The "hysterical personality" was erroneously considered a condition found only among women. There has since emerged abundant clinical evidence to support the existence of Casanovas and bons vivants.

Early psychology gave various labels to the histrionic pattern, such as the "choleric character" (Heymans & Wiersma, 1867), the "fickle temper" (McDougall, 1932), as well as the "extroverted-intuitive type" (Jung, 1921).

The perspective that most accurately foresaw today's clinical consensus cites "a preference for theatrical pathos...to dream themselves into big purposes in life, the playing with suicide, the contrast between enthusiastic self-sacrificial abandonment and a naive, sulky, childish egotism, and especially a mixture of the droll and tragic in their way of living" (Kretschmer, 1926, p. 141).

Mind

Storyteller thought processes are typically insubstantial and lacking in insight. Suffering from cognitive dissociation, there is difficulty integrating facts as well as remembering them. Scattered thought processes can result in blocking on people's names, forgetting appointments or where the car is parked, losing personal items, and telling the same story multiple times. These memory problems get converted into new material for dramatic storytelling.

Histrionics are usually motivated and cooperative in therapy because they need to make a vivid impression on the therapist. This works to the advantage of the therapist who is flexible enough to participate somewhat in a histrionic-like dialogue—that is, to interact with a measure of excite-ment and energy, adding a touch of drama to the therapeutic conversation. The histrionic may well terminate therapy that is too cognitive, dry, or boring. The effective therapist is lively enough that this does not happen.

Once you have demonstrated that you possess humor and spontaneity, you can integrate important cognitive informa-tion into the therapy by functionally representing the part of the histrionic counselee's brain that needs upgrading: the neocortex.

For instance, while listening with rapt attention and re-sponding with animation, you begin to interlace cognitive rationale for logical causes underlying distressing social events. You review the pros and cons of hyper-emotionality, especially highlighting how to handle negative emotions constructively. You model how to weigh evidence that sup-ports or challenges the counselee's life assumptions. You add new factual information about how one's behavior in a fam-ily of origin can overlap with and contaminate one's current behavior, encouraging the counselee to reflect on such con-nections. You offer insight into how a greater balance of love and assertion, or weakness and strength, can enrich the counselee's emotionally significant relationships.

In proceeding this way, you are stimulating cognitive growth that builds a developmental bridge for sizing up situations and thinking before acting. As Millon and Gross-man point out, "No intervention plan is complete without providing (the counselee) with alternative behavioral possibilities and an understanding of their possible advantages over current patterns" (2007b, p. 109).

A related strategic goal involves helping histrionic counselees get out of the moment enough to develop an overview of a situation or relationship in which they are enmeshed. You literally help them to discover, activate, and benefit from the power of their neocortex to solve problems, gain overviews, and plan ahead.

Reformulating Cognitive Self-Talk

Within the rhythm of emotional empathy and cognitive interpretation, you can utilize typical Storyteller automatic self-talk, most of which is unconscious, which you help to reconfigure as therapy proceeds:

- ✦ Unless I captivate people's attention I am nothing.

- ✦ I am irresistible and deserve special love.

- ✦ It's not my fault I'm forgetful and disorganized. I just get caught up in the spontaneity of life!

- ✦ People will abandon me if I'm not the life of the party.

- ✦ If I don't entertain people or flirt with them, they'll find me boring.

- ✦ I am very intuitive about people.

These automatic thoughts contribute to a diminished spiritual core, low frustration tolerance in the face of difficulties, and a lack of interpersonal wisdom that keeps the histrionic from becoming more mature.

Here is an example of new thoughts you might offer for the counselee's assimilation. Notice how several are framed toward enhancing the marketing appeal the person already possesses:

- ✦ "One of the ways to really get and keep people's attention is to develop a rhythmic conversational style that lets them feel as significant as you like to feel. Does that make sense to you?"

- ✦ "Here's an intriguing fact about human interaction: the more you reveal your weakness in balance with strength, the more lovable people find you."

- ✦ "Here's an idea for remembering where you left your car keys. You can develop a habit of touching them and visualizing them in your mind—things you're very good at—and then concentrate on where you place them as you're leaving the car. This lets your unconscious mind form a vivid impression of their location; then your unconscious will spontaneously retrieve this image when you return to the car. Would you care to try this out for homework and see how well you do? I'll give you a cheer if you pull it off."

- ✦ "I know that flirting is fun and that you're good at it, but have you ever realized the downside—that people can view you as adolescent-like and incapable of having a mature relationship?"

- ✦ "I agree that you're intuitive about how to pick up on people's interests and appeal to them. It's kind of exciting to realize that the Self Compass will not only make you more intuitive, but also add stability to your relationships."

Histrionic Storytellers are masters in the fine art of eliciting stimulation and captivating the attention of others (Riesenberg-Malcolm, 1996). Compass Therapy builds on this histrionic emotionality and reduces its negatives by teaching counselees how to restrain feelings as well as express them, a form of emotional modulation crucial to therapeutic progress. This is like showing someone how to adjust the volume control on a radio, emphasizing that low to moderate levels allow for more effective reception than high volume alone.

Further, counselees need help in recovering emotionally-laden memories that they would prefer to avoid. This standard work of psychotherapy can help them uncover buried emotions that would otherwise haunt current relationships.

A useful approach for tackling the histrionic pattern's emotional dynamics focuses on integrating the LAWS of a counselee's whole Self Compass. I will present some examples of possible interactions as though you are doing the counseling in the present moment.

Love Compass Point

Therapist: "You are a dynamic and talented communicator. I propose that we enrich your interpersonal skills by helping you develop emotional self-sufficiency."

Counselee: (Pleased by the compliment and surprised with the concept). "What does that mean?"

Therapist: "Emotional self-sufficiency means that you learn how to love yourself reliably enough that you don't need others to do it for you."

Counselee: (Laughs). "Isn't love something people give you? It would ruin everything if I had to do it for myself!"

Therapist: "Does it ruin dining out with people if you use your own knife and fork?"

Counselee: "Okay. So how am I supposed to love myself?"

Therapist: "Well, you have absolutely convinced me that you are an intriguing, humorous, and fun-loving person. The next step is to internalize this perception of yourself so that it can seep deep down into the feeling level and register in your heart."

Counselee: "I'm not usually at a loss for words. I guess no one has actually described me like that."

Therapist: "But isn't that what you've spent your life trying to convince people?"

Counselee: "Of course. But don't get too psychological. Just tell me how to do this and I'll give it a try."

Therapist: "Just repeat these words: 'I am an intriguing, humorous, fun-loving person.'"

Counselee: (Blushes slightly and speaks slowly). "I am an intriguing...humorous...I forgot what comes next!"

Therapist: (Smiles). "Fun-loving person."

Counselee: "Oh yes...fun-loving person."

Therapist: "And I love myself."

Counselee: (Bites lip). "And I love myself."

Therapist: "Even when I'm weak and can't control people's reactions the way I'd like to."

Counselee: "Even when I'm weak and things fall apart."

Therapist: "You're doing great. Just one more part."

Counselee: "Okay."

Therapist: "I love myself and don't need to pressure people into loving me."

Counselee: "That would save a lot of work, wouldn't it."

Therapist: "Good insight. Can you say it?"

Counselee: "I love myself and don't need to make other people love me."

Therapist: "Wow. I'm impressed. Now how about putting it all in your own words."

Counselee: "I can't remember all that!"

Therapist: "That's okay. Just try giving the gist of what you've been saying."

Counselee: (Takes a deep breath). "I am a really great person who tries her best even though I can make a mess out of things, and I love myself anyway. Is that right?"

Therapist: "You've got it. Now how are you feeling as you say this?"

Counselee: (Looks down at her body. Relaxes her hands in her lap). "Warm. Good. Peaceful."

Therapist: "My commendations. You really are learning about emotional self-sufficiency."

In other sessions the therapist visits each compass point, seeking to stimulate emotions pertinent to that quadrant of the Self Compass, and to help the counselee learn how to identify emotions, savor them without impulsively acting, and think about how to communicate with others with fewer emotional displays.

Weakness Compass Point

Here are some examples of how the therapist might explore the Weakness compass point:

1. "I wonder if you can remember the most humiliating experience you've ever had. Can you talk about it so that we discharge the unconscious emotion surrounding it and make that memory objective—like a photograph in a scrapbook." Here you are bypassing emotional catharsis in favor of teaching the concept of intellectualization, where a person learns to think objectively about an event without getting overwrought.

2. "How do you know when you are feeling empty inside? Have you ever thought about how everyone feels hollow from time to time, only some people just cover it up better than others?" This normalizes the inner emptiness that histrionics typically push out of awareness, and provides a safe context for exploring it.

3. Over the course of therapy you can unpack and sort out a spectrum of weakness-oriented emotions relevant to a particular counselee. These include: confusion, frustration, anxiety, shame, helplessness, terror, abandonment, rejection, betrayal, jealousy, envy, or loneliness. Here Compass Therapy agrees with Psychodynamic Therapy that "making the unconscious conscious" is crucial to therapeutic success. It is like spring-cleaning a bedroom closet. You provide a trash bag and enough clothes hangers so that the counselee

can decide which memories to throw away and which ones to hang up in the closet of meaningful experiences. This enhances their ability to discern the trivial from the valuable, which cleans up their daily perceptions of life events, and also helps to integrate past experiences instead of repressing them.

Assertion Compass Point

"It seems that you have angry flare-ups from time to time when somebody disappoints you, or when you feel that they have acted disrespectfully. Let's talk more about what anger means to you, and how you can communicate it diplomatically without shocking people."

This provides a natural opportunity for the therapist to model a non-inflammatory way to disagree with someone or stand up for one's self without resorting to excessive melodrama. Compass Therapy stands in strong alignment with Psychodrama in using mirroring, role-playing, and role-reversal to teach these practical lessons.

In *mirroring*, you play back to the counselee how they look, sound, and act in a particular behavior you are focusing on. You match their tone of voice, body language, and words as closely as possible, and then ask what they noticed as you mirrored the sequence of behavior. Make sure you don't exaggerate their behavior, or else they will feel rightly humiliated and become self-conscious.

In *role-playing* you create a situation the counselee has described and play it out spontaneously as though it is happening in the present moment. Then you talk over what the counselee has discovered.

In *role-reversal* you become the counselee and they become a person they are having difficulty communicating with. Then, in your role as the counselee, you model more actualizing behaviors drawn from a whole Self Compass. This lets them tap into a new behavioral repertoire by seeing how they, too, can engage others more effectively.

For an in-depth discussion of these and other psycho-drama techniques, I refer you to *Christian Counseling That Really Works: Compass Therapy In Action* (Montgomery, 2006).

Strength Compass Point

Paradoxically, histrionics remain quite unconvinced of the strengths they try to convince everyone else they have. So it is appropriate to commend them when they stick to a task, complete a train of thought, express what they want and need, and follow through to completion of a goal.

You want to reinforce strength-oriented activities, since the histrionic would normally zip past them, diving into some surface whim or digression. Giving the counselee an emotional boost of "congratulatory affirmation" encourages their development of persistence, competency, and independence (Montgomery, 2006, pp. 175-176).

Body

The tendency to repress genuine emotions in favor of superficial behavior often results in psychosomatic symptoms like migraines (Benjamin, 2003). The inability to handle solitude can lead to panic attacks, especially when feeling rejected or abandoned. The need to maintain an artificial aura of excitement creates a vulnerability to alcohol or drug abuse.

The single most useful therapeutic technique to diminish these symptoms and increase inner serenity is muscle relaxation. This can be accomplished in two ways.

The first method of *whole body muscle relaxation* involves taking about twenty minutes to lead the counselee in relaxation procedures that involve eight major muscle groups throughout the body. These muscle groups include: a) tightening the hands into fists; b) flexing the biceps of the arms; c) tightening the throat by pressing the chin down onto the chest; d) making an ear-to-ear grin; e) tensing the brow into a frown; f) arching the legs with the toes pointed away from the head; g) contracting the legs with the toes pointed toward the head; and h) contracting the stomach and buttocks muscles.

You introduce the technique by saying, "We're going to help you melt your muscles so that any time you feel anxiety, you can shift into a state of relaxation and serenity."

Then you say, "I'm going to count slowly from one to five as you gradually tighten the muscles that we are focusing on. At five, you are to relax completely, and enjoy the sensations of pleasure and serenity that flow through your body." After guiding the counselee to tighten and then relax each muscle group, you say, "Feel the difference between tension and relaxation in this area, and enjoy the sensations of relaxation and serenity in your body."

Upon completing this sequence many counselees report it as the first time they have ever felt completely relaxed.

You can initiate the second method of *differential muscle relaxation* at any point in a session when the counselee shows excessive body tension. Taking only a minute of targeted focus, you might say: "I just noticed that you raised your shoulders a couple of inches when we were discussing how you used to feel around your mother. Let's pause to relax those muscles. Take a moment to raise your shoulders up toward your ears. Hold this tension while I count to five." At five you say, "Now relax completely, letting your neck and arms become as loose as wet noodles. Take two deep breaths. How do you feel?"

These physical exercises are instrumental in teaching the histrionic-patterned counselee how to counter situational and interpersonal anxiety with serenity and muscle melting.

Adjunct treatment with psychopharmacological agents may well improve confidence, impulse control, and frustration tolerance, contributing to the counselee's ability to respond to psychotherapy (Joseph, 1997). If notable depression accompanies the histrionic pattern and the therapist feels convinced that this is not merely an attention-getting device, then treatment with an antidepressant should be considered as part of the therapeutic strategy. If there are periodic mood swings that remain unresponsive to counseling, a medical evaluation might uncover rapid mood cycling, a bio-genetic condition that responds well to medication.

Spirit

To avoid feeling deflated or depressed by negative thoughts and feelings, histrionics repress large segments of memory and emotion (Crawford et al., 2001). This repressed material is converted into muscular tension in order to keep it partitioned from consciousness. It is no wonder, then, that histrionics formulate fuzzy and spacey accounts when trying to recall their past.

But there is a further unforeseen consequence. This compartmentalization of past from present eclipses the spiritual core, or "I am" center of selfhood. This vacuum at the center of existence results in living like an actor who has no coherent personal life or history apart from the current theatrical production. The actor feels alive and animated on stage before a live audience, but as soon as the curtain goes down and the theater empties, the actor faces a sense of meaninglessness—the dark, existential aloneness of an empty life (Overholser et al., 2002).

Lacking a center of gravity that holds, the greatest fear for histrionics becomes "falling apart at the seams," or "coming unglued," a spiritual dilemma indeed, since this is what frequently happens. Even friends and acquaintances grow tired of the frenetic performance and fickle shallowness of the Storyteller's masquerade as a vibrant person.

The early psychoanalysts discovered the intense reservoir of repressed emotion that would explode in the form of an emotional catharsis when the counselee followed the sequence of free association down into the catacombs of the unconscious. They also found that bringing cogent interpretations of past events removed much of the anxiety and distress that troubled the histrionic, and helped the person live more authentically in the present.

Compass theory agrees with psychoanalytic theory that the conversion of repressed energy into actualizing growth constitutes an emotional re-education (Alexander, 1961). The non-manipulative bond established with the therapist helps ground the person in reality, diminishing the pressure to distract the self by getting attention from others. Awareness of a counselee's own desires, needs, and preferences gradually replaces the insatiable quest for love, leading to inner-directed need gratification (Rogers, 1995).

By choosing to live from the spiritual core, the counselee finds core-centeredness and interpersonal mutuality freed from the Love compass point alone. The new organizational center of the spiritual core coordinates the self-regulating rhythms of love and assertion, weakness and strength, in ways unique to the counselee. Newfound spiritual tranquility allows for the development of adaptive behaviors and the ability to learn from negative or painful situations rather than taking flights into histrionic fantasy.

Now the counselee can combine their liveliness with the resiliency of an actualizing Self Compass.

8
PARANOID ARGUER PATTERN

You can recognize when someone with the paranoid arguer pattern has entered your practice because you feel uneasy, as though someone is sizing up your weaknesses to use against you. Paranoid Arguers exaggerate the Assertion compass point to the exclusion of the Love compass point. They exude an attitude of suspicion and testiness that reflects their penchant for blaming and attacking others (Montgomery & Montgomery, 2008). Just as a shark snaps up a mackerel, the paranoid pattern will take a bite out of the naïve therapist.

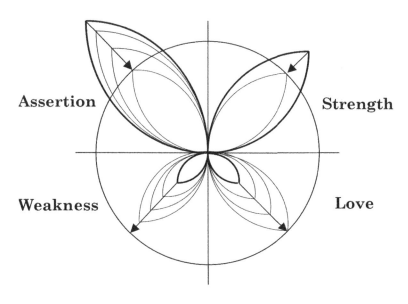

You can grow apprehensive if there are several paranoid Arguers in your practice, because they try to make you walk on eggshells, revealing their hidden agenda that the one who is going to change is you. Their edgy tension, abrasive irritability, and sarcastic humor contribute to a formidable defensive armor (Sinha & Watson, 2006).

The Pattern's Interior

Fearing the vulnerability that accompanies love, Arguers harden their hearts to the needs or suffering of others, ruling out the possibility of intimate bonding (McHoskey, 2001). Instead, the Love compass point is used to manufacture displays of fake charm. Likewise, the humility and soul-searching of the Weakness compass point are twisted into self-pity, where Arguers berate people, institutions, or life itself as unfair to them. The Strength compass point inflates the Arguer with airs of self-importance and invincibility, even illusions of omnipotence (Noonan, 1999), and a burning need to get their way (Reid, 2005).

The paranoid pattern exists as a pure prototype of fixation on the Assertion compass point with aggressive trends. It is also found in combination with the adjacent compass points of either Strength or Weakness. In the case of Strength, paranoid aggression combines with narcissistic pomposity or compulsive obsession; with Weakness, the paranoid develops avoidant depression or schizoid detachment. In all instances, the opposite polarity of Love is shut off and prohibited expression.

These compass distortions mean that paranoid Arguers believe people are out to get them, and that they are justified in the hostility and bullying they direct towards others (Coolidge et al., 2004). They levy castigating remarks with impunity because there is no remorse. Antagonism and suspecting the worst in others color everything they do (Sheldon & Stevens, 1943). This pattern is expressed on a continuum from mild to moderate to severe levels, as are all personality patterns. This means that actualizing individuals need a mild dose of paranoid suspicion for healthy skepticism about advertising claims, product guarantees, smooth-talking sales tactics, and conning or cajoling behavior from other people. But the paranoid Arguer congeals these self-protective strategies into a mistrustful worldview that pervades the Mind and Heart, Body and Spirit.

Arguer Pattern

Compass Point: Assertion

Manipulation: Blaming & Attacking

Thoughts: Distrustful to Delusional

Feelings: Sullen to Hostile

Actions: Contrary to Vicious

Growth Needs: Caring & Trusting

Origins

The paranoid Arguer pattern finds its origin in a lack of basic trust. There is evidence that "in many cases the paranoid person has received sadistic treatment during early infancy and (as a) consequence, has internalized sadistic attitudes toward self and others...(The person) is exquisitely sensitive to traces of hostility, contempt, criticism or accusation" (Cameron, 1963, p. 645; 1974).

Much research considers hostility as a primary descriptor of this pattern. Blum (1982) notes that this hostility stems from the bullying behavior children experienced during early development. Children who are prone to future paranoid inclinations remain deeply ambivalent about attachment to others. They feel a desperate need, yet sense the danger in such a commitment. They develop a history characterized by "difficulty in bonding that is accompanied by an underlying fear of betrayal and loss" (Blum, 1982, pp. 331-361).

A study with aggressive boys found that their hostile behavior initiated a cycle of parental anger that in turn furthered their aggression. The parents finally withdrew, thereby reinforcing the boys' initial aggression. Withdrawal of parental authority short-circuited the boys' ability to learn more controlled and adaptive behaviors later in life (Patterson, 1976).

Studies support the role of early experience, showing verbal abuse (Johnson et al., 2001), emotional neglect (Johnson et al., 2000), and child-parent conflict (Klonsky et al., 2000) as contributing to the paranoid aggressive mindset.

Clinical Literature

Paranoia is a term characteristic of the Arguer pattern meaning "to think beside oneself." The term "paranoia" is of Greek origin, found in medical literature 2000 years ago, and precedes the writings of Hippocrates, capturing the notion of a delusional belief system that emphasizes both suspicion and hostility. Unwilling to follow the lead of others, and accustomed to trusting only themselves, the paranoid Arguer pattern requires the reconstruction of reality in accordance with its dictates.

Freud (1938) termed paranoia a "neuropsychosis of defense," highlighting how this pattern wards off reality through the defense mechanisms of denial and projection. Shapiro (1965) added that the projection of unacceptable feelings and impulses onto others both eliminates guilt and accounts for the lack of intrapsychic conflict.

Unwilling to acknowledge their faults or weaknesses, Arguers shore up their self-esteem by projecting personal shortcomings onto others, believing that it is others who are malicious and vindictive. This pattern is expressed in a variety of forms. They include: the "combative type" who wants to fight the world, the "eccentric type" who withdraws yet harbors persecutory delusions, or the "fanatic type" who recruits others into secret sects (Schneider, 1950).

Horney (1950) observed that paranoid-patterned persons exhibit "sadistic trends" that distract them from their hidden inferiority. By blaming and attacking they build a counterfeit self-esteem. This obnoxious behavior acts to isolate them from meaningful or intimate relationships, further confirming their suspicion that the world is against them and that "the blame for their failure (lies) solely on external hindrances" (Kraepelin, 1921, pp. 268-271).

Compass theory has selected the term "Arguer" to stand for the perpetual contrariness and automatic argumentation that dominates the paranoid's perceptual field. There are endless ruminations or "subliminal arguments" about past injustices or wounds to their pride; current quarrelsomeness with family members, work associates, or strangers; and plans-in-preparation for arguing their case in the immediate future. Like a disputatious defense attorney, they are always on the job, considering no detail too trivial for possible use in winning a battle in the courtroom of daily life.

Mind

Treating paranoid-patterned counselees involves embracing a paradox: the best therapeutic strategy is to give up the need to help them. Why? Because their radar will translate any conscious or unconscious need of yours as a devious attempt to influence them. If you want to help them, they will see this as condescension—that you're really only interested in taking their money or building your ego at their expense.

In other words, they come in armed to the teeth to defend themselves against dependence upon you or learning anything from you. Fritz Perls (1989) called this the bear-trapping game, by which he meant that aggressive-oriented counselees lay out traps that spring into action when you least expect it. They may cajole you with questions about your qualifications, your personal life, or your intentions for them, then place your words or actions into a distorted context that is aimed at your humiliation (Harper, 1996). Or they may jump on a phrase you use and put you on the hot seat.

You would not be human if you didn't feel the occasional sting from these machinations. Yet you can foresee and avoid most traps by developing modest expectations for the therapy, engaging the counselee at a more objective than subjective level, and, when appropriate, uncovering the structure and function of the paranoid Arguer pattern with calm aplomb (Montgomery, 2006, pp. 35-46). Equally important is keeping the motivation for every aspect of therapy squarely on the counselee's shoulders.

One might wonder why paranoid Arguers are willing to seek therapy, let alone pay for it.

The most common answer is that they are motivated to recruit a mental health professional into agreeing with them that someone in their interpersonal world is stupid, devious, and argumentative because they are not doing what the Arguer wants them to do (Lee, 1999).

If they can convince you to agree with them that the other person (usually a spouse, child, or work associate) is guilty and they are innocent victims, then they can use your expert opinion as a hammer for battering the other person.

Understanding the Paranoid's Mental Territory

By thoroughly mastering the paranoid mentality, you develop immunity from various paranoid tactics that could otherwise leave you rattled. If you know their pattern as well as they experience it from inside themselves, and yet don't use your knowledge to blame and attack them, they detect that they can't manipulate you. Their trust and respect for you as a therapist increases.

Here are a few points to keep in mind. Paranoid Arguers are stubborn and proud of it. Their views are always right. Criticize them and they become vindictive. Threaten them and they become stronger. Attack them and they make vengeful plans to make your life miserable.

Their thought patterns run along these lines:

⊕ People can't be trusted because they are devious and will side against you.

⊕ I am honest in saying that my philosophy of life is how things really are.

⊕ I must test those around me to see if they are loyal.

⊕ Other people want to interfere with my freedom, put me down, and discriminate against me. I have never received the good treatment that society owes me.

⊕ If people seem friendly, they're only trying to manipulate me. I need to be constantly on guard against adversaries who want to take advantage of me.

⊕ I am hard-nosed and proud of it. People make me angry because they are untrustworthy and exasperating.

Arguers' independence isolates them from social feedback, so they hear only the marbles rolling around in their own heads. Nothing else is relevant; nothing else matters. Over time their thoughts can take the form of delusions in which they are captains of fate struggling against formidable forces, a theme strengthened by selectively interpreting most stimuli to fit this internal scenario.

Their highest ongoing priority is to maintain freedom in a world of their own making—a mentality that shares much in common with schizoid, schizotypal, and schizophrenic ideation. On the other hand, they share with the histrionic pattern ideas of reference whereby they interpret insignificant or innocuous events in ways that suit their dictates and confirm their suspicions (Porcerelli et al., 2004).

Compass Therapy suggests this explanation for paranoid Arguers' stubbornness and vainglorious pride: they have desensitized themselves to the Love compass point as a defense against caring, and to the Weakness compass point, where hurt, shame, and self-doubt are barred from consciousness.

This decommissioning of Love and Weakness reduces their interpersonal connection with humanity to a defensive vigilance against perceived threats. The short-term gain is a remarkable lack of intrapsychic conflict achieved through an aggressive reflex-arc that utilizes the mid and lower brain stem—what I call the "reptile brain"—to create a psychology of hate, suspicion, and retribution. The neocortical functions are recruited to verify these assumptions by sifting for evidence to build a case that other people have ulterior motives.

In every vocation paranoid Arguers vent their malevolence on those under their control. They train underlings to walk on eggshells to reinforce their power over others, criticizing them over nothing as a form of stimulation. And, of course, there is not the slightest remorse for dressing someone down because "if he (or she) had done the right thing, I wouldn't have had to blow my stack."

Understanding these features helps the therapist selectively empathize with the pain the counselee has known in life, while at the same time feeding back a certain amount of truth serum about the toxic effects of the paranoid Arguer pattern. While taking care to speak in a diplomatic and non-inflammatory way, you nevertheless remain firm about how pattern recognition can serve the counselee's self-interest better than the paranoid pattern itself.

You identify with their pride, yet suggest that a realistic integration of both strengths and weaknesses will increase their capability to understand motivation. You temporarily align with their grudges against others, while suggesting that this narrowed perceptual field creates a vulnerability all its own. You compliment their no-nonsense realism, while delicately pointing out that the reason they are in marital therapy (or some other difficulty) is related to a general lack of empathy and caring (Montgomery, 2006, pp. 37-46).

Over time you construct the mental possibility that the world might be a friendlier place than they assume, and that other people could find them interesting and attractive if they'd quit baring their fangs. Many paranoids are genuinely surprised to learn that there are people in the world who want to like and love them, but have never been given the chance.

Heart

An undercurrent of irritability flares up at a moment's notice. The Arguer magnifies minor slights and takes sudden offense. Suspicious of domination, they stay on guard against any attempt to rob them of power. They frequently intimidate others with icy glares, raised eyebrows, pointed fingers, cold shoulders, and stern lectures. Beneath the hard veneer that conveys grandiosity and self-importance, paranoid Arguers shelter a fragile self-image (Dimaggio et al., 2006).

Arguers stay in control emotionally by making mountains out of molehills and launching arguments when people least expect it. They are capable of verbal or physical abuse when rage escalates out of control, yet remain convinced that others ask for this treatment. As masters of barbed-teasing, they keep people off balance, launching impromptu interrogations designed to justify resentments and test the loyalty of anyone who is close to them (Harper, 2004).

The paranoid Arguer "expects to be misunderstood and misused, so if someone shows the slightest annoyance, he or she responds with a perceptive, fierce, well-focused rage. They can attack harshly with virtually no justification because of the belief that he or she was about to be attacked by the target" (Benjamin, 2003, pp. 322-326).

They enjoy making people feel uncomfortable. Paradoxically, paranoids are bored by a healthy relationship. They will act provocatively if a relationship is peaceful, cynically if love is expressed, and contrarily if communication flows naturally. An Arguer recalled, "When I was a kid, I always liked to bat balls against the wall. They'd bounce back and then I'd hit them harder and harder. That's what I do to people. I get them all upset and then I bat them around. It makes me feel powerful, like I can defeat everybody but nobody can defeat me."

Rarely does the undercurrent of envy and contempt subside. They must remain ready to pounce on anyone whose abilities or attitudes evoke their ire. Under the guise of self-justified ventilation on others lies a feeling of being overlooked and cheated by life.

The Yell

Here is a portion of a transcript from a session I had with a military officer and his wife of twenty years. John had a pattern of harshly interrogating Leila about money she spent on their college-aged son. Yet John was spending a significant portion of their savings on recreation vehicles and fishing trips without consulting her.

In an earlier session I had presented the Self Compass for discussion. John had described himself as a commander and a warrior, which Leila had translated to mean, at least in terms of his treatment toward her, a "glorified jerk." He had stomped out of that session and sat stewing in the car, whereupon I asked her what life would be like if he was no longer her center of gravity. She had answered that from the beginning of their marriage she had taken a submissive role, but now was questioning whether marriage was worth the treatment she received.

Now we were in the fourth session:

John: "Leila's been acting weird all week, like she's hiding things from me. If there's one thing I can't stand, it's someone doing something behind my back and hiding it from me."

Dan: "It's like you need to be in total control and she's not allowed to have an independent thought."

John: "I don't mind her thinking as long as it's what she's supposed to think."

Leila: "I'm glad you said it that way in front of Dr. Dan. You do try to control my thoughts and my moods. If I'm not this pretty little housewife who hovers around your every need, then you become a whiny baby."

Dan: (I noticed that John's face reddened and tensed with anger). "Let's slowdown for a moment, so that I can catch up. John, you mentioned fearing that Leila is hiding something she's done from you. Would this be like how you hid the purchase of the recreational vehicle from her?"

John: "I never said I didn't buy it."

Leila: "But you totally hid that you bought it with our retirement funds."

John: "So I'm not supposed to enjoy life?"

Leila: "Not when you leave us vulnerable financially and drive those things full speed all over those mountain trails."

John: (He slapped his hand against his thigh). "Leila, when I want your opinion I'll tell you what it is."

This is a good example of how couples counseling dialogue can meander all over the place, even while revealing crucial dynamics of the relationship and of each person's personality pattern. The conversation reflected that Leila was outgrowing the dependent Pleaser pattern she had exhibited in their marriage. She was the one who had forced the issue of counseling by mentioning she was thinking about divorce. This floored John and he felt angry and vindictive about it because he thought they had a great marriage. That is perfectly understandable in that while paranoids seldom experience discomfort themselves, they create substantial pain and turmoil in their spouses.

Dan: "So we have a difference of opinion here about how money should be spent, and about who should control the marriage. Let's focus on one goal for this session in our remaining time. I'd like each of you to tell me what is most important to solve today."

John: "That's easy. There's something new I want her to do sexually. She's not willing to do it. That's not fair."

Dan: (I noticed Leila blanch). "Okay, and what is it for you, Leila?"

Leila: (She looked at John). "I want you to stop pounding the dashboard of the car like you did before this session—and yelling at me with such fury. It absolutely terrifies me!"

John: "I barely tapped it. You should know I didn't mean anything by it. You want me to be honest about my feelings don't you? Besides, you've always been too thin-skinned."

Notice the masterful delivery of the whole paranoid Arguer agenda in this one response. Denial. Rationalization. Blame-shifting. Accusation. I chose this moment for a compass intervention.

Dan: "John, you are a big muscular man who is in excellent condition, aren't you?"

By appealing to his glorified self-image with a compliment framed as question, I neutralized his contrariness and garnered his cooperation.

John: "I can still bench press 250."

Dan: "And do how many pushups?"

John: "At once? Sixty. Seventy-five if I push it."

Dan: "So you are still a formidable warrior."

John: "I've still got my moxie."

Dan: "And yet it puzzles you that Leila becomes physically afraid of your power when you whack your fist on the dashboard?"

John: "I've never, ever, hit her yet. And I never will."

This is a perfect paranoid response, because even though it sounds like an innocent disclaimer and complete assurance of trustworthiness, there is something menacing about it.

Dan: "You may know that. But all she's got to go on is your behavior. And pounding the dashboard is very demonstrative behavior."

I knew even as I said this that I'd stepped in a bear-trap because his eyes locked onto mine like a laser beam.

John: "Dan, if your wife wouldn't give you sex even after all the decent things you did for her, wouldn't you let off a little frustration? There's not a man alive who wants to be pussy-whipped by his wife and turned into a wimp who has to go play with himself because she keeps her legs shut!"

By now John's eyes were boring holes into mine, and with his last comment he slapped the arm of his chair for emphasis. Leila had brought a hand to her lips and sat there looking ashen.

Dan: "That's very descriptive, John," I said. "I like how you bring me and every other male in as a case-in-point to prove how unfair your wife is, and how totally she deserves the demonstration of anger you gave her in the car."

John: "How else is a wife to know what a man needs and how he feels about it?" He glanced at his watch.

I could tell by John's calming down and giving a self-satisfied smirk that he felt he had delivered the coup de grace of the session. I could imagine his mind saying, *Case closed. Point proved. Now I'll get sex and keep my physical expressions, terminate therapy, and not pay this dopey psychologist another cent.*

Dan: "Well, we've only got five minutes left. But, say, John, I wonder if you'd be willing to try a little experiment before you leave today."

John: "No problem."

Dan: (I stood up and walked to a nearby wall mirror). "Could you join me here?" He did so. "Now, I want you to make the most fearsome warrior face you've ever made. Let out a war cry if you can. Then it will be my turn."

John: "This is the nuttiest thing I've ever been asked to do, but here goes." He let out a loud yell, his eyes bulging out, and contorted his face into a combat grimace. When he'd finished he smiled triumphantly. "Pretty good, huh."

Dan: "Yes, I am very impressed. Now I want you to do something that takes as much courage as going into battle. I want you to step inside your wife's skin for one minute, and look at me in the mirror, as though I am Colonel John."

John: (His face softened. I could see he was trying to find some internalized representation of his wife within him; his blank look showed that it was to no avail).

Dan: "Just pretend you are her and you feel great admiration for the warrior who is your husband. You're thinking that John is strong. He's fearless. And he's about to communicate with you."

John: (Looking encouraged from the positive description of himself, he gazed into the mirror.) "Okay, I'm Leila, and I'm feeling those things."

Dan: "Great, now I'm going to role-play John in the car a while ago."

Locking my eyes onto his in the mirror, I screwed up my face like a gargoyle, letting molten lava erupt from my eyes, and exploded with a bloodcurdling yell. When I finished howling, John's face had turned ashen and his jaw had dropped. I guided us back to our seats.

Dan: "We've got a minute left. Any discoveries either of you'd care to share?"

John: (Looking abashed). "I never knew I looked like that."

Leila: "My heart is pounding. This is exactly why I'm so afraid of John."

Dan: "John, is there anything you'd like to tell Leila before we call it a day?"

John: (He spoke in a very low halting tone of voice). "Ah. Leila. I don't know how to say this. Umm. I really love you. I am shocked that this is what I've looked like over the years." He looked at me.

Dan: (I nodded supportively). "Well done, John. I'm going to let you two finish this conversation in your car. I'll see you next week."

This kind of social feedback helps Arguers challenge the paranoid template that has ruled them unchallenged for so many years. In John's case, we were now building an emotional bridge to Leila that could help repair years of damage to the relationship. And though that bridge was tenuous and the path before us uncertain, at least now this couple had a chance to cross it.

Body

Because anger is overused as the primary mode of reacting to life, an Arguer can become unconsciously addicted to adrenaline. The adrenaline rush of excitement generated by the "fight" response typical of this pattern results in a speeded-up pulse, accelerated breathing, and increased oxygenation of the brain and skeletal muscles, leaving the body pulsing with energy (Schneider & Tarshis, 1975). Compass theory proposes that this "adrenaline high" is a secondary gain of the paranoid pattern's generalized alarm-hostility reaction. It is possible that an Arguer looks for opportunities to get angry so as to offset inner emptiness with intermittent episodes of physiological excitement (Montgomery & Montgomery, 2008).

Notable among quieter type paranoids is the poker face that offers no hint of inner thoughts or feelings that might give others the upper hand. For more aggressive paranoids, however, there is a considerable use of facial muscles and probing eyes that send a signal to others: "Don't mess with me."

Quick body movements are common, like raising the hands in self-defense if the paranoid Arguer hears or sees something out of the ordinary. They are ever ready to defend themselves by launching a first strike. The gait reveals an edgy rigidity that inhibits grace and blocks kinesthetic enjoyment of movement or sensual appreciation of their surroundings.

Adjunct pharmacological treatment may enhance the receptivity to psychotherapy in some paranoid Arguers. A low dose of antidepressant medication that incorporates anti-anxiety and anti-compulsive features may considerably reduce the aggressive tension that pervades the Mind and Heart, Body and Spirit (Triebwasser & Siever, 2006). Neutralizing compulsive ruminations can diminish the paranoid's chronic re-processing of negative social memories and allow the learning and development of more socially constructive behavior.

Compass Therapy suggests that some paranoid Arguers experience agitated depression—an undercurrent of unhappiness and discontent that manifests itself as a need to lash out. Reducing physiological anxiety through relaxation training can facilitate enough wellbeing to allow repressed feelings of vulnerability and inferiority to surface, promoting the integration of the Weakness compass point. This in turn can open up the Love compass point for experiments with love, forgiveness, and belonging.

When the counselee has shown sufficient psychological and spiritual stability for at least six months, the therapist can oversee an experimental attempt to wean off any psychopharmacological agents. However, if the original underpinnings of the paranoid pattern start to manifest— restlessness, irritability, distrustfulness, hypervigilance, rumination, and angry aggression—then there is a good chance the counselee may need medical support for a normal life. The therapist can frame this in the same category as needing reading or distance glasses in order to have 20/20 vision.

Spirit

For the paranoid pattern, therapeutic techniques recede to the background and the human relationship itself takes the foreground. You might say that even psychology plays a secondary and supportive role to ontology: the existential encounter between two persons searching for a truth that can be lived and not just talked about.

The Arguer begins therapy on the most dubious of terms, like an ice skater who sticks to the shoreline because of massive fears and urgent beliefs that skating toward the center of the pond will necessarily result in falling through the ice and drowning. In other words, the paranoid has never experienced a human relationship that worked out well, a relationship where trust led to self-disclosure that developed reciprocal caring and grew into a reliable companionship.

While the therapist gives up the need to change the paranoid's mind or lifestyle, the therapist nevertheless offers a relationship that can grow into a positive bond. How do you do this with someone who is negative, suspicious, and just looking for an excuse to nail you to the wall? You seek to establish a calm, objective, and genuine respect for the counselee as a person, while keeping in mind that the paranoid pattern limits prospects for health and happiness (Meissner et al., 1996).

The first movement of therapy involves tentatively taking the counselee's side in their need to blame others for their state of distress. At the same time, you plant new seeds of awareness about the restrictive nature of the paranoid pattern. I call this dual dynamic the rhythm between *conditional alignment* and *collaborative implantation* (Montgomery, 2006, pp. 167-171).

Counselee: "The people I supervise at work are a bunch of lazy bastards who need me to spy on them and crack the whip when they're slacking off."

Therapist: "You feel put out by these sluggards and get a bit nasty to keep them in line."

Over time the Arguer learns that you don't buy their whole spiel, especially about painting themselves as innocent characters, and that you are confronting them while at the same time respectfully identifying with them. Paradoxically, this increases their trust in your judgment as one who cannot be hoodwinked, but who is sympathetic to their concerns.

The next movement involves probing into what childhood and adolescent experiences they remember as especially painful, humiliating, and demonstrative of people's untrustworthiness. You do this indirectly, so as not to engage their defenses.

Counselee: "I've timed my wife before when she's gone grocery shopping and it usually takes her thirty minutes to get everything. But the last two times she's gone shopping she didn't come back for forty-five minutes."

Therapist: "I'm curious about something. This feeling you get inside, this overwhelming sense that you can't trust her...When was the first time you recall having that feeling about someone?"

In this way you help the counselee bypass their defenses and begin talking about the emotional pain of earlier years. It won't be long before they are reliving and releasing those feelings—shame, terror, rejection, betrayal, jealousy, envy, or helplessness—the very emotions that made them decommission the Weakness compass point.

Yet because you are standing with them in these cathartic moments, they are internalizing new experiences of trust, vulnerability, and caring that are not used against them. This shows them that they can face and process negative feelings with another person in a positive way that brings relief and inner peace. It's not long before they begin sharing current anxieties about new situations more openly.

Then it's time to talk about the paranoid pattern itself. The little tidbits of information and interpretation you've been offering selectively all along begin to take hold. Now the counselee can hear directly about the pattern without reacting defensively in denial or hostility.

Counselee: "So after I asked for the raise I sat there for a full minute. I figured he was thinking of all the ways he could deny the raise and put me down. I almost stomped out of the office to beat him to the punch. But then I thought, 'Quit trying to read his mind. Let him say whatever he wants and then you can deal with it.'"

Therapist: "That's impressive. Here your old paranoid pattern was trying to talk you into judging the guy and stampeding out to show him up, and then your new insights kicked in and gave you the courage to hear him out."

Counselee: "Yeah, and I'm glad I didn't push it, because when he spoke up, he said he'd been thinking of several reasons I deserved the raise, and was glad I'd brought it up."

The next movement has to do with health psychology and spirituality. Here is what I said to the man I've been describing in this case:

Dan: "Evan, you've come a long way in learning to trust your spiritual core and process what's happening in relationships without jumping to conclusions. I wonder if you might consider adding a few moments of meditation or prayer to your life each day, asking for discernment between times when you can benefit from some of the paranoid's honest insight into people's motives, and times when the paranoid pattern is about to shoot you in the foot."

Evan: "I've never thought much of prayer, but I'll keep it in mind."

The final movement deals with consolidation of therapeutic gains. Here you reinforce Self Compass principles when you hear the counselee using them. You seek to cognitively, emotionally, and spiritually strengthen the compass points in order to help make the transition from short-term memory to lifetime learning, employing a light touch.

Counselee: "I got my wife some flowers this week just for the heck of it. She's really warmed up to me now that I don't bug her about her time away from home."

Therapist: "That's a creative use of your Love compass point. And I like how you're developing a better integration

117

of Strength and Weakness. It's made you more relaxed and trusting of her."

Counselee: "It's sure made a difference in her."

Working with a counselee stuck in the paranoid Arguer pattern can feel exasperating at the beginning, but once you establish boundaries that let you speak honestly about the pattern, and once the Arguer begins to see that what you say has merit, the therapy moves forward much as with any other counselee. Just keep your relaxed vigilance intact, so you are prepared for any sudden attacks on your insight, motives, or credibility, because these are likely to occur even though the counselee is making decent progress.

9
ANTISOCIAL RULE-BREAKER PATTERN

Compass Therapy holds that the antisocial Rule-breaker pattern functions on a continuum from mild to severe. Many creative individuals break rules when they favor innovation over social conformity. However, hardened antisocials exaggerate Assertion (which leads to guilt-free aggression) and Strength (which leads to cockiness) at the expense of caring from Love and humility from Weakness (Mitchell et al., 2006). The therapeutic growth strategy, then, involves increasing Love and Weakness to neutralize and balance the otherwise reckless use of Assertion and Strength.

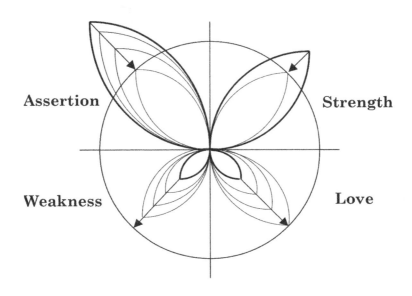

The Pattern's Interior

Compass theory employs the term "Rule-breaker" as a significant feature of the antisocial mindset because it reflects a willful stand to live outside the boundaries of custom and the rule of law, and because counselees readily understand the term.

On the positive side, most children and adolescents normally experiment with breaking rules as part of their coming of age, discovering their personal power over-and-against the socializing forces of a tribe, family, religion, or schooling. Carl Jung (1989) experienced this phenomenon as a child, when he carved a little manikin and hid it under an attic slat where no one could find or harm it. He later wrote that the ability to possess and keep this secret helped provide him with a personal identity.

Antisocial persons know how to play their cards close to their chest, and though they often trust no one but themselves, as was true for Beethoven, they can also band together to challenge tradition, express rebellion, and break the law, as did the writers of the Declaration of Independence. During therapy I often compliment an antisocial Rule-breaker for their resistance to enculturation, which Abraham Maslow (1971) considered a prerequisite for the pursuit of self-actualization.

A healthy dose of antisocial sentiment fosters the willingness to take risks, test boundaries, think outside the box, and not take someone else's "no" as the last word on a possible goal or action. Einstein's biographer explains that Einstein so hated formal schooling that he devised a scheme by which he received a medical excuse from school on the grounds of a potential nervous breakdown. He convinced a mathematics teacher to certify that he was capable to begin college studies without a high school diploma (Frank, 2002).

However, these positives reach the point of diminishing returns when an aggressive trend constricts into a rigid template. Now the antisocial Rule-breaker pattern overtakes the personality. Callous adventurism eclipses compassion or sensitivity to others (Raine et al., 2004).

Suspicion and hostility are common to both the Rule-breaker and Arguer patterns, the clear indication of an exaggerated Assertion compass point. But Rule-breakers are more opportunistic, impulsive, and shamelessly exploitive than Arguers. Nor do Rule-breakers cultivate secretive persecutory delusions, since they are quite open about touting "the law of the jungle" as the wisest philosophy of life.

While paranoid histories can include humiliating failures that reveal the discrepancy between their glorified self-image and lack of personal development, antisocial Rule-breakers are notably resourceful. They learn from life experience that little will be achieved without substantial effort and cunning, and that desired goals must be accomplished by one's actions (Kotler & McMahon, 2005).

If Rule-breakers overly use the upper quadrants of the Self Compass, what happens to the lower quadrants? The Love compass point is warped into a façade of charm that masks the hidden intent to exploit. The Rule-breaker represses feelings of tenderness, for this would give others the edge. The avoidance of healthy Weakness keeps them from empathizing with other's pain or admitting any faults. It is precisely this lack of empathy combined with entitlement that creates a "superego lacunae"—a massive deficiency in social conscience (Kernberg, 1984). Thus a Rule-breaker is streetwise, glib, and able to lie convincingly, and is well equipped to exploit people's weaknesses or trust.

The antisocial pattern sometimes combines with narcissistic, histrionic, or schizoid patterns, which serve the antisocial by adding features of grandiosity (distorted Strength), extroverted charm (distorted Love), or lone wolf cunning (distorted Weakness). Antisocial Rule-breakers use their creativity to assimilate characteristics drawn from other patterns in order to better manipulate others while camouflaging their true intent.

Rule-breaker Pattern

Compass Point: Assertion

Manipulation: Deceitful & Exploitive

Thoughts: Callous & Defiant

Feelings: Cool to Malicious

Actions: Irresponsible to Belligerent

Growth Needs: Caring & Trusting

Origins

Either extreme indulgence or excessive harshness can influence a child's rejection of social values. Children who do not internalize parental values are disposed to seek immediate gratification through impulsive behaviors. This leads to low frustration tolerance, indifference to people's welfare, and actively deceiving others for personal gain or pleasure.

Infants who experience neglect or abuse have difficulty developing an attachment bond. If this persists, children can develop an active mistrust in others, concluding that relationships offer more pain than gratification. They can abandon the quest for intimacy in favor of manipulating parents and siblings to meet their needs.

Those antisocial children who become overtly aggressive are often either modeling a parent's behavior and/or rebelling against what they consider intolerable conditions at home. Usually bright, these children take over control of the family (Benjamin, 2003). They feel little remorse because they have not developed a solid attachment to anyone. As youths, they can develop a rebellious mindset, showing reckless disregard for their own or other's safety, vindictive gratification in humiliating others, delight in challenging taboos, defiance in the face of threats of punishment, and repeated verbal insults and/or physical assaults. Corollary behaviors can include truancy, vandalism, stealing, sexual promiscuity, and substance abuse. Such children seem addicted to risk and excitement, flouting social convention and breaking rules (Dadds et al., 2005).

One study cites the best predictors of adult antisocial behavior as callous/unemotional conduct, depression, and marijuana use (Loeber et al., 2002). Other studies list alcohol and substance abuse as prominent contributors that intercept normal development by promoting the progression toward an antisocial lifestyle (Myers et al., 1998; Bauer, 2001; Bahlmann et al., 2002). The increase in published reports of violence committed by adolescents shows that therapists need to pay special attention to antisocial pathology among their adolescent counselees. The combination of drugs and alcohol may cause these adolescents to engage in more violent acts as adults.

Of note are results from the Greifswalder Family Study that correlate the negative modeling of parental drinking with the incidence of antisocial personality disorder among their children (Barnow et al., 2007).

Clinical Literature

The pattern of behavior that *DSM* nomenclature presently defines as the antisocial personality disorder was described in nineteenth century clinical literature as "moral insanity," in which "the moral or active principles of the mind are strangely perverted or depraved" (Pritchard, 1835, p. 85).

The original perception concerning the term "psychopathic personality" later came to include a broader definition that encompassed such traits as guiltlessness, incapacity for love, impulsivity, failure to learn, untruthfulness, and superficial social charm (Cleckley, 1964). Others described the antisocial pattern as the "manipulative personality" (Bursten, 1972), the "impulse ridden character" (Reich, 1976), and "pure interpersonal hostility" (Kiesler, 1996).

More recently, the term "sociopathic" has replaced "psychopathic" to reflect the social rather than the purely psychological origins of the pattern. In agreement with Millon, I view the current *DSM* designation of the "antisocial personality disorder" as overemphasizing delinquent and criminal behaviors (Millon & Grossman, 2007b). A number of contemporary studies focus on the organizing principle of nonconformity rather than criminality as the defining trait of the antisocial pattern (Vasey et al., 2005; Vien & Beech, 2006).

Mind

The therapist can offer reflections and interpretations that not only show empathy for Rule-breaker counselees, but also help them become aware of the cognitive self-talk that underlies the antisocial pattern:

+ I disdain traditional ideals and hold conventional ethics in contempt (Blair et al., 2005).

+ I have no guilt about using and discarding others when I no longer need them.

+ I take pleasure in shrewdness, calculation, and the transgression of social codes (Martens, 2005).

+ I can wear a mask of helpful civility to hide my true intentions (Salekin et al., 2005).

+ Openness and caring are signs of weakness. If I run into a kind and attentive psychotherapist, I'll "take him (or her) for a ride" (Benjamin, 2003, p. 212).

✦ I don't mind escalating into verbal threats or physical violence if it gets me what I want.

✦ I will never be caught. I'm always ahead of the law, the regulatory boards, and the gatekeepers.

✦ I think people should have access to all the alcohol and drugs they want.

Antisocials typically block a therapist from any transactions that resemble moralizing, yet respect tough-minded challenging that resonates with their strong-willed posture (Glasser, 1965, 2001). In a way akin to Reality Therapy, Compass Therapy meets the antisocial at the level of concrete operations, where they are cognitively fixated, and nudges them forward toward abstract thinking.

By connecting behavior with its logical consequences, and developing interpersonal perspective that anticipates their behavioral impact on others, counselees learn how to increase non-exploitive exchanges with individuals and institutions in daily life. This growth strategy is very similar to coaching a rebellious teenager into a more proactive life.

Heart

Because antisocials are quickly bored with normal routines, they often have difficulties in relationships, marriage, or at work (Blair et al., 2006). Having little or no frustration tolerance, they seek immediate gratification of needs and instincts. This impatience is partially why they develop an independent existence outside of social networks and disdain conventional pathways that lead toward education, employment, and achievement.

Likewise, they are prone to cheat on tests, job hop, seek extramarital flings, and illegally generate income through embezzlement, credit card fraud, tax evasion, selling drugs, prostitution, get-rich-quick schemes, or borrowing money from friends and relatives with no intention of paying them back.

This self-serving attitude leads to an emotional truncation that prevents them from learning how to handle normal anxiety or interpersonal emotions. Life boils down to pleasure versus pain and the ardent pursuit of hedonistic short-term thrills. Yet this quick-fix quest for continuous ecstasy backfires because it builds a backlog of turbulent emotions that remain raw and unprocessed. There is no way to successfully beat down the ominous anxiety that accompanies living a double life, keeping track of one's lies, struggling with unpaid bills and legal repercussions, or being haunted by surreal dreams. Primal emotions of terror and rage nip at the heels of consciousness as Rule-breakers use all their energy to keep one step ahead of others and have a good time.

While every therapist goes about this differently, a major dimension of therapy consists of helping antisocial counselees cathart their pain from the past, develop healthy ways to handle anxiety and anger, and take new risks in relationships that generate enough mutuality to give them a first emotional taste of love, trust, and companionship.

This process of becoming more human gradually overcomes their deficits in emotional processing (Habel et al., 2002). Beck et al. (2007) suggest that therapist qualities particularly valuable when working with antisocial counselees include self-assurance, a relaxed and non-defensive interpersonal style, a lively sense of humor, and a clear sense of what you will go along with and what you won't.

The ultimate goal of therapy with antisocial Rule-breakers centers around forming a collaborative nurturing attachment that is nevertheless immune to their wiles.

Body

Bio-psychological characteristics that correlate with antisocial personality disorders in childhood and adolescence include reduced excitability, decreased behavioral inhibition, low autonomic baseline arousal, low orienting reactions, accelerated habituation, and increased thrill seeking (Vloet et al., 2006).

The use of psychotropic agents targeted at particular symptoms such as aggressive outbursts, hyperactivity, impulsivity, and mood can increase the overall effectiveness of therapeutic intervention. Antidepressants, antipsychotics (risperidone), mood stabilizers, antiepileptic drugs, stimulants, and adrenergic drugs can provide effective options for individuals with conduct disorder (Tcheremissine & Lieving, 2006; Hirose, 2001; Mulder, 1996).

Despite the cool exterior and superficial charm, an antisocial's body is riddled with muscular tension. Studies show that the antisocial Rule-breaker is the most frequent personality disorder among alcoholics, perhaps a consequence of self-medicating their chronic bodily discomfort (Hesselbrock et al., 1985).

Once sufficient therapeutic trust is established with the antisocial counselee, muscular relaxation exercises and abdominal breathing techniques are effective in establishing a physical wellbeing that is not chemically dependent. Though an antisocial counselee will at first fend off these exercises, calling them ridiculous and unneeded, the persistent therapist may find an opening to complete a relaxation-training procedure that provides the person with a first-hand experience of the intoxicating pleasure of visceral serenity.

By developing a baseline of physiological relaxation through psychological techniques and/or pharmacological support, the antisocial can begin to actually feel emotions instead of steeling the body against them. Buried memories of interpersonal anxiety can find admission to consciousness by exploring constructive ways of integrating sensing, feeling, and thinking.

Counselee: "When Mom called I didn't just hold the phone away from my ear and let her go on and on."

Therapist: "You mean you actually attended to what she was saying?"

Counselee: "Well, like we've been working on here, I didn't just hear her, but I felt the feelings that were building inside me."

Therapist: "That's quite an advance. What did you discover?"

Counselee: "That I've always been irritated by the one-sided conversation she has with me. She just talks about herself and never asks about me."

Therapist: "And so the emotion you were feeling was—"

Counselee: "Anger. But I didn't let her have it."

Therapist: "Oh?"

Counselee: "No. I put together inside myself what I wanted to say. Then I took a couple of deep breaths. I stopped her at the end of a sentence, and said, "Mom, I don't like when you just talk about yourself. If you want me to stay on the phone, then ask something about me."

Therapist: "That was brave of you. I can see where you were showing sensitivity too. It's like you were actually laying out new guidelines for how to have a successful conversation together. How did she react?"

Counselee: "She must have got really mad, because there was silence for about thirty seconds. Then she said, 'Okay, what is happening in your life?' I told her a couple of things and then we hung up. But that was the first two-way conversation we've ever had."

Therapist: "I am amazed how well you handled your temper with her, and also how in touch you were with your inner feeling. What did you feel like after you hung up?"

Counselee: "I was kind of jittery, I guess from the anger, but also because we actually made some kind of emotional connection, and that's really new."

Spirit

Antisocial Rule-breakers harbor a dark secret. They are locked in mortal combat with all humanity, yet in every crowd they are alone. An inner void bleaches out life even around close family. How tedious is the life sentence of passing time on planet Earth with other human mammals that are no more to you than objects in the food chain of a dog-eat-dog world.

Orlando came into therapy as a referral from his pastor. During our first three sessions he seemed distant and determined to keep our conversation at a surface level. About the only thing I knew for sure was that he was under a court order to see a therapist or go to jail.

Halfway through the fourth session, I said, "Orlando, you are very skilled at not disclosing anything important about yourself. I want to respect this. I know you want me to write the judge to say you are making progress in therapy, but ethically I cannot do this. If you don't want us to go deeper, then we can end this session now and I won't charge you for it. Then you can handle the judge however you want. What would you like to do?"

Orlando looked distraught and shifted into a tactic:

Orlando: "Please, Dr. Montgomery, don't go and make me leave therapy. The judge will send me to jail. You're my only hope of staying free."

This maneuver was designed to make Orlando appear innocent about his non-disclosure and make me feel guilty about sending him to a terrible fate.

Dan: "If you want to do therapy, then let's get to it. But superficial chitchat doesn't cut the mustard."

Orlando: "Okay, I'm here because I got mad at my girlfriend and restrained her in a cabin for an afternoon. She called the police when I let her go and they took me to jail for false imprisonment even though I meant no harm by it."

Dan: "How did you feel when she reported you?"

Orlando: "I wanted to knock her head off but I was afraid she'd cause me even worse trouble, so I kept my mouth shut. My attorney worked out a deal with the judge because I don't have a record and because I served in the army. The judge said to see a therapist or go to jail, and the attorney said, 'Don't talk to your girlfriend until you get some anger-management training.' That's it."

I felt impressed with the plausibility of Orlando's story, but more than that, I sensed traces of genuine human feeling as he shared it.

Dan: "Okay. That's a decent start. Can we agree that your goals are to learn to handle your anger, to develop man/woman communication so that you don't commit major crimes on your dates, and show the judge good reason to keep you out of the slammer?"

Orlando: "I can go for that."

After this delayed launch we set about forming a tentative therapeutic alliance. Before long I found out that a sadistic older brother had verbally abused Orlando for years, and that in self-protection he had adapted a survival strategy of keeping everything to himself while hating his brother intensely.

After high school, he joined the army as a way of leaving home. But with that move he jumped from the proverbial frying pan into the fire. Harsh treatment in boot camp by a sadistic sergeant intensified his inward rage. He perfected his skills for fortifying a façade of cooperation to keep off the sergeant's radar. However, nothing worked to save him from the terror of military combat. In a particular series of sessions he relived the horrors of being trapped in a foxhole with bombs bursting all around, being sent on reconnaissance missions where he knew a bullet could strike him at any moment, and the deaths of fellow soldiers.

He was deeply moved one day when I said he had showed true heroism in surviving his brother, the sadistic drill sergeant, and the enemy soldiers who had sought to kill him. Then I asked how far he was willing to go to regain the humanness they had conspired to take away.

Orlando: "I never thought of myself as a hero of anything," he said with tears in his eyes. "I always thought of myself as a coward who couldn't face up to life."

It is this kind of vulnerability that reflects an antisocial counselee's first fearful contact with the Weakness compass point. I wasn't about to let this go unrewarded.

Dan: "Not only are you a brave man, Orlando, but there's a deep strain of humility in you. Somehow you feel embarrassed about taking legitimate credit for your courage and resourcefulness."

Orlando: "But I'm not resourceful. I still hate everybody. I don't trust anybody. I'm just out for myself."

Dan: "What about your girlfriend. Do you hate her?"

Orlando: "That's the hell of it. I love her but when she doesn't do what I want, I treat her really bad. I don't blame her for calling the police."

It took these two months of therapy before Orlando was able to straightforwardly take responsibility for his original arrest. He still had no contact with his girlfriend for fear of getting into worse trouble. My counsel in the matter had been that premature conversation with her would likely prove disastrous, but that if he established a track record of anger-management and interpersonal savvy, she might be amenable to a more mature companionship.

Having experienced several emotional catharses to exorcise the psychic wounds of his military experience, we turned to the issue of his brother who was in a local hospital dying of cancer. It was here that I introduced the topic of spirituality as a possible resource.

Dan: "It sounds like your brother is on his last legs. Is there any unfinished business with your brother that you'd like to take care of before he dies?"

Orlando: "No. He's a bastard and I hate him. I'm glad he has cancer."

Dan: "I can understand that. He treated you like dirt all those years and you wanted to strangle him. My only concern is that you're dying of the cancer of hatred right along with him."

Orlando: "What do you mean?"

Dan: "The revenge you feel, the gloating over his condition. These are understandable emotions. But if they get forever trapped inside you, then they'll poison you and your girlfriend and increase the darkness inside you—that feeling that life has no meaning except for triumphing over others."

Orlando: "But he hates me too!"

Dan: "How about if you pray for him? That you wish him well in his last hours of pain and torment."

Orlando: (Laughing). "I'm not about to do that. God might go over there and heal him!"

Dan: "I'm thinking that maybe God will heal you."

Orlando told me later that he not only prayed for his brother, but also had decided to pay him a last visit in hospital. They were very wary of each other at first, but then tears came to them both. The brother died three days later.

There were many other issues that Orlando had to face and develop new responses for handling: the anger that could so easily flare up and threaten his evolving social existence; the freedom that the judge finally awarded him; the interpersonal communication with the girlfriend who continued dating him once she saw evidence of more stable behavior; the awkwardness and impatience he felt in holding down a new job; and the ever-present temptation to bail out of real human relationships and pursue the abyss of manipulation and conning.

In one of the last sessions of our ninth and last month of therapy I suggested that he might keep a daily spiritual vigilance to remind himself that he was not in this life alone—that there were other people who cared about him and knew of his bravery, and that included me.

Don't be afraid of the antisocial Rule-breaker counselee, and don't open yourself to a full level of trust either. Remember that this counselee is well practiced in deceit and has an unconscious agenda to pull the wool over your eyes as they have done with a long line of others. On the other hand, you can develop enough "cash and carry" trust to conduct meaningful conversations, forming a positive transference that creates an opportunity for the counselee to bond with you successfully enough to let you move within their psyche with significant healing agency.

Also keep in mind a referral to a local Twelve-Step group if substance abuse is part of the picture. Because of its nature as a spiritual fellowship, Twelve-Step participation is found to improve psychosocial functioning and increase the commitment to change, as well as reduce drinking and drug use (Emrick et al., 1993; Tonigan et al., 1996).

10
AVOIDANT WORRIER PATTERN

Weakness is built into the human condition. While most people learn to accept their weaknesses and work to overcome them, counselees stuck in the avoidant Worrier pattern do not. Persons become stuck on the Weakness compass point because they are trapped with a pervasive fear of life and overriding sense of being in danger. The solution, from the weakness-stuck person's point of view, is to pursue safety at all costs, and this requires taking no risks. Naturally, the resulting lifestyle of arrested development is inflexible and socially impoverished (Grilo, 2004).

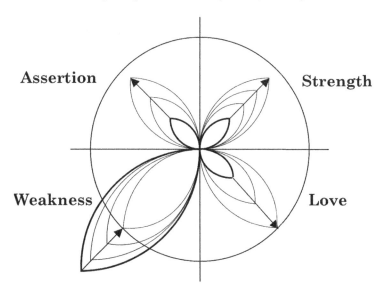

The paradox is this: though avoidant Worriers possess the capability for a fulfilling life, their interpersonal anxiety compels them to avoid opportunities for growth, discount compliments, and minimize accomplishments (Grant et al., 2004). Unfortunately, this only increases their ruminations about their undesirability and painful isolation (Johnson et al., 2005; Skodol, Oldham, et al., 2005).

The Pattern's Interior

The exaggeration of weakness, accompanied by an abandonment of the Strength compass point, locks the Worrier-patterned person into a lifestyle of helplessness and incompetence. Worriers see themselves as inadequate and boring, lacking enough skill or intelligence to succeed.

Although the longing for intimacy remains strong, they do not build successful relationships because fear of rejection or ridicule overwhelms them. Therefore they hold back from friendships and avoid social encounters to guard against the risk of disappointment. Nor do they stand up for themselves, preferring to retreat instead.

The avoidant pattern exists as a pure prototype of fixation on the Weakness compass point with withdrawn trends, but in some cases bonds with an adjacent compass point of either Love or Assertion. In the case of Love, the Worrier develops dependent submission to another person. In the case of Assertion, the Worrier develops paranoid prickliness or antisocial hostility. In every instance, however, the opposite polarity of Strength is shut down and prohibited from expression.

For the Worrier counselee, potential energy from the Strength compass point collapses into the sinkhole of a failure mentality. Avoidant persons bring this mindset with them into therapy. It is challenging for the therapist to initiate growth stretches from the Weakness compass point into the Strength, Assertion, and Love compass points, since Worriers reflexively reject change.

When the therapist begins to offer assistance, the Worrier can manufacture excuse after excuse to sabotage any growth steps. Eric Berne (1994) termed this game, "Why don't you—Yes, but...." The novice therapist says, "Why don't you try (this or that)...." The counselee replies, "Yes, but I did that once and it didn't work," or "Yes that's a good idea, but it feels too scary to try." In essence, this is the same kind of foot-dragging that has exasperated a long line of people who have listened sympathetically to the Worrier's woes and sought to offer help.

Even though the avoidant Worrier's personality pattern sabotages growth and development, it appears to Worriers as if other people's frustration with them is confirming their fundamental assumption: "People don't like me. I can't do anything right." This self-blame for their lack of social connection intensifies the self-alienation that reinforces their isolation from others (Huprich, 2005).

To break out of this avoidant cycle of restricting choices requires actualizing growth toward the LAWS of a whole Self Compass. The therapist works patiently to find entrée into the person's self by stimulating small steps into other compass points, creating movement within the personality that equals aliveness rather than fearfulness. Only slowly through the warmth and encouragement of the therapeutic relationship does the spiritual core show new signs of life. A synergistic momentum helps to overcome deficiencies in experiencing the pleasures of life by opening doors for love, hope, achievement, and joy (Hans et al., 2004).

For Davies, the avoidant needs to build co-operation (Love), confidence (Strength) and aggressive forms of behavior (Assertion) to develop their intellectual ability, aptitudes, and motivation (1991).

Initial Reflections

As a therapist you can't go wrong offering initial reflections that capture elements of the Worrier's inner perceptual field. You work at first to restate exactly what the counselee is disclosing. Only gradually, as rapport deepens, do you respond with an interpretative edge, making the avoidant pattern more ego-dystonic by disclosing how the rigid pattern opposes the person's wellbeing.

In this regard Compass Therapy resonates with the spirit of Motivational Interviewing (Miller & Rollnick, 2002), a client-centered, semi-directive method of engaging intrinsic motivation to change behavior by developing discrepancy between a counselee's self and what is harming them, and then exploring and resolving this ambivalence by helping the counselee formulate healthier growth aims.

Here are some possible interpretations for the Worrier:

+ "So from what you are saying, your avoidance has created difficulties for you when people are around, but by yourself you think clearly. Could it be that you have more relational intelligence than you imagine, but just haven't felt motivated to develop it?"

+ "Are you afraid that longing for love will result in a repetition of the pain you've experienced with someone in the past, when actually you'd like to feel close to someone now?"

+ "Who do you suppose had so much power over you that they helped cause you to retreat from all relationships? If this person vanished from your history, would you feel free to try again?"

+ "You've said you live marginally to avoid risks. But could it represent an even greater risk to stay the way you are?"

+ "If you had interpersonal confidence, what would you do differently this week?"

```
╔══════════════════════════════════════════════╗
║  ┌──────────────────────────────────────────┐ ║
║  │           **Worrier Pattern**            │ ║
║  │                                          │ ║
║  │  Compass Point: Weakness                 │ ║
║  │                                          │ ║
║  │  Manipulation: Helpless & Passive        │ ║
║  │                                          │ ║
║  │  Thoughts: Deprecating & Foreboding      │ ║
║  │                                          │ ║
║  │  Feelings: Guarded to Anxious            │ ║
║  │                                          │ ║
║  │  Actions: Lethargic to Avoidant          │ ║
║  │                                          │ ║
║  │  Growth Needs: Assertion & Confidence    │ ║
║  └──────────────────────────────────────────┘ ║
╚══════════════════════════════════════════════╝
```

Origins

Worrier-patterned persons usually experience loving nurturance from their family of origin during infancy. They develop an attachment bond that motivates them to want social contact with others. But subsequently they are subjected to regular humiliation. An overly judgmental parent can criticize them for not doing things perfectly, or mock them for making mistakes.

Research indicates that some children are over-sensitive to criticism from their parents because they are born with a genetic predisposition toward inhibited and fearful responses (Kagan, 1994). They withdraw or cry when faced with new or strange situations. If their parents respond by ridiculing them, it reinforces an already preferred response of avoidance. They receive a defeating message from their family: "You are flawed and nobody out there will like you. Stay with us, where it is safe" (Benjamin, 2003, p. 293).

Learning theory suggests a "learned helplessness" to explain avoidant behavior. This can develop by repeatedly experiencing fearful events over which persons perceive they have no control, resulting in helpless behavior (Meyers, 1995).

Clinical Literature

Avoidant Worriers retreat from human interaction even though they are often creative and emotionally sensitive. Their hypersensitivity is demonstrated by "affects (that) are so powerful...they must avoid everything which might arouse their emotions," notes Bleuler. "The apathy toward the outer world is then a secondary one springing from a hypertrophied sensitivity" (1950, p. 65).

Philosopher Sören Kierkegaard recorded in his journal how he viewed himself as "melancholy, soul-sick, profoundly and absolutely a failure in many ways" (Dru, 1959). The burden of this sorrowful existence is captured in Emil Kretschmer's (1925) description of the "hyperaesthetic type." "There is a constant self-analysis and comparison: 'How do I impress people? Who is doing me an injury? How shall I get through?' This is particularly true of gifted, artistic natures...They are (people)...whose life is composed of a chain of tragedies, a single thorny path of sorrow."

Karl Menninger (1930) described the avoidant Worrier as the "isolated personality" who is prone to failure in social situations—as "wistful 'outsiders' who long to dive into the swim of things and either don't know how or are held back by (inculcated) restraining fears."

While Worriers may be talented in solitary endeavors, the interpersonal anxiety that plagues them causes an overload of core fear. Kurt Schneider (1950) called the avoidant pattern the "aesthenic personality," citing "a deeply rooted insecurity and the lack of any robust self-confidence. This type is continually ridden with a bad conscience and are the first to blame themselves for anything that goes wrong. They are people forever dissatisfied with themselves through life."

Portrayals such as these affirm the present day perspective that a biological predisposition to generalized anxiety and depression can exist within the avoidant Worrier pattern. In fact, the characteristics of the avoidant Worrier are frequently cited in the literature on depression (Skodal et al., 2005).

Mind

The automatic self-talk of Worriers is self-deprecating. Yet the therapist need not fall under the spell of grimness, but can respond in innovative ways that invite the counselee's exploration into the Strength, Assertion, and Love compass points. Playful exploration in itself, as long as empathic rapport is constantly replenished, provides part of the antidote for bringing a spirit of risk-taking and adventure into the counselee's life. By showing trust in the counselee's ability to handle what you are saying, you are expressing a respect for the counselee's strength that is contagious.

Worrier: "I'd like to be accepted, but I know that people are out to ridicule me." Therapist: "An interesting motto you might try out is, 'A stranger is a friend I haven't made yet.'"

Worrier: "No matter how hard I try, nothing works out. Sometime I feel like just giving up." Therapist: "I think most of humanity knows that feeling. What do you suppose can help someone who feels that way to eventually succeed?"

Worrier: "Dreams and fantasy are better than reality." Therapist: "The imagination is a wonderful tool for creative living. I agree that you're very talented that way."

Worrier: "No one is as scared and embarrassed as I am." Therapist: "You might have to include me in that category. I faced several situations last week where I felt some anxiety."

Worrier: "I'm always the last person to arrive somewhere and the first to leave." Therapist: "That's an amazing accomplishment. What would happen this week if you arrived first somewhere and left last? Would people die of shock?" (This introduces humor to de-catastrophize the negative mindset).

Worrier: "I can't stand disappointment." Therapist: "That puts you into the same category as most of the inventors in human history." (This reframes a habitually disempowering perception into a potentially empowering one. It might take time for an idea like this to register, but the counselee's unconscious does take in what you are suggesting).

Though Worriers are typically unwilling to face or discuss their negative thought patterns, when you interact with them in surprising ways, they can smile inside and loosen their tight hold on negativity.

Heart

"Shyness, feelings of inferiority, lack of self-confidence, hypersensitivity, pathological feelings of guilt, emotional instability, panic, and indecision maintain a feeling of weakness which provokes further weak reactions" (Tournier, 1963, p. 27). Worrier-stuck counselees hope for grace but feel guilty. They pine for friendship but feel estranged. They long for success but assume it is out of reach.

It is important to understand that the Worrier-patterned person experiences a confusing undercurrent of sadness, tension, and tentativeness—the logical consequence of being stuck on the Weakness compass point. They feel anguish at every turn, whether it is unrequited desire for affection or terrible fear of rebuff. Since they are so introspective, they are acutely aware of these painful feelings. More often than not, their solution to this turmoil is a self-protective state of numbness and fantasy. Worriers often substitute daydreams about a wish-come-true life for direct involvement in life. But ultimately such a fantasy life only serves to widen the discrepancy between one's imagined life and daily reality. However, the therapist can enlist this use of imagination as part of the therapeutic strategy.

Nora: "I wish I could write children's books so that kids who read them wouldn't have to suffer as much as I do."

Dan: "Fascinating idea. I can just see you holding your first book next to your heart, brimming with pride. Then you get asked to the local elementary school to talk to a third grade class about it and all these kids get to feel your interest in their lives."

Nora: "That can never happen because the teacher in the writing class I'm taking really hurt my feelings this week."

Dan: "I'd like to hear exactly how that happened, but I can't help thinking that this is the very thing that can help you become an emotionally sensitive author."

This dialogue actually occurred during therapy with a counselee who had scored in the 95% range of the avoidant personality disorder, as assessed by the *Millon Clinical Multiaxial Inventory*. She had been committed to a psychiatric unit after a second attempt to slash her wrists, where she read my book *The Self Compass* in the hospital library. Upon release, she entered into psychotherapy with me. We worked through intense memories of sexual abuse in childhood that had left her hating her body and loathing her self. Once she passed through this valley of healing, she went on to author five children's books that provide tender insights into childhood pain.

Sometimes it is helpful to enter into a counselee's perceptual field in order to make adjustments that they can never make by themselves. Compass Therapy supports the Gestalt Therapy principle that by shifting a counselee's inner experiencing of an event, you can facilitate a change in how they will handle a similar event in the future.

This next technique focuses on helping to remove the Worrier's fear of ridicule by facilitating growth stretches toward the Assertion and Strength compass points. Compass Therapy calls this *projection withdrawal* (Montgomery, 2006).

Therapist: "Tell me about what you fear when entering a room filled with people."

Counselee: "I'm afraid they're all looking at me. Judging me. Thinking I'm ridiculous."

Therapist: "Okay, close your eyes and visualize a room full of people. Can you describe a recent social event?"

Counselee: (Closes eyes). "Yeah. Thanksgiving dinner."

Therapist: "Good. Now begin reliving the dinner scenario. What are you feeling?"

Counselee: (Body tenses): "My brother has invited some friends. I feel mortified. I can't wait to get out of here."

Therapist: "So you're frozen like a statue because..."

Counselee: "Because I know they'll hate anything I say and think I'm ridiculous like my brother does."

Therapist: "Now try an experiment. It's safe here. No one can judge you. In your mind's eye look around the table and judge each one of these people, including your brother. Say exactly what makes them look ridiculous to you."

Counselee: "This is hard...Okay, Stevey, the guy across from me, is wearing a ridiculous shirt."

Therapist: "Tell Stevey directly."

Counselee: "Stevey, anybody knows that purple and pink clash. That's the most ridiculous shirt I've ever seen."

Therapist: "Now go to the next person."

Counselee: "Zach, you're fat. Gobbling all the mashed potatoes and pumpkin pie isn't going to help you out!"

Therapist: "Very good. Next person."

Counselee: "There's just one more. Bob, your scruffy beard looks like a mouse lives in it."

Therapist: "And your brother."

Counselee: "Timmy, you're a bully and I hope you fall on your face someday so you'll quit picking on me."

Therapist: "And is there anything ridiculous you'd like to mention to Timmy?"

Counselee: "Your front teeth are crooked."

Therapist: "All right. Now open your eyes. I want to compliment you on completing this experiment even though it took you into unknown territory. What did you discover?"

Counselee: "Well, it was interesting because I started out scared to death like I usually do. But then when I started judging the other people I felt calmer. I even felt excited at the end. But isn't that a terrible thing I just did?"

Therapist: "It was an experiment in withdrawing your projection of strength and assertion from other people and owning these compass points in yourself. In strength you really can make judgments about people and situations. And in assertion, you really can protect yourself by seeing other people's foibles for a change."

Counselee: "That's cool how that worked. I think I'll try thinking that to myself next time."

Therapist: "I look forward to hearing how it goes."

In contradistinction to the active approach just mentioned, a therapist sometimes has to take an opposite tack to keep from becoming enmeshed with the Worrier's passivity. The *joining technique* lets you occupy the Weakness compass point with the counselee, and therefore makes it difficult for the counselee to remain there.

Dan: "So Lester, you're saying that you really want to move out of your parents' house but are afraid to get a job. Right?"

Lester: "I know it's wrong to live there without paying rent, especially now that I'm thirty. But I feel too much anxiety around people to go out and get a job."

Dan: "And what is your current evidence for saying that?"

Lester: "Well, it's not current, but I worked for a bank several years ago and I got very nervous. I know that'll happen again."

Dan: (Because I've tried unsuccessfully to stimulate a willingness to take new risks with this counselee, I shift into joining). "I see your dilemma. You don't want to live at home with your parents, but it's completely impossible to get a job and move out."

Lester: "I wouldn't say it's impossible, but it's something I just can't do."

This slight admission that moving out is not completely impossible signals the beginning of an unconscious shift into the Strength and Assertion compass points. I go even deeper into his Weakness compass point.

Dan: "Exactly. The bank job that made you nervous proved once and for all you can never hold a job."

Lester: "Well, not exactly. I did okay with the math that was involved. And the vice president said I was very reliable. It's just that I got really nervous around certain customers."

Dan: (Now I can offer more support). "So would it be fair to say that if you combine the strengths you showed at the bank with learning how to handle certain people, you might land a new job and move away from home?"

Lester: "I feel some anxiety about it, but it's possible."

Body

Many counselees caught in the avoidant Worrier pattern are made doubly self-conscious by physical symptoms that are activated by an overly aroused sympathetic branch of the autonomic nervous system (the "fight or flight" response) that occurs in the presence of others. These include blushing, sweaty palms, trembling and other physical symptoms.

When asked to speak up, speech can become halting, which only accentuates their self-consciousness and sometimes triggers visceral panic that causes their minds to go blank (Haller & Miles, 2004; Farmer, Nash, & Dance, 2004).

To make matters worse, Worriers absorb every subtlety of other people's voice inflexions, eye movements, and hand gestures, often misinterpreting these as somehow derogatory. This isn't always fantasy, since many Worriers were mercilessly teased in elementary, middle school, or high school. Or they may have experienced comparable humiliation in other social contexts that resulted in keen alertness to any possible sign of ridicule (Dimic et al., 2004; Zimmerman et al., 2005).

There is evidence from physiological psychology that avoidant personalities may experience aversive stimuli more intensely and frequently than others because they possess an especially innervated neural substrate in the "aversive center" of the limbic system. The possible dominance of the sympathetic nervous system can account for the excessive release of adrenaline into the bloodstream, resulting in hyper-vigilance and an easily provoked state of alarm. This hypersensitivity, in turn, creates a mental bias that often misreads even innocent comments or events as somehow critical of the Worrier (Shea et al., 2004).

Such indicators support the notion of a biological predisposition underlying the avoidant pattern. When indicated, an antidepressant can reduce social anxiety and promote a physiological stability that creates a more even playing field for the development of self-confidence (Strength), self-expression (Assertion), and friendship with others (Love) (Scott, 2006; Seedat & Stein, 2004). Additionally, non-addictive minor tranquilizers or beta-blockers can relieve symptoms of autonomic excitation such as blushing, sweating, or trembling (Marchesi et al., 2005).

Paradoxical intention is a therapeutic technique that counters the discomfort from sympathetic system arousal. You might use it, for example, with a counselee with a severe blushing problem that inhibits his participation in a college classroom.

Therapist: "So your greatest fear right now is turning bright red if one of your professors calls on you to speak?"

Counselee: "Yes. I may drop out of college."

Therapist: "Yet if there's a way to overcome this, you'd like to know about it, right?"

Counselee: "Yes. But I need something to help me by to-morrow. It's my turn to give an oral report."

Therapist: "Okay, are you willing to try an experiment?"

Counselee: "Anything's better than the blushing."

Therapist: "Good. I'd like you to pretend right now that tomorrow has arrived and you're about to give your report."

Counselee: (Pauses. Grimaces. Cheeks start to flush). "I'm starting to feel hot."

Therapist: "Excellent. That's just what I want. Now try as hard as you possibly can to start blushing...that's right...start blushing right now so much that *Newsweek* will hear about it and send a reporter to investigate the young man who turned so crimson that the whole world wants to read about it."

Counselee: "That's not fair. You're making me smile and it's hard for me to blush."

Therapist: "I'm sorry. I just want you to concentrate with all your might right now on turning so red that students in the class are afraid they're going to get sunburned. They start passing out sunscreen lotion while you're giving your oral report."

Counselee: (Strains as though trying to push blood into his head).

Therapist: "That's good, but you're not red enough. Try harder to sweat buckets of perspiration that absolutely drench your shirt. I'll personally pay for the dry cleaning bill, but I want the cleaners to testify that this is the most soaked and sweaty shirt they have ever seen."

Counselee: (Frowns with concentration for all he's worth, but then his face relaxes into a grin). "I'm getting a little sweat going, but not as much as usual."

Therapist: "Now this is your last chance in our dress rehearsal for your blushing and sweating performance in class tomorrow. Give it all you've got. Blush with greater radiance than the sun. Pour out buckets of sweat from your armpits—enough to drown the whole U. S. Navy!"

Counselee: (Face turns from red to normal). "I don't know what's wrong. I just can't do it."

Therapist: "That's okay. I appreciate you participating so fully in this experiment. What's going on is that you are consciously interrupting a normally unconscious blushing and sweating response by deliberately willing it to happen. The harder you consciously try to exaggerate the physical symptoms to a comical extreme, the less your autonomic nervous system can manufacture them."

Counselee: "So I'm actually supposed to try very hard to blush in class even if I'm scared to death that I will?"

Therapist: "Exactly. Look at it this way. You have an overly sensitive nervous system that moves into panic at the least sign of embarrassment. So normally, without this technique, your fear that you will blush and sweat plays right into out-of-control blushing and sweating. But when you deliberately take charge of these symptoms and try on purpose to make them even worse to a comical extreme, then paradoxically your nervous system calms down. Before long, the blushing and sweating that have occurred begin to subside."

Counselee: "What if I do start blushing?"

Therapist: "We already know that you will start blushing. Once it starts, your job is to make the blushing redder than ever on purpose. The intention to actively will the symptom is what makes paradoxical intention work."

Counselee: "Okay, I'll give it a try."

Therapist: "Good. Take my voice with you tomorrow."

Spirit

Here are some actualizing affirmations for integrating Strength, Assertion, and Love with healthy Weakness:

- ✦ I'm as intelligent as the next person. The weakness I've known has made me very sensitive to others who suffer. I can exercise this empathy by reaching out to individuals who are still stuck on the Weakness compass point.

- ✦ I may as well press on. Everyone feels scared once in a while. There is growth in the valley. I'll come through this just fine.

✦ I can enjoy both solitude and interaction with people.

✦ I can learn how to handle and express my thoughts and feelings, and to let other people express theirs.

✦ I don't have to sit on the sidelines any longer. For this I am thankful.

✦ I can call upon God and others who love me when I'm feeling especially unlovable.

The main thing to remember in working with avoidant Worriers is not to get caught up in worrying for them. They are used to worry; their lives are steeped in worry. And that worry, like the common cold, is highly contagious.

Just as a physician treating a person with a bad cold washes his or her hands after every examination, so you should wash your hands psychologically and spiritually after every counseling session. I do this by giving the person up to God, saying, "Please guide this Worrier to outgrow the habit of worrying. I will engage them during sessions, but you take it from there. Thanks. Amen."

11
SCHIZOID LONER PATTERN

Actualizing persons interact with the world through rhythms of contact and withdrawal, involvement and detachment, activity and passivity. Contact, involvement, and activity require action to engage in work, relationships, or self-development. Withdrawal, detachment, and passivity allow for resting and sleeping, solitude, and recharging one's batteries. But the schizoid cuts this rhythm in half, fixating on withdrawal, detachment, and passivity. The word schizoid derives from the Greek word *schizoid* and means "split off." All the compass points are collapsed, except for Weakness, which intensifies into nothingness (Kretschmer, 1925).

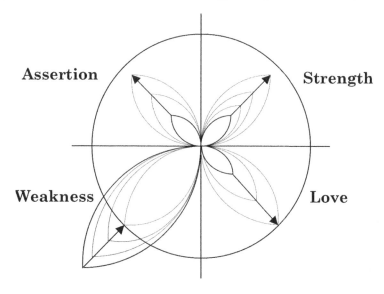

The Pattern's Interior

While the schizoid Loner and avoidant Worrier patterns are both trapped on the Weakness compass point, they distance themselves from people for two different reasons. Worriers are shy and sensitive, yearning for intimacy yet held back by fears of ridicule and rejection. By contrast, Loners withdraw because of "an indifference to everything—to friends and relations, to vocational enjoyment, to duties or rights, to good fortune or bad" (Bleuler, 1950, p. 40). The rewards and pleasures of companionship mean nothing, confining them to inescapable loneliness (Martens, 2010).

Karen Horney noted that schizoids actively "move away from people" by forming an impenetrable shell that makes others fade out of consciousness (1945/1994). The phrase, "Out of sight, out of mind," is not just a credo. It is a daily goal.

Not only do others disappear off their radar screen (West et al., 1995), but their emotions evaporate as well (Haznedar et al., 2004). This life plan has its merits in that schizoid Loners maintain simple lives, untroubled by feelings, impervious to relationships, and undisturbed by inner conflicts. In fact, if a person wants to live an ascetic life that is celibate and single, the schizoid pattern offers the structure and function for doing so. Perhaps this accounts for the secret superiority often noted in schizoid counselees (McWilliams, 1994). Compass theory posits that this tendency reflects the psychodynamics of a tightly repressed Strength compass point that acts out in the form of unconscious narcissism (Montgomery & Montgomery, 2008). Millon notes: "Fantasy in a schizoid-like person sometimes betrays the presence of a secret grandiose self that longs for respect and recognition while offsetting fears that the person is really an outcast" (2004, p. 390).

While everyone needs a rhythm that includes occasional withdrawal and detachment, the schizoid Loner's selection of isolation as a long-term coping pattern leads into dangerous territory: a solitary confinement that begins as a retiring lifestyle, but can spiral into schizotypal eccentricity, possibly leading to several types of schizophrenia (Collins et al., 2005; Giesbrecht, 2007). For this reason Rollo May has described the schizoid life as existentially hollow (1969/2007).

This hollowness reflects the interpersonal truth that human beings need social stimulation, and when they isolate from the rewards and consensual validation society normally provides, their psyche begins to create its own media show: excessive daydreaming, voices that speak from illusory entities, and the formation of an alternate reality that is light years away from normalcy.

In other words, the psychospiritual energy for actualizing growth, when not pursued, doesn't just disappear; unconscious forces convert it into the landscape of the Loner's version of the universe. In Self Compass terms, the Loner-patterned person lacks esteem for self or others (Strength compass point), love for self or others (Love compass point), and courage to take risks for self-development or the bettering of circumstances (Assertion compass point). The energy from these compass points is shunted into exaggerated weakness, creating a barren existence rather akin to the hermit crab.

By applying techniques that balance a healthy Weakness compass point with an awakening of the Strength, Love, and Assertion compass points, therapeutic intervention generates enough aliveness to jump-start the Loner's motivational engine and develop the LAWS of personality.

Loner-Patterned People:

- ⊕ Regard human relationships as messy, problematic, and undesirable. They avoid self-reflection and introspection by living simple lives.

- ⊕ Prefer nonsocial activities like computer games, surfing the net, watching television, or collecting things.

- When social demands at work or at home make them uncomfortable, they retreat and draw into themselves.

- Do not like intrusions on their time or energy. They have a tendency to drift through life.

- Possess a vague and tangential philosophy of life.

- Are content to live within narrow borders by earning a meager livelihood or living parasitically off parents or relatives.

Loner Pattern

Compass Point: Weakness

Manipulation: Detached & Indifferent

Thoughts: Obscure to Barren

Feelings: Solitary to Isolated

Actions: Lethargic to Avoidant

Growth Needs: Involvement & Caring

Origins

Schizoid Loners most likely learned to wall off from others because they perceived their family as distant and aloof. They experienced fragmented family communications from an emotionally unresponsive parent with whom they identified, leading to a weak attachment bond with others in which little was expected or given. While basic physical and educational needs were met, there was little liveliness or fun in family life.

"No one ever talked to me as a child," reports a young woman. "I felt completely invisible, so I got into the habit of watching life go on around me. Eventually I withdrew and quit caring."

Another source of the schizoid pattern lies in a childhood or adolescence steeped in peer rejection or bullying (Beck et al., 2007). One counselee recalled having been rolled up in a gymnastics mat after physical education class in middle school. The bullying boys simply left him there. He wasn't found for almost an hour. This was but one of many such memories that he finally opened up about in therapy.

Children who develop the Loner pattern are disinclined to interact with other children or participate in active games. They prefer to isolate themselves and do their own thing. Awkward in large motor coordination, they draw ridicule from peers that trigger further retreat into a cavern of aloneness.

It is possible that the Loner-patterned person experienced a particularly unsatisfactory emotional relationship with the mother, "who fails to convince her child by spontaneous and genuine expressions of affection that she herself loves him as a person" (Fairbairn, 1940, p. 13). As a result, Loner children become unable to give and receive love (Love compass point).

In addition, either through lack of parental modeling or lack of social motivation, schizoid adolescents stick so much to themselves that they miss out on a whole host of normalizing social skills. These include how to introduce yourself to others, how to begin and end conversations, how to respond reciprocally in a friendship, how to respond emotionally to good news or bad news, and how to set goals for achievement and merit. These personal, emotional, and social deficiencies knock out any learning experiences from the Strength, Love, and Assertion compass points, rendering Loners socially inert and incapable of bonding.

Clinical Literature

In early clinical literature, this pattern was referred to as the "shut-in" personality to describe behavior that defended against anxiety by "shutting out the outside world, a deterioration of interests in the environment, a living in a world apart" (Hoch, 1910). The term, "autistic personality" highlighted Loner tendencies to "narrow or reduce their external interests and contacts" and develop a "preoccupation with inward ruminations" (Kraepelin, 1919).

Eugene Bleuler coined the word "schizoid" and observed that such individuals were "incapable of discussion" (1924, p. 441.) Carl Jung developed his concept of "introversion" in part to describe the social detachment of Loner-patterned persons, remarking that "they have no desire to affect others, to impress, influence, or change them in any way...which may actually turn into a disregard for the comfort and well-being of others" (1921, p. 247).

The current view holds that the schizoid-patterned life is a solitary one characterized by dissociation of the mind from the body and feelings. The result is emotional deadness and social apathy.

Mind

You enhance therapeutic communication with schizoids by understanding the inner workings of their mind and putting into words what they typically think, albeit in their semiconscious and unreflective way. The automatic self-talk of the Loner pattern sounds like this:

⊕ I can do things better when people aren't around.

⊕ I am a loner and an oddity.

158

- Relationships interfere with my freedom.

- People are replaceable objects.

- People should talk only when there's something to say.

- When people are out of sight, they are out of mind.

- I am safe when I am alone.

- I sometimes feel depressed about my boring life.

- I feel lethargic and fatigued much of the time.

- Sometimes life is meaningless. I am nothing.

Heart

There is a fear-based paradox in the schizoid pattern that reflects the unmitigated tensions between a Strength compass point that is deeply repressed and a Weakness compass point that is deeply embraced. The schizoid seeks the pseudo-strength of isolation in an attempt to solve the fear of engulfment and obliteration that enmeshment with others might bring (McWilliams, 1994). Yet this very isolation results in a fear of non-being (that is, total insignificance in the universe) that stems from their inner barrenness (Raja, 2006).

Events that provoke joy, anger, or sadness in others evoke a blank response in the Loner-patterned person. Since they avoid emotional investment, they possess no repository of learning and memory from which to draw intuitive hunches about emotional interactions with others (Collins et al., 2005). This is reflected in their lack of empathy for anyone and completely objective orientation to humanity; that

159

is, people are as significant as chairs or rocks or trees. Emotions, whether positive or negative, are muted to the point of flat affect. "Nothing moves; nothing is alive; everything is dead, including the self. The self by its detachment is precluded from a full experience of realness and aliveness" (Laing, 1960, p. 87).

The Loner views emotional needs or expressions as unnecessary and bothersome. They can go through a day without saying a word. Festive occasions like holidays and birthdays are frequently deadened by their apathy. Family matters are left to coast without direction or communication.

Body

Generally, Loners are so disembodied that they barely breathe, causing a chronic shortage of oxygenated red blood cells to the brain and musculature. This shallow breathing contributes to physical lethargy, mental barrenness, and a clammy handshake. Speech is typically slow and sometimes barely audible. The face is unexpressive and mask-like. Movements lack rhythm or grace.

With such individuals the biogenic component of behavior looms large. Talking therapy is severely limited by the schizoid's low energy level and activation deficiencies that can typically reflect chronic shortages of catecholamine neurotransmitters in billions of neurons throughout the brain and body.

Psychopharmacologic treatment as a form of adjunct therapy can experiment with trial periods of a number of stimulants to see if they increase the counselee's energy and emotional expressiveness. For instance, antidepressants such as bupropion (Wellbutrin) can effect a transformation from apathy into vitality, and anhedonia (the absence of pleasure) into a fuller enjoyment of sensing and feeling. When feelings and drives that were formerly inhibited are activated in the counselee's awareness, they can be processed through an expansion of the schizoid's Self Compass

160

and coupled with behavioral experiments now fueled with motivational energy.

Spirit

The schizoid Loner pattern requires of its host a disconnection to the spiritual core and brings with it a consequent depersonalization of the self. The self, then, becomes not a living soul, but a stream of consciousness in a void. Early analysts detected this interior soulless void (Kretschmer, 1925).

The lack of a vital self inhibits feeling connected to humanity and to God. The therapist can suggest that the counselee experiment with making conscious contact with God as a loving personal presence. Or if the counselee has a philosophy of life that excludes faith in God, the therapist can suggest the value of participating in a service group that sponsors volunteer work while providing fellowship for members. The therapeutic bond itself is an invitation to awaken the spiritual core from its Rip Van Winkle slumber into meaningful dialogue about life, values, and purposes.

If the counselee had childhood or adolescent roots in a particular faith, it is productive to examine why they may have left it, and whether they might explore the possibility of visiting a faith-community once again. Many religious communities embrace schizoid Loners who show the slight-est interest in joining a singles group, prayer fellowship, or couple's retreat. This healing love—something the Loner gave up on in childhood—may well kick-start a social learn-ing curve that pulls the person into a friendlier version of the world than they have ever known.

Suggestions for Compass Intervention

The therapist begins a session with a warm interpersonal welcome, as though inviting someone out of a wintry night into the hearth of one's home, where fireside chats can occur.

By embodying a spirit of cordiality and expressing genuine interest in the schizoid Loner's journey, a message is given: "Though you have received cold rebuffs when growing up, and though you have formed a warranted skepticism about the bother of being human, I am interested in hearing your story. I am not put off by your aloofness and catatonic-like indifference. I care what happens to you."

Therapeutic dialogue will be one-sided and halting. Normally when counselees pause in a conversation it is because they are processing their feelings and gathering thoughts. But when the Loner pauses it is because nothing is happening: no arousal, no concern, and no motivation to keep the conversation going. If you just let this happen, the energy of therapy will die an early death. On the other hand, if you talk too much or try to make small conversation, the schizoid may feel spooked by over-stimulation and terminate therapy to return to hibernation.

What to do? You relax your body, stay curious about the person's life, and break the silence with thoughtful observations, or summaries that initiate a new direction.

Carl, a fifty-year-old man with a responsible job, entered therapy with a presenting problem of lack of motivation to get up in the mornings and go to work. An associate had told him complaints had been aired regarding his remoteness.

Carl's energy was so low in the first two sessions that we could hardly keep a conversation going. By the third session he had begun a course of Wellbutrin after a psychiatrist validated my observation that his arousal level was close to nil. In this fourth session he showed improvement, but the long pauses characterizing the schizoid pattern still persisted. This exchange occurred near the end of the fourth session.

Dan: "I am curious how you handled childhood friends."

Carl: "I didn't have any." (He stared into space).

Dan: (I let a minute pass to see if he'd say more). "I'm kind of imagining what it would have felt like to have no playmates, no kids to run around the neighborhood with."

Carl: "It was fine."

Dan: "Did you have a pet?"

Carl: "A dog. Mother made sure I'd take him outside at night to empty."

Dan: "To empty?"

Carl: "To pee. But Mother would never use a word like that." (Long pause).

Dan: "So with your dad living across the country, it sounds like Mom and the dog were very significant to you."

Carl: "No. The Black Knight was important to me."

Dan: "You've not mentioned him before. I'm intrigued. Tell me about the Black Knight."

Carl: "He defied King Arthur's Court. He didn't care what they thought of him. He didn't need anyone."

Dan: "I kind of like this guy. Sounds like he was a real maverick with guts to stand up for himself. Was he a boy in your neighborhood?"

Carl: "No. He was a piece in my knights and castle toy set. He was actually grey like all the pieces. Only I painted him black."

Dan: "And how did you feel about him?"

Carl: (Shrugged shoulders). "He was okay."

Here we see a fluid reality that shifts back and forth from fantasy to history, from persons to objects, all revelatory of Carl's inner life. I wanted to reinforce that there was a time in his childhood when he actually felt attraction and interest toward an object that represented a person. Maybe we could import those memories into the present, and thus energize some of the connections between Carl and other people.

Dan: "I can see that the Black Knight was very special to you. To think that you selected him from all the rest and gave him the honor of being close to you...wow."

Carl: (Made eye contact). "I painted a gold cross on his shield."

Dan: "Gold on black is a stunning color combination. Did the cross have a special meaning?"

Carl: (Shrugged shoulders). "I'm Catholic. I figured he was too." (Pause of one minute).

Dan: "So here we have three beings: Mom, the dog, and the Black Knight. And there is the Catholic faith somewhere in the mix. Now tell me, where do you fit in?"

Carl: (Long pause. Glanced up at the wall clock). "I don't know." (Rubbed his chin with his hand. Took a deep breath). "I just know that no one could defeat the Black Knight." (Eyes glazed over).

Dan: "I appreciate your sharing these things today. You are narrating a story about an anti-hero with a destiny that's not quite clear yet. Narrators are very powerful. They create and destroy worlds by their fiat. So what part did you assign to the Black Knight—is he a dispenser of life and death?"

Here I was engaging him as though he was not schizoid, as though he could follow and comprehend my questions. This constituted an indirect self-fulfilling prophecy in that it would translate into his unconscious as though he possessed a normal capability for conversational responsiveness. It might eventually help him crawl out of the foxhole of the schizoid Loner existence. I had to be careful, though, not to overload him to the point of confusion and withdrawal.

Carl: (Grinned wryly). "Funny you should say that. Maybe my job as a federal court judge means that I became the Black Knight."

Dan: "Remarkable insight you're seeing here. Let's both give it some thought. I'll look forward to hearing what you come up with next session."

Drawing the session to a close in this fashion validated Carl's fledgling psychological mindedness and reinforced the interpersonal camaraderie between us. It also provided an indirect suggestion to his unconscious to do further archival searches in seeking a meaningful continuity between the Loner maverick childhood, his current work life, and his yet-to-be-chosen destiny.

At the beginning of the next session Carl had lapsed back into his apathetic mindset. But once our conversation turned toward the topic of putting together childhood fantasies, adult career choices, and the merging of the Black Knight with his work as a judge, Carl came alive.

Carl: "I did notice something this week. You know, I still keep that Black Knight in a small box of old toys. I suddenly remembered why I identified with him. I was ignored in elementary school, and though I was smart, other students thought I was dumb since I didn't play with them at recess. (Pause of thirty seconds). They made fun of me but I didn't care. Then in middle school I got pimples really bad and looked like a pepperoni pizza."

I could tell from the depth of this response that the therapeutic dose of Wellbutrin was providing Carl with a level of physical and mental energy that he had probably lacked for a lifetime. He didn't seem to notice this, which is normal for schizoid-patterned counselees until they develop more self-awareness.

Dan: (Laughed). "That's a good analogy. You're very talented with words. So you were a smart fellow in a pre-adolescent body, and you withdrew from everyone so their comments wouldn't hurt you. Is that right?"

Carl: (Nodded). "I had this secret world where I was the powerful one and they were scummy minions."

Dan: "Is that where the Black Knight comes in?"

Carl: "I think so. I can see now that I was like the Black Knight, because I put a wall between me and people to make them leave me alone."

Dan: "So how did this connect with becoming an attorney and a judge?"

Carl: (Paused) "I lived in the library at law school. Then when I was practicing I took cases and built airtight arguments. (Paused). I think I was appointed a judge because no one could influence me in any way. All I cared about was the objective standard of law. I didn't pay attention to people's excuses."

Dan: "A valuable attribute. Yet if I might use terminology from Compass Therapy, I'd suggest that you became a high-functioning schizoid Loner, positioned in a socially sanctioned niche that gave you superiority while assuring that you were untouchable."

Carl: "I like that. It sounds a lot like Darth Vader, my other hero."

This awareness helped to strengthen the continuity between the past and present. Now we could focus more on what was happening each week in Carl's life and relationships, and do psychological archeology only when pertinent.

In the next phase of working with schizoids, you listen for current issues that are related to the presenting problem and engage them in these areas.

Here is Carl in the fourth month of therapy.

Carl: "Dr. Dan, I have a new problem. Now that you've got me thinking about how other people experience me, I'm starting to feel nervous. I don't like it."

Dan: "Actually, that's great news. It used to be that you had so much rigor mortis that you couldn't feel your body or your emotions. Now you're feeling both. That means you're alive!"

Carl: "But it's distracting, not just in court, but in restaurants and walking downtown. I can't get out of my mind what you said about me scaring people off because I look like an undertaker."

Dan: "What's happening is that we are renewing your developmental history, only this time there are new possibilities. When we started therapy, you were a fifty-year-old man with a highly responsible job, who processed information about relationships at about the level of a seventh-grader. But now you're making good progress, and your social perceptions are more akin to a high school sophomore. The next thing you know, you'll start thinking about dating."

I knew I had given a great deal of information and ran a risk of overloading Carl, so I sat back in my chair and relaxed, signaling that the ball was in his court.

Carl: (Paused for one minute, then shifted in his chair and made eye contact). "That's funny to think of myself as high school age. But it fits. I've been starting to think about girls. There was this waitress who bent over and gave me a view of her bosoms and I thought to myself, 'Whoop-tee-do.' But then I thought, 'Shame on you!'"

Dan: "Sounds like even your hormones are coming out of deep freeze."

Carl: "I don't know if I like all this. My life used to be simple. This is uncomfortable."

Dan: "Do you suppose you can handle a little discomfort on the way toward becoming an emotionally and psychologically mature man?"

Carl: (Paused thirty seconds. Set his chin a little higher than usual). "Yes, I can."

Now comes the phase of therapy in which you enter the counselee's life as a living presence, a docent, a coach. Yet you realize they are still vulnerable to the voice and familiarity of the pattern that saved them from anxiety in the past. Don't feel put off when the schizoid pattern rears up to protest the actualizing growth. Just stay aware that this phase of growth-consolidation can trigger a relapse based on conflict with an emotionally significant person who doesn't like the changes they are seeing in the former schizoid. The other person can precipitate a crisis by giving the Loner an ultimatum that unconsciously says: "Either go back to your old pattern so I can feel comfortable with you again, or take your chances and leave me behind."

In the seventh month of therapy Carl received such an ultimatum. He came to the session looking like death warmed over. His handshake was limp. He took his seat and said nothing.

Dan: (Waited for about a minute, then heard Carl sigh). "My gosh, Carl, you seem to have the world on your shoulders."

Carl: "It's not the world. It's Mother."

Dan: "What's happened?"

Carl: "I told her on the phone last night that Stella and I have been dating and getting pretty serious." (Paused, eyes staring at the carpet).

Dan: "Yes?"

Carl: "She said, 'You can't do that. I'm about to retire and need to move in with you.'"

Dan: "That's a pretty bold announcement on her part. What are you feeling inside?"

Carl: (Paused). "Nothing. All my feelings went away. I didn't go to work today. Almost didn't come here."

Dan: "If you had a feeling, what would it be like? A butterfly? A blade of grass?"

Carl: "A lawnmower." (With that, I noticed that he sat more upright in the chair).

Dan: "Expand that feeling. What does the lawnmower want to do?"

Carl: "To cut the grass and mow down a big weed."

Dan: "And your mother is..."

Carl: "The big weed that won't let me get on with my life. It's not that I don't care for her, but I can't stand the thought of being in the same house with her. She'll want everything her way, like she always did."

Dan: "Excellent observation. Where would you say that the two of you were stuck on the Self Compass in your grow-up years?"

Carl: "That's easy. She was off the scale on strength. And I hid from the world in weakness."

Carl suddenly looked back over his shoulder with all the apprehension of a child about to get a tongue-lashing.

Dan: "You are courageous to describe your mother accurately as a full-blown top dog. It's okay to describe people's behavior, even a parent's. You're not being disloyal. You are judging objectively."

Carl: "Then why do I feel so nervous?"

Dan: "Apparently because she's standing right behind you. Is that what it seems like?"

Carl: (Looked over his shoulder again). "I know she's not really here, but it feels like she's listening to every word."

Dan: "What is she wearing today?"

Carl: "Her old green dress."

Dan: "Does she have any makeup on?"

Carl: "She quit wearing makeup the day my dad left."

Dan: (Looked behind Carl and made a gesture of welcome). "Mrs. _____, would you please join us and have a seat on the chair across from your son?"

Carl: (Carl's eye movements followed the imaginary mother around his chair and to the chair where I had gestured for her to sit down. He looked at me with lips pursed and eyes wide).

Dan to Carl: "While we are pretending that she has joined us, there is a sense in which she is psychologically here. She lives within your spiritual core, and this is a good time for a direct conversation with her. I'll help you out. Can we go ahead with this experiment?"

Carl: "What do I do?"

Dan: "I'm going to talk to your mother, and I'd like you to provide her with a voice to answer me."

Carl: "But I don't know what she thinks."

Dan: "Your unconscious knows a great deal about her." (Turned toward the mother's chair). "Mrs. _____, I'd like you to tell me about Carl, what kind of boy he was, and what kind of man he became."

Carl as Mother: "Well, Dr. Montgomery, Carl was a well-behaved boy who kept to himself a lot. We lived in a big house and I had to work for a living. He became very responsible at an early age." (Paused, as though finished).

Dan: "Did he play with other kids?"

Mother: "He had to take care of the dog—to make sure he emptied properly. He couldn't go running ragtag around the neighborhood like the other boys did." (Paused, as though finished).

Dan: "And the relationship between you?"

Mother: "I knew I could count on him."

Dan: "What about the man that Carl became?"

Mother: "I'm proud of Carl. He lives alone and has responsibility. I'm going to retire and go live with him so we can be together again."

Dan: "Anything else you'd like to tell me?"

Mother: "Nothing else is necessary."

Dan: "All right. Thank you for speaking with me."

In this dialogue I tapped into Carl's unconscious reservoir of knowledge and experiences about his mother, comprised of hundreds of thousands of impressions upon his psyche about her thoughts, values, body language, habits, moods, and Self Compass location. The same information conveyed through a rational interview would lack the vividness of her real presence that Carl captured through becoming her voice in interaction with me. If Carl had shown the slightest confusion about the role-playing sequence, I would have immediately stopped and clarified the part he was to play. But probably because of the history of our sessions, and the fact that we had used role-playing before, he was able to engage in the scene with full concentration.

Now I wanted to ratchet up the stakes of this therapeutic encounter with Mother by letting him speak for himself. The advantage of doing this in a session was that he would unconsciously draw strength and assertion from my presence as a supportive power.

Dan: "Now, Carl, I'd like to hear what was going on inside you as I talked with your mother."

Carl: (Paused). "I was struck by how confident she was. She's not nervous around people like I am."

Dan: "Anything else?"

Carl: "Yes. That she has my whole life planned out without consulting me. That's why there's no room for Stella. She would be competition."

Dan: "Wow, I think you just hit pay dirt. Now I'd like to invite you to role-play a new conversation in which you share your current insights and feelings with your mother. Want to give it a try?"

Carl: (Shifted in his chair and breathed deeply). "I've got to talk to her tonight on the phone, so I might as well start now."

Dan: "Okay. Here's how we'll do it. I'm going to sit in Mother's seat and become her. You need to deal with me, because I'm going to say things that will definitely rattle your cage and try to control your present and future."

Carl: (Loosened his collar). "I don't know if I can do this."

Dan: "Do you want to have a life that includes Stella?"

Carl: "Yes."

Dan: "Then you've got to stand on your own two feet and learn to handle Mother."

Carl: "All right. Go ahead."

Dan as Mother: (I moved to the mother's chair). "I want to know, young man, why you were hesitant when I said I was going to retire and come live with you."

Carl: (Momentarily relapsed to all his old body language, with arms that dangled, vacant eyes, and wooden posture). "I...I...I...."

Dan as Mother: "Speak up, son. Don't keep your mother waiting."

Carl: (Made unsteady eye contact with me as Mother). "I am not a young man. I am a judge and my decisions count for something."

Dan as Mother: "Are you correcting me? Where have your manners gone?"

Carl: "You are speaking quite clearly, Mother. Why shouldn't I?"

Dan as Mother: (Changed my tone to a more conciliatory one). "Now, Carl, dear, we mustn't let the things we learn in therapy disrupt our family loyalty. All we have is each other. That how it's been. That how it's going to be."

Carl: (Set jaw squarely). "That's how it was. That's not how it's going to be."

I stood up, moved out of the mother's persona, and sat back down in my therapist's seat.

Dan to Carl: "I'm speaking as myself now. How are you doing with this conversation?"

Carl: "My mind keeps wanting to cloud over. I keep feeling a voice inside me say, 'It's no use. She'll never change. Retreat and let her do what she wants.'"

Dan: "This is a truly wonderful moment. We've just heard with absolute clarity the voice of your old schizoid Loner pattern inviting you back into numb withdrawal, and promising you that this will make everything okay. What do you think about that?"

Carl: "I could hardly resist. But something inside me said, 'Dr. Dan is with you now. I'm not alone. I can deal with this.'"

Dan: "I believe that is the voice of your spiritual core, and I celebrate your courage for listening to it. Now is there anything else you need to tell your mother before she leaves?"

Carl: "Yes, there is."

I exchanged seats and assumed the mother's persona, gazing at Carl with my chin raised. I said nothing, but let my eyes convey both entreaty and a warning to behave.

Carl: "Mother, you've worked hard all your life, and you deserve a good retirement. But I am a grown man now, with a woman I want to date and probably marry. I've got to concentrate on that relationship. I can't have you telling me what to do anymore."

Dan as Mother: "But I don't have any real friends. My whole life is centered on you. How can you let me down this way?"

Carl: (Sat still, seemingly deep in thought. The pause went beyond his normal haltingness, and I sensed he was genuinely stuck).

It can be productive to guide counselees to the threshold of new decision-making, and coach them to try something new. But in this case, I felt that Carl was on the verge of overextending himself, and if I let that happen, he could later collapse into his old void. So I made an adjustment.

Returning to my therapist seat, I spoke gently to Carl.

Dan: "Carl, you've shown genuine strength and assertion today, and said significant things to your mother for the first time. This might be close to a good stopping point, so that you can reflect this week on the best way to proceed with her."

Carl: (Breathed a sigh of relief). "I'd like to do that."

Dan: "In getting closure for this conversation with her, is there anything else you'd like to say to me?"

This approach provided Carl with a less threatening avenue of expression that would help get him up to date with himself.

Carl: "Yes. I want to say that I feel sorry that Mother has not made friends all these years. I don't think I ever realized that she's not a very friendly person. She always seemed so decisive. (Paused). But I also know that it feels unhealthy to have her move in with me. Maybe I can find her an apartment or condo a few blocks away. That would leave Stella and me space for our relationship, while still visiting with Mother from time to time."

Dan: "I'm struck by how you're combining compassion from your Love compass point with enough Strength and Assertion to separate from her and establish your own identity. This is crucial for building an intimate relationship with Stella. You are not your mother's little boy any more. You're a fully grown man."

Carl: (Sat up and prepared to leave). "It doesn't feel as bad as I thought it would, standing up to her. I think I can do this."

The third movement of therapeutic intervention took place over the next several months; that of consolidating Carl's gains while he kept learning how to trust his emotions and express them in relationships.

Though he often felt tempted to numb himself by withdrawing, he gradually learned the wisdom of staying in psychological contact with people that he cared about. This meant learning to express anger or annoyance as well as love and caring. When communications went awry, he learned both how to apologize and how to forgive. I watched with appreciation his transition from psychological adolescence to a maturing personhood.

By the one-year mark and final phase of therapy, Carl had married Stella, relocated his mother to an apartment a couple of miles away, and established boundaries with her that were cordial but firm.

Fortunately, Carl's mother had been warm enough to Stella not to alienate her at their first meeting. So Carl and Stella would regularly invite the mother to dinner or to church and cultural activities. The few times she tried to lay a guilt trip on Carl or punish him with silence, he didn't bite, but rather proceeded to carry on the relationship under the revised terms that he had developed in therapy.

I knew that Carl, Stella, and the mother-in-law would face hurdles and challenges for the rest of their lives. At the same time, I was thankful to see this formerly schizoid Loner develop a warmly human universe where those he cared about were invited to share life's enjoyments with him.

12
NARCISSISTIC BOASTER PATTERN

With omnipotent self-assurance (Britton, 2004) Boaster-patterned persons follow the lead of their namesake, Narcissus, a mythological figure who fell in love with his reflection, an apt metaphor for the grandiosity of the narcissistic pattern (Campbell et al., 2002). While actualizing persons balance self-esteem with humility to form a rhythm of Strength and Weakness, narcissists repress Weakness, denying self-doubt by creating a compensatory persona based on Strength (Beck et al., 2007). They lack caring from the Love compass point (McWilliams, 1994) and use Assertion to resent those who fail to respect them (Patton, 1996).

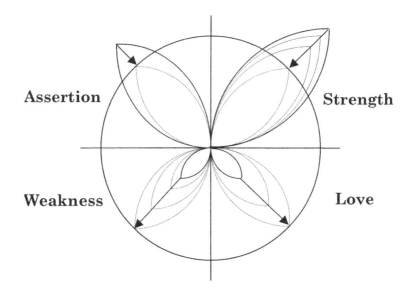

The Pattern's Interior

Compass Therapy employs the term "Boaster" to describe the narcissistic pattern because whether verbally or through body language, Boasters constantly display their achievements and strive to appear as better looking, more confident, wealthier, more brilliant, more accomplished, and more important than others (Witte et al., 2002; Twenge et al., 2009). But like Narcissus, their self-glorification reflects more illusion than fact, since narcissists usually lack the motivation, discipline, and skills required to ground these attributes in reality (Aizawa, 2002).

By contrast, the healthy use of the Strength compass point found in actualizing persons comes from realistic self-appraisal and demonstrated talents, achievements, and relationships. They esteem others as they do themselves, without getting sidetracked by envy or jealousy. Corrective feedback from others does not trigger the dramatic threat to self-esteem experienced by the narcissist.

Narcissists puff up their self-image to avoid activating fears of inferiority (Beck et al., 2007). They frequently wound spouses, children, friends, and associates by placing themselves on a pedestal from which they pass judgment on the perceived imperfections in others, secretly seeking to safeguard their aura of positive superiority (Gosling et al., 1998), and can show an aggressive edge (Tracya et al., 2009).

The Boaster pattern shares with the Storyteller pattern a need for admiration. But while Storytellers actively solicit attention from others, Boasters disdain this dependency, feeling that it would limit their power and imply that they are incomplete. Instead, the Boaster employs a nonchalant, coolly superior style to elicit other's admiration.

The Strength compass point is exaggerated with the need to be right about everything, which they share with compulsive Controllers. But their entitlement, a central defining trait of this pattern, lifts them above the rules of convention and engenders haughtiness and huffiness (Montgomery & Montgomery, 2008).

A paradox worth noting is that while Boasters show remarkable indifference to the needs, feelings, and wellbeing of others, they nevertheless feel extremely vulnerable to criticism or being ignored, together with a strong desire for loving support and admiring deference from others (Benjamin, 2003). This leads to unbalanced relationships in which the narcissistic Boaster remains emotionally immature and incapable of sustaining the rhythmic reciprocity required for intimacy. It is common for narcissists to experience several divorces over the course of their lives (Beck et al., 2007).

Boaster-Patterned People:

⊕ Like to make powerful first impressions.

⊕ Give constant attention to how they look, what they wear, and what they say.

⊕ See their time as valuable. Others should give them the right of way in traffic, allow them to cut into lines, and serve them immediately in restaurants.

⊕ Feel exempt from difficult or dull tasks, seeking special assignments that lead to recognition.

⊕ Think that people should be happy to wait on them, follow their lead, and take their advice.

⊕ Assume that no one has a right to criticize them. It is understandable if they react with anger at such insolence.

⊕ Believe that others should be glad to give to them without expecting anything in return.

Boaster Pattern

Compass Point: Strength

Manipulation: Self-absorbed & Entitled

Thoughts: Patronizing to Grandiose

Feelings: Calm to Cocksure

Actions: Suave to Snooty

Growth Needs: Humility & Caring

Origins

Freud hypothesized about the origins of narcissism in his investigation of dreams: "I have found that people who know that they are preferred or are favored by their mother give evidence in their lives of a peculiar self-reliance and an unshakable optimism which often seem like heroic attributes and bring actual success to their possessors" (1933, p. 398).

Yet while a certain degree of parental praise contributes positively to children's self-esteem, overblown praise inflates it, sowing the seeds of narcissism (Benjamin, 2003). Overindulgence leads children to the conclusion that the world revolves around them, well past the stage of normal egocentric thought.

Parental longings for self-glorification can be fulfilled through the creation of perfect, brilliant, or beautiful offspring. As a consequence, such children are not loved as persons in their own right, nor encouraged to accept weaknesses as well as strengths. They become psychologically addicted to unmerited adoration and so develop little frustration tolerance. Put off by hard work, they expect life to unfold with ease. They develop a pattern of superficial dabbling, flitting from one activity to another, driven more by narcissistic needs for recognition than for mastery of the task at hand. A notable exception occurs with the "Nobel Prize Complex" phenomenon (Tarkatoff, 1996) where narcissism and the compulsive pattern unite in an extraordinarily disciplined effort to achieve.

Boaster traits can develop from parental indifference or neglect as well as pampering, in which "a child may develop an exaggerated desire for 'greatness' by way of shoring up a sense of self-worth in the absence of the ordinary parental praise...The neglected child may present an outward sense of (compensatory) specialness covering an inward sense of worthlessness" (Stone, 1993, p. 260). There is also research supporting either highly permissive or highly authoritarian parenting that results in adult narcissism (Ramsey et al., 1996).

Compass theory adds another source of narcissism based on the psychology of the obvious: extravagant success in life through the sudden rise to power, fame, or wealth can trigger the formation of the Boaster pattern. A person is seduced into believing the myth of their greatness, a belief that is reinforced by fawning peers and a hero-worshipping public (Montgomery & Montgomery, 2008).

Clinical Literature

Narcissism is a well-founded concept in clinical literature. Freud described the "narcissistic libidinal type," focusing on how easily this individual assumes social leadership: "The main interest is focused on self-preservation; the type is independent and not easily overawed...They readily assume the role of leader, give a fresh stimulus to cultural development or break down existing conditions" (1931/1950, p. 249).

Horney employed an effective metaphor in conveying the essence of narcissism as "self-inflation," which, "like economic inflation, means presenting greater values than really exist" (1939, pp. 89-90).

The "phallic-narcissistic character" captured the essence of this pattern for Reich, whose colorful description conveyed his view: "If their vanity is offended, they react with cold disdain, marked ill-humor, or downright aggression. Their narcissism is expressed not in an infantile but in a blatantly self-confident way, with a flagrant display of superiority and dignity" (1949, p. 217-218).

For Leary (1957), the narcissist pattern showed self-confidence based on "adjustment through competition" that sought superiority and feared inferiority.

Kiesler employed concrete adjectives to create a vivid picture of the narcissistic pattern as brazen, cocky, boastful, pushy, egotistical, self-enthralled, and unable to ask for help with anything (1996, p. 21).

Recent research supports the prevalence of the narcissistic personality pattern in the general U.S. population and its association with considerable prevalence among men, whose rates exceed those of women (Stinson et al., 2008).

Mind

Narcissistic counselees do best with a therapist whom they respect and a therapeutic explanation of their difficulties that impresses them while keeping their dignity intact. It empowers the therapist to know in advance the basic themes of Boaster-patterned thinking, while keeping in mind that some of this self-talk represents unconscious assumptions about life:

⊕ If I am powerful enough, I can be totally confident and eliminate all self-doubt.

⊕ I am superior to others and they should grant me special privileges.

- I am above the rules. I can do whatever I wish to reinforce my superior status and to expand my aura of influence.

- I am entitled to admiration and people should feel grateful to have me around.

- If you love me, you'll do whatever I want, when I want.

- I have no use for people who don't hold me in high regard.

- I don't like it when someone else in a group gets special attention.

- All that matters is what I want, feel, or think.

- Very few people are worth my time; the rest bore me.

- I must succeed in order to prove my superiority.

- You are present in my life to admire me.

The distinguishing feature that separates narcissism from highly successful and confident individuals rests in the belief that without superior success and distinction, the person is insignificant and worthless (Beck et al., 2007).

Like compulsive Controllers, who are also stuck on the Strength compass point, narcissistic Boasters are prone to black-and-white thinking in assessing themselves and others. They are either entirely worthy or entirely worthless, and in order to rule out the latter, they stubbornly cling to the former. To sustain their ascendancy, they don't think twice about revising their personal history to transform failures or to justify their current position.

The narcissist pattern distorts the Love compass point into an exclusive admiration of one's self. Narcissists expand this distortion by coolly assuming that others should love them as they love themselves and that others should give them the same preferential treatment they give themselves. The idea of loving others is lost on those stuck in the Boaster pattern. When their expectations are not met, narcissists can find themselves easily offended and reluctant to let go of perceived infringements of their rights (McCullough et al., 2003).

Thus underneath the facade of superiority lies self-doubt, envy of others, and an inability to love (Akhtar & Thompson, 1982). The entitlement inherent to the pattern makes narcissists wise in their own eyes, blind to how they take others for granted, using people to gratify ego needs for adulation and power.

Because the Love and Weakness compass points are repressed, narcissists unconsciously experience interpersonal vulnerability, underlying emotional distress, difficulty in regulating affect, and interpersonal competitiveness (Russ et al., 2008; Cain et al., 2008)—and they don't know why. Without Weakness, they lack the reality testing of understanding their weaknesses and the humility of a teachable spirit. Without Love they are unable to express compassion, nurturance, or forgiveness. This brings up an important point that is useful, even vital, to address in therapy.

Conflicts and misunderstandings in relationships require forgiveness in order to heal emotional wounds and restore harmony and trust. However, the structure and function of narcissism makes this rhythm of reconciliation impossible, leaving the narcissist skeptical about emotional closeness and ever more reserved over the lifespan about opening their hearts to anyone.

Compass Therapy seeks to ferret out and expand awareness of this unwillingness to forgive, so that the counselee can develop a merciful heart. Research shows that entitlement predicts unforgiveness, where the narcissist easily takes offence, bears grudges over real or imagined slights, and loses the little trust they had in others, all of which cycles into further levels of entitlement and unforgiveness (Exline et al., 2004). This pattern saps energy that otherwise could be invested in building and maintaining intimate relationships. Narcissism takes a costly toll on the interpersonal life of the Boaster as years go by.

Here is a compass intervention offered in a third session with a counselee whose presenting complaint revealed a grudge against her mother and her mother's new husband of two years.

Counselee: "When my mom married again I didn't like how she gave my new step-dad the attention she always gave to me."

Therapist: "You felt that her new spouse was laying claim to special treatment that historically belonged to you."

Counselee: "Exactly, and when I asked if I could fly to Hawaii with them for their honeymoon, they didn't seem enthusiastic."

Therapist: "How old were you at the time?"

Counselee: "Twenty-three."

Therapist: "So this happened two years ago and it still grates on you."

Counselee: "I just don't see why they can't include me in their activities. Or why they won't come to my family birthday parties with my biological dad and all the rest of my relatives."

Therapist: "You're perplexed why your mom and her new husband seem standoffish toward your father and relatives on your mom's side. Like, 'Hey, you two, quit sticking together and come celebrate my special occasions like parents are supposed to.'"

Counselee: "Exactly. I know my real dad feels a little uncomfortable around them and my step-dad doesn't feel close to any of my relatives. But shouldn't they put all that aside when I need them to be there for me?"

Therapist: "It's like their universe should revolve around you, even though your mom and her new husband need to build a life of their own. Is that right?" (This mild level of confrontation seeks to make the counselee's underlying narcissistic pattern more visible).

Counselee: "Well, that makes me sound selfish and spoiled, which maybe I am a little bit. (Tears up). But people should care about my needs and not be so selfish about theirs!"

Therapist: "May I give you more of an overview as a professional psychologist?"

Counselee: "Okay."

Therapist: "It sounds to me like you were raised with a lot of attention directed your way. This is good to a point, because it helped you feel special as a human being. But what we experience in childhood and adolescence must often be surrendered in the rite of passage to adulthood. What do you think this means for you?"

Counselee: (Pauses. Wipes tears away). "Well, I guess it means I need to grow up emotionally. Maybe that I should be less focused on getting attention from my mom and step-dad, and more focused on getting my life together. Is that it?"

Therapist: "That's it."

Counselee: "But what should I do when I feel annoyed that Mom won't come over and do things like we used to do: shopping at the mall, helping me fix up my apartment, things like that?"

Therapist: "Do you have any peer friends?"

Counselee: "My boyfriend, who just became my fiancé last week." (Smiles).

Therapist: (Smiles back). "Congratulations on your engagement. What would happen if you reduced expectations toward your mom and invested this energy into your boyfriend and any new couple friends the two of you enjoy?"

Counselee: "That sounds like a mature thing to do. But part of me wants my mom and my boyfriend to dote on me."

Therapist: "Sometimes when you walk through one door, another door necessarily closes. Can you forgive your mom for needing to move forward with her new life, and for needing to invest her primary energy toward her husband so they can build an emotionally intimate marriage?"

Counselee: "I'm going to have to work at it. But since you put it that way, I suppose I can help her out by not making so many demands."

Therapist: "Then you are indeed a very special daughter."

Body

Boaster-patterned persons tend to hold the body stiff with pride. "The head is held fairly high, the backbone straight. These would be positive traits were it not for the fact that the pride is defensive, the rigidity unyielding" (Lowen, 1975, p. 166). Spontaneous self-expression is held back in favor of calculated self-presentation to ensure that one never looks foolish. This guardedness takes the form of holding back feelings of affection or impulses to reach out to others. Holding back is translated anatomically as "holding in the back."

Apart from prideful self-containment, there is a general aliveness in the body. Bright eyes, good skin color, and animation of voice and gesture reveal the strong confidence of the narcissist. However, if extremely rigid arrogance has set in, the grace of movement is sacrificed, the eyes lose their luster, and the skin tone may be pale from an overabundance of muscle tension throughout the body (Lowen, 1975, p. 168).

Research seems to indicate "no distinctive biophysical precursors...We must trace the roots of this pattern to psychogenic influences" (Millon et al., 2004, p. 343).

Alcohol or drugs can find a place in the counselee's life because they enhance feelings of grandiosity (Calsyn et al., 1996; McMahon & Richards, 1996). The warm glow of a chemical high can all too easily become a permanent substitute for relating to others with real feelings.

Spirit

The most "grievous cost" of narcissism is a "stunted capacity to love" (McWilliams, 1994, p. 175) that arises from a decommissioned Love compass point. This lack of nurturance, forgiveness, and caring is strongly related to causing pain and suffering to others (Miller et al., 2007).

The therapist can approach this difficulty by walking a delicate line, reflecting both the interpersonal strengths of the narcissistic counselee, which are easy for the counselee to recount, and then asking for some of the ways the counselee has let others down or hurt them. This builds awareness of the Love and Weakness compass points, and the exploration process in itself provides a spiritual opportunity for the counselee to experience remorse and regret.

Dan: "I'd like us to focus on a polarity swing between the Strength compass point, where you are most comfortable, to the Love and Weakness compass points, where you tend to avoid experiencing memories and feelings. Are you willing to try this growth experiment?"

Ken: "Sure, go ahead."

Dan: "I'd like you to tell me about some experiences where you felt absolutely superior to others in the years since college to your present job as market analyst."

Ken: "Okay. I was a natural for basketball, making the varsity my sophomore year and then starting every game until I graduated. There were championship games where I could hardly miss a shot. I got a lot of press coverage. The cheerleaders were wild about me."

Dan: "I'm just curious, but how did you treat these cheerleaders?"

Ken: "I screwed half the squad, and that was a real accomplishment because usually girls will tell other girls in time and you won't get to make the rounds. It may have had to do with being the most popular guy on campus. Even professors passed me when I only did half the work. Who wanted to flunk the star player?"

Dan: "So you had this incredible way of using your strength and confidence not only against opponent ballplayers, but against your own college family."

Ken: "I wouldn't go that far. They were just people, and I've always been able to snow people to get what I want. That's why I'm the top sales guy where I work."

Dan: "So that's a very good recounting of your accomplishment and glories. Now let's explore the Love compass point. How do you rate your experiences there?"

Ken: "Hmmm. That's challenging. I can say I've had two or three dates a month ever since I left college. I sweet talk them and take them back to my condo and do the dirty deed. But love? I don't think so."

Dan: "How many women are we talking about here, that you've had sex with?"

Ken: (Paused thirty seconds). "I would say about 2.5 per month, year around, for ten years. That comes out to about three hundred."

Dan: "That might qualify for the Guinness Book of World Records. How do you suppose each of those individuals felt the morning after?"

Ken: (Laughed). "Probably like I did. Hung-over."

Dan: "Now just for fun, let's pretend you're one of the girls that falls for Ken's pitch at the bar scene, goes to his condo for sex, and wakes up the next morning in his bed hung-over. What do you feel toward Ken?"

Ken: "I don't have much of a clue what she would feel. I haven't ever cared what the women I date feel about anything. I suppose she might think, "I wonder if Ken is a low life who's just broken my heart or a stand-up guy who's open to getting married."

Dan: "And which kind of guy are you?"

Ken: (Stuck out the fingers on his hand and wriggled them). "I see a university ring on this hand, but, guess what, no wedding band. Marriage is for the weak guys who don't know how to play the game. Conquistadores don't need marriage; they take the spoils and look for the next victory."

I could sense that I may have lost my way in the strategy I was seeking to employ. I had hoped to evoke some sign of human feeling for the hurt Ken had caused. But he was having none of it. I decided to personalize the conversation even more.

Dan: "So it seems like the cheerleaders and the ladies you meet in bars are fair game. You mesmerize them with your spiel and knock them off as a way of passing time. What if one of these girls was your sister and the cock-of-the-town was having her. Any feelings?"

Ken: (Eyes narrowed). "Funny you should say that. My sister is one of the few people I haven't taken advantage of. I guess it's because she was a SID's baby and we almost lost her. I've always been kind of protective. But last year she was having trouble with her husband. She asked me to come over and baby-sit so they could go out and sort things through. I made up a few lame excuses and never showed up. Now they're divorced."

I noted that the joviality and cavalier attitude were gone.

Dan: "So she was turning to you for help in trying to make her marriage work. And you—"

193

Ken: "Ignored her. Lied to her. Abandoned ship."

We sat in silence to let the words sink in.

Dan: "I want to commend you for saying that so honestly, even compassionately. What does it feel like to be aware of a loving feeling?"

Ken: (He looked down, brow furrowed). "It doesn't feel loving. I feel ashamed. I didn't even return her last calls. I just distracted myself with working at the office and chasing women at night. It's like I wanted her to disappear until she didn't need me anymore, and then I could come back and act like nothing had happened."

Dan: "Do you regret that approach now?"

Ken: (Shrugged his shoulders). "Regret, regret. I regret losing almost a million dollars on the stock market last year. I regret being alone on certain weekends. (Paused). I guess I regret not being there for Sis when she needed help."

Dan: "Can you focus on that last sentence and see what feelings come with it?"

Ken: "I avoided her when she needed me most and I'm..."

Dan: "Go ahead."

Ken: "I'm very sorry."

Dan: "That sounds sincere. Like you feel it in your heart."

Ken: "Yeah. I wish I had helped her out."

Dan: "If she were sitting here, what could you say to get the guilt off your chest and somehow make amends?"

Ken: "I could say, 'Hey Sissy, I'm really sorry that I didn't pick up on your calls last year. I know it left you in the lurch. And I'm really sorry that you and Brian went your separate ways. I just want to say I love you. If you need me to come out and baby-sit the kids, you can have my cell number. Just give me a day's warning so I can arrange things at the office. But I'll be glad to help you out.'"

Dan: "There's so much beauty in what you just said. Any discoveries inside yourself?"

Ken: "Well, at first I felt like the world's lowest scumbag. But after I got it out, I felt lighter. I guess I've been carrying it around without knowing it."

Dan: "Is there a name for the feeling you're having right now?"

Ken: "Peace. I do love her and I am sorry. I think I'll call her this week and ask her out for lunch."

Dan: "Good plan. I appreciate your courage."

This session had developed a beginning rhythm between Assertion and Love in Ken's personality. In a session the following month, I saw an opportunity to introduce Ken to the rhythm of Strength and Weakness.

Dan: "So you like how your sister is responding to you."

Ken: "Yes, we were never all that close. But since I apologized and took care of her kids a couple of times, she's really warmed up to me."

Dan: "This strikes me as significant, like you are learning how to integrate an actualizing principle. I wonder if we might form it into a concept that you can master."

195

Ken: "What is it?"

Dan: "Well, ever since you had that huge financial reversal, you've been in crisis mode. Depression. Self-doubt. Inferiority. Fear of never being on top again."

Ken: (Looked uncomfortable). "It's been really bad. I've never felt like this before. I just sit in my office pretending I'm making calls to new clients. But all I can think about is, 'Why didn't I withdraw all my money before the market tanked? I'll never make that much money again.'"

Dan: "That's the material side of the equation, that you might not become as rich as you had hoped, but there is a spiritual side that seems important to address."

Ken: "How do you mean?"

Dan: "I say this with the greatest respect for all you've accomplished, but it seems to me that the humble acceptance of your shortcomings is a quality you've never been willing to experience. Now by a strange turn of events, it may be the one quality that can help you now."

Ken: "The guys at the office would laugh at that. No one ever admits a weakness. Especially me."

Dan: "Are you laughing inside at what I've suggested?"

Ken: (Paused). "No, I'm not. It sounds all too true. But doesn't giving in to weakness make you a loser?"

Dan: "Yes, giving into the weakness of your fall from greatness will render your narcissistic pattern impotent."

Ken: "Okay, how's this. 'I'm broke and stupid and will never be rich again.'"

Dan: "That's pretty graphic and certainly the opposite of grandiosity. But it's also a way that the top dog narcissism can beat up and blame the underdog human weakness—the fact that you and millions of other investors could neither foresee nor control that sudden market downturn. Now how could you say the same thing, only with compassion for yourself?"

Ken: (Took a deep breath). "Well, I guess I could say that Ken didn't know as much as he thought he did about controlling global finance, and that he took a huge loss…"

Dan: "That's good. Go ahead, and don't forget to give Ken some dignity even when he's at the bottom of the heap."

Ken: "He took a huge loss, but maybe that's what he needed in order to quit worshipping himself and get his feet on the ground."

Dan: "Wow. I feel the humility in that. Any other insights from the Weakness compass point? Any wisdom there?"

Ken: "This is a lot harder than being in charge of things."

Dan: "Exactly, it takes a lot more courage to be humble than to strut your strengths. Now give it a try to find new words for any benefits that come from your experience on the Weakness compass point."

Ken: "Don't laugh, but the first thing that comes to mind is that I'm not as big of an ass as I used to be."

Dan: "Excellent. Go on."

Ken: "That I've done a lot of soul-searching, especially now I know I've been a narcissist all my life. No wonder I feel so lonely, even in the bar scene."

Dan: "So you're planting your feet more in reality, getting off your high horse, and beginning to see that sincerity has more value than pretension. Is that right?"

Ken: (Paused, then nodded). "And that I can be close to someone like my sister, or maybe even someone I date, if I can stay human enough to watch out for their needs like I do my own."

In working with counselees stuck in the narcissistic pattern, keep in mind that despite all appearances, they actually do want to grow up and benefit from the LAWS of actualizing health.

13
COMPULSIVE CONTROLLER PATTERN

The compulsive personality pattern employs behaviors often rewarded by society: promptness, organization, work, discipline, and self-control. In moderation, any person benefits from the industry these traits afford. But the compulsive pattern makes moderation impossible. The "Controller" exaggerates the Strength compass point in an all-or-nothing effort to control thoughts, emotions, work projects, spouse and children, relationships, and if one is religious, even God. The Assertion compass point is drawn upon to ferret out and judge imperfection. The Love compass point is sterile. The Weakness compass point is exiled from consciousness.

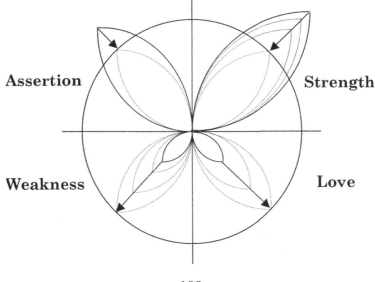

The Pattern's Interior

Though it masquerades as socially sanctioned and virtuous, the compulsive Controller pattern more accurately functions as a micromanager that sizes up any situation or person as falling short of an inner ideal of perfection (Pretzel & Hampl, 2009). Even a therapist is in for trouble when suggesting that compulsives could enjoy life more if they surrendered this grim rule-keeping existence.

What we have here is a neurotic paradox: the very personality pattern that promises society the most stable, responsible, and consistent behavior actually poisons self and others through critical judging and emotional reserve. Without developing awareness of the pattern, the counselee can never outgrow it, nor rise above its deflating impact on those around them.

The skilled therapist discerns how the compulsive convincingly invokes custom, logic, morality, family rules, and past behavior in similar situations to strengthen their conviction about what "should" happen in a given situation, and how they pose as masters of control when they are really filled with anxiety about any prospective change, especially in their own personality.

The Strength compass point forms the underlying girder for the compulsive Controller pattern, with secondary support from the Assertion compass point when opposition occurs. This makes compulsive control a top dog pattern, since it favors controlling others over being controlled by them. The Weakness compass point is denied and converted into doubly energizing its opposite compass point: Strength.

The Love compass point is stripped of heartfelt feelings and turned into doing one's duty. The nurturance, patience, and forgiveness that love requires are displaced by criticalness, impatience, and grudge bearing. Controllers busy themselves attending to what they consider of utmost importance: striving, achieving, and staying organized (Shostrom & Montgomery, 1978).

Though the compulsive pattern exists as a pure prototype that is fixated on the Strength compass point, it can combine with the adjacent compass points of Assertion or Love. In the case of Assertion, the compulsive displays the argumentativeness of the paranoid pattern, except the focus lies with legalistic points about the "rightness" of their judgment. In the case of binding with the Love compass point, the compulsive displays conscientious "goodism," striving to be perfectly good at rescuing everybody. In all these instances, the opposite polarity of Weakness is avoided at all costs, save for the fact that it haunts the unconscious with anxiety.

Defense Mechanisms

Most baffling to the novice therapist is the defensive armor that guards the Controller pattern from emotional experiences in therapy. Millon notes that compulsives use more ego defense mechanisms than any other personality pattern (2004). These include reaction formation, splitting, introjection, confluence, and repression, each of which will be dealt with as the chapter progresses.

The primary defense mechanism is *reaction formation*, which quashes impulses of vulnerability or uncertainty by fortifying a socially acceptable façade of self-righteous strength. This process dissociates the Weakness compass point from the rest of the Self Compass. Thus the compulsive loses touch with and even disdains experiences of sadness, hurt, anxiety, and need in self and others. To live this way, the compulsive must doubly exaggerate the Strength compass point in a continuous effort to make life seem safe and under control.

The compulsive pattern also subverts the Assertion compass point through reaction formation. Because showing anger or disagreement with parents was prohibited in childhood, the person learned to safeguard the self by inwardly forbidding impulses of defiance (Berman & McCann, 1995). So the adult Controller has become a master of disguising anger as criticism "for a person's own good" or judgment against perceived rule violations (Stein et al., 1996).

If someone doesn't follow the "shoulds, oughts, and musts" of the Controller's mindset, the Controller feels a righteous duty to point out this shortcoming and offer a moralistic chastisement to drive the point home. Thus, when a compass point, in this case Assertion, is camouflaged by a defense mechanism, it still exerts a force in behavior, even though that force is converted to manipulation.

The therapeutic disengagement of reaction formation involves expanding the counselee's affect whenever any trace of anger or resentment is shown, working toward that time when the person comes into direct contact with anger, defiance, or assertion. By normalizing these primal feelings, and giving a compass interpretation of Assertion as a healthy aspect of human functioning and key ingredient of autonomy, the reaction formation loosens its hold. Gradually the counselee integrates diplomatic assertion into their behavioral repertoire. Likewise, the therapist makes it safe for the counselee to reveal and integrate the contents of the Weakness compass point, learning that they are not humiliated for showing vulnerability and uncertainty, but rather warmly complimented for their humanness.

The defense mechanism of *confluence* is a further outcome of overweening Strength. For the compulsive, this means identification of the self with the greater power of one's workplace, religion, or membership in an organization. By aligning with the strength of this greater power, compulsives fortify their authority. They make others conform to precise standards that are unworkably stringent and all-pervasive, gaining unconscious satisfaction from making others as burdened as themselves.

A third defense mechanism is called *splitting*, in which a primary portion of the person's life energies are invested in strength-oriented activities (discipline, follow through, planning), while a fragmented secondary portion is invested in an unconscious cover up of the fears and doubts that under-lie decision-making. This has a geyser-like effect, in that the Controller pattern attempts to keep everything under control, even while the chaos derived from procrastination is building toward an inevitable eruption. That eruption comes in the form of a sudden psychosomatic complaint—a pain in the neck, lower back, solar plexus, forehead, or bowels—that is actually more acceptable for the compulsive to deal with than facing the internal cleavage within the Self Compass.

In Summary, Controller-Patterned People:

+ Believe that work, duty, and moral perfection are the most important things in life. They emphasize self-discipline, emotional restraint, and the letter of the law.

+ Are preoccupied with how life should be and uncomfortable about how life really is.

+ Insist that subordinates or family members adhere to their "correct" way of doing things.

+ Resist novel ideas or anything unfamiliar: "They have surrounded themselves, as it were, by a protective wall...A constant 'no' is the almost automatic defense against intrusion" (Fromm, 1947, pp. 65-67)

+ Are workaholics who feel guilty about taking vacations, spending money, or relaxing and having a good time.

+ Have difficulty seeing past details and grasping the larger picture.

- Consider introspection a fruitless waste of time and resist the notion that there are unconscious forces at work within personality.

- Come across interpersonally as formal and emotionally distant precisely because they choose safe topics about which they view themselves as fully informed, while taking care not to self-disclose.

Controller Pattern

Compass Point: Strength

Manipulation: Righteous & Rule-bound

Thoughts: Critical to Obsessive

Feelings: Impatient to Perturbed

Actions: Compulsive & Tense

Growth Needs: Humility & Playfulness

Origins

The defense mechanism of *introjection* emerges in childhood as a response to feeling judged and overwhelmed by guilt and anxiety. The child identifies with the voice of the critical parent and "swallows it whole" as an intact superego that tells the child how to behave well at all times (Perls, 1992). The child gives up normal curiosity and adventure in favor of a safe existence that concentrates on the perceived Strength of adherence to rules (Sullivan, 1956). Compass theory adds that introjection bypasses the risks and learning opportunities of normal child and adolescent behavior, leaving an adult without practical experience in integrating the Love, Weakness, and Assertion compass points.

The budding Controller usually models a parent's controlling pattern. Parents overly socialize and micromanage the child, who becomes the model of adult orderliness. Parents set expectations for perfect performance without considering the child's developmental level. Rather than commending successes, parents take progress for granted and watch for errors with a critical eye.

The child's spontaneity and playfulness is squelched and replaced by a solemn hyper-maturity. With it forms an underlying guilt, a sense that one can never do enough "to secure parent approval" (Millon & Davis, 2000, p. 189). Instead of playfully interacting with toys and other children, the controller-in-training is too worried about getting messy or making a mistake to enjoy the adventure of childhood.

Clinical Literature

Freud described the compulsive personality pattern as the "anal character" which is manifested in people who are "exceptionally orderly, parsimonious, and obstinate" (1925).

In an expansion of this concept, Abraham described the "obsessional type" as experiencing "pleasure in indexing and classifying...in drawing upon programs and regulating work by timesheets...The forepleasure they get in working out a plan is stronger than their gratification in its execution." And regarding a judgmental attitude toward others, he wrote: "They are inclined to be exaggerated in their criticism of others, and this easily degenerates into carping" (1927, pp. 148-152).

Reich (1949) emphasized the presence of emotional repression and rigid body armor in "the compulsive character." He noted that compulsives are reserved and self-possessed, hiding their emotions from themselves and others.

Shapiro (1965) observed the rigidity of the Strength compass point with its self-conscious control in "obsessive-compulsive" types: "These people not only concentrate; they always seem to be concentrating." The underlying motivation that drives this pattern is control of oneself and external circumstances, a control that is achieved by assuming an "omniscience and omnipotence (that) can give one a false illusion of certainty" (Salzman, 1985, p. 19).

An explanation of the near synonymous terms "obsessive" and "compulsive" may prove helpful. In the nineteenth century Von Krafft-Ebing (1868) introduced the German word for compulsive, "Zwang," to refer to patients with compulsively constricted thinking. A year later Griesinger (1869) used the word compulsive or "Zwang" to describe patients who incessantly cross-examined themselves about what to do and how to do it. By the early twentieth century this German word had found its way into American translations as "compulsion" and British translations as "obsession" (Millon et al., 2004).

Today obsessive-compulsive symptoms refer to specific repetitive thoughts and acts that are beyond volitional control; e.g., washing one's hands frequently. When applied to a personality style, the obsessive-compulsive personality disorder is essentially the same as the compulsive disorder.

To simplify this duplication of terms, Compass Therapy defines the compulsive Controller personality pattern as a rigid style of functioning in which a counselee is obsessed with perfection and compelled to emphasize control above all else. They must appear to others as strong and decisive in every situation. The key word here is "appear," because the overblown Strength is founded upon a reaction against ever-present anxiety (Weakness).

Mind

Given their developmental history and formidable super-ego, the fundamental category of mental beliefs for the compulsive is "I should" (Beck, et al., 2004). Their minds govern behavior by words like "always," "never," "ought," and "must" in order to reduce the ambiguities of life into knowable certainties. This results in a "curse of perfectionism" that commands the compulsive to never make mistakes or to admit them when they inevitably occur (Montgomery, 2006, pp. 59-69). To carry off a perfectionist life, compulsives split the personality into an idealized self that is scrupulously conscientious, and a disowned self that is real but repressed from consciousness.

This cognitive-behavioral split between the rational "I should" and the secret "I fear" can pair the compulsive pattern with disorders from every compass point (Villemarette-Pittman et al., 2004). Thus, aggressive compulsives are self-righteous in a mean-spirited way. Schizoid compulsives are superior and aloof in their loner existence. Dependent compulsives strive to express perfect love to everyone all the time and judge themselves harshly for failing. Narcissistic compulsives flaunt their compulsions in a spirit of self-glory.

All these combinations share an interpersonal ambivalence (Warner et all, 2004) as evidenced by ingratiating behavior toward "superiors," or a dictatorial attitude toward "inferiors" (Pollack, 1987, pp. 249-250).

The automatic thoughts of the compulsive pattern express absolutes that leave little room for growth. Here are some examples:

- I must always be in control.

- I must do everything right the first time.

- People should do things my way.

- Thinking is always superior to feeling.

- There's a correct solution for all problems.

- You ought never throw anything away because you might need it later (Steketee & Frost, 2003).

- You should organize each day with a to-do list that must be completed before bedtime.

- To make a mistake is to deserve criticism.

- You can keep yourself from making a mistake by always being careful and thorough.

- People should do better and try harder and never shrink from duty.

- I have to enforce high standards on others because otherwise they will fall short.

- Criticizing people helps them avoid future mistakes.

- Enforcing rules is the best way through life.

Even when compulsives successfully achieve a goal, they ruminate about whether it was done well enough: "I should have done a better job. I should have planned more thoroughly. Why did my boss only praise me once? What did I do wrong?" And they fixate on the future: "How am I going to organize this so it will come out perfectly?" One mother worked so hard preparing every detail of her daughter's wedding that she collapsed from exhaustion right before it began.

There lies in this pattern an illogic that the Compass Model helps to explain. The compulsive drive for perfection leads to frequent procrastination and occasional paralysis of the will that derives from all-or-nothing thinking (Maslow, 1998; Egana et al., 2007). Since the outcome of every circumstance must be perfect, compulsives often hesitate to make decisions, for fear of a mistake. Eventually, these procrastinated choices add up to the considerable baggage of guilt and worry, which are exiled to an unconscious storage bin on the Weakness compass point.

The Self-Image Diagram

The Self-Image Diagram can assist compulsives in understanding how to free up their rule-bound thoughts and integrate them with emotion, relational intimacy, relaxation, and the actualizing power of a balanced Self Compass.

The therapist explains that the Perfectionist Self houses all the rules introjected from childhood—the critical top dog part of the self that demands perfection, represses emotions, and exiles unacceptable impulses to the unconscious.

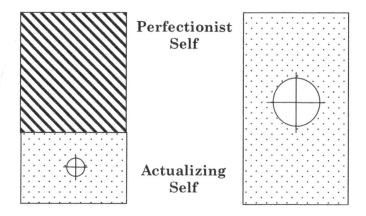

On the left side, the diagram shows how the Perfectionist Self presses down on the Actualizing Self, making the person top heavy with a "tyranny of shoulds" (Horney, 1945).

The Perfectionist Self operates within the very structure of the compulsive dynamics by accusing the Actualizing Self, which, if given the chance, would enrich the personality with flexibility, emotional discernment, bodily relaxation, and spiritual serenity.

The truth is that the contents of the Actualizing Self cannot be released for exploration and discovery, let alone for actualizing growth, until the pressure from the Perfectionist Self is dismantled.

On the right, the diagram shows how the Actualizing Self is freed for expression, yet incorporates those aspects of the Perfectionist Self now balanced by the Self Compass, such as interest in a job done well enough, not perfectly.

Because growth happens slowly over the course of therapy, the gradual liberation from the compulsive pattern comes from many small adjustments that eventually transform the compulsive template into the personality and relational health of compass living.

As a way of warming up to these concepts, the therapist encourages the counselee to unpack the contents of the rule-laden Perfectionist Self, exploring how they first learned to associate perfectionist control with security and loss of control with catastrophe. When they voice fears about becoming a reckless, irresponsible person if they let their guard down, you offer assurance they will only strengthen their integrity and increase their capability by exchanging black-and-white thinking for a wider range of behavioral options. This way of framing growth uses healthy Strength to outgrow compulsivity itself.

Heart

Though compulsives are usually agreeable and wanting to impress the therapist at the beginning of therapy, it won't be long until the therapist runs into the brick wall of the pattern's intrinsic stubbornness and tendency to get lost in details (Holaway et al., 2006). Further, there is an edge to the communication that arises from the counselee's inner pressure to always be right. A distrust of change quickly reveals itself as a resistance to new ideas (Jovev & Jackson,

2004) and a reluctance to enter into a corroborative therapeutic relationship.

Yet progress comes by drawing out the compulsive's high expectation for other people's behavior, a topic they can talk about with a degree of emotional enthusiasm. In listening to how frequently they are disappointed by other people's lack of discipline or laziness, you can expand the feelings of frustration and anger that lie buried in the unconscious. These feelings of critical discontent will surface first because it feels less vulnerable to express anger than to express hurt or anxiety.

Over time, though, as the therapeutic conversation deepens, you reflect other feelings that the compulsive has completely disowned, which are enlightening to them when framed in a communication that preserves their dignity.

Therapist: "So it's not just discontent you feel with your wife, it's also some anxiety about feeling so alone."

Counselee: (Pauses to reflect). "I think that's probably accurate, although technically I don't like thinking of myself as an anxious person. But I did feel alone during childhood, even though I was very involved in activities and organizations. People looked up to me but I didn't feel close to anyone."

Therapist: "And you had hopes that this marriage would bring that closeness?"

Counselee: "Well, everybody says how happy you should be in marriage, and that having kids should bring love to your life. But I just feel left out and kind of ignored."

Therapist: "That's an excellent expression of a feeling. It helps us both understand that you really want more love in your life, and really feel its absence."

211

By expressing empathy for the counselee who is trapped within the compulsive pattern, you are giving the counselee a new emotional experience of feeling deeply accepted and understood. This is the very form of love that was missing in the counselee's upbringing. You are also reframing the emotional dimension of the counselee's human nature as something to be cherished and approached with curiosity rather than condemned.

This growth process encourages the development of spontaneity and flexibility so characteristically absent from compulsives (Mudrack, 2004). For once you have helped the counselee to own and express loneliness or sadness, you are opening the door to other more edifying feelings.

Let's say that in another point in the session the counselee expresses frustration about being late to work that week.

Therapist: "When you knew you would arrive at work ten minutes late, what were you feeling inside?"

Counselee: (Takes a deep breath). "I felt like my life depended on getting there on time, and that people would think I was irresponsible for being late."

Therapist: "That's when you got the speeding ticket?"

Counselee: "Yes. I tried to tell the officer what a good driver I am, but I still got cited."

Therapist: "So the compulsive pattern created fear about being late, and this pressured you to speed up?"

Counselee: "Exactly."

Therapist: "It's like the pattern made you feel as though you were going to appear on the cover of *Time* with the caption, "Accountant Late for Work: Office Falls Apart.""

Counselee: (Laughs). "I think maybe the pattern makes me exaggerates things."

Therapist: "Good insight."

Body

What compulsives don't know but are often intrigued to find out is that the defense mechanism of *repression* actually represents as much a physical phenomenon as it does psychological. Repression occurs at a given moment in time when a particularly strong emotion is perceived as threatening and immediately converted by bioelectrical innervations into muscular tension. This takes physical effort at the molecular level, for it involves stopping the emotion in its tracks, freezing its motion by tightening both smooth and striated muscle fibers. Because of this muscular contraction, the emotion no longer flows as a feeling that can be processed and understood.

An arrested emotion creates an unfinished state in the psyche, like an incomplete circle with a gap blocking its completion. It is normal in human development to repress certain feelings in threatening or uncomfortable situations, but in the history of the compulsive there is a steady formation of many unclosed circles, so many that it becomes a way of life to exist with a tense, shutdown body to keep emotion under control.

No wonder the compulsive counselee is afraid to relax the body, or to have unstructured leisure time. To do so risks loosening up an uptight body and releasing into consciousness a flood of feelings that are messy and uncontrollable.

However, repression of emotions and physical memories is a labor-intensive activity with an unforeseen consequence, again a fact of life that the compulsive may want to know about. Negative emotions that are converted into physical tension cause pain: muscle spasms and muscular exhaustion in the form of headaches, backaches, pains in the neck, gastroenteritis, joint pain, insomnia, and a host of other psycho-somatic complaints that plague the compulsive child and adult, as though trying to shout, "Pay attention to me. I am an emotion and I have an important message for you about how you are feeling right now."

So continued repression in the here-and-now is required to stay numb to emotions. Living an overly busy life with constant mental distractions assures that these emotions are kept out of consciousness. Compass theory suggests that over the long haul compulsives, even though they strive so hard to put up a front of propriety and discipline, feel secretly exhausted. But even this is kept from awareness by soldiering on.

It makes perfect sense, then, that eating disorders are quite common among compulsives (Sansone et al., 2005; Halmi, 2005). Compass theory offers this explanation: the compulsive Controller bans relaxation, leisure, play, and laughter from life, and judges them as unnecessary wastes of time. If exercise or hobbies are pursued, it is in a compulsive manner that is serious and takes work. This ascetic existence leaves the body craving stimulation and pleasure in order to feel alive rather than dead. Many compulsives discover the physiological fact that food, and especially carbohydrates, can create a rush of arousal upon ingestion and tranquilize the body as an afterglow.

It isn't long before the body develops a psychological and physical craving for more. This sets up a perpetual battle between willpower to control weight and urges to eat compulsively, followed by remorse and self-disgust. Twelve-Step groups like Overeater's Anonymous are valuable as an adjunct to psychological counseling, as is assistance from a medical facility if spiraling weight gain or weight loss become a danger to health.

Relaxation training, biofeedback, abdominal breathing, and clinical hypnosis are beneficial techniques in that they reduce overall muscle tension, helping the counselee learn how to shift from compulsive beta wave thinking to mellow alpha wave serenity.

Compass Therapy concurs with Behavior Therapy that guided behavioral practice can generate and reinforce new learning. What follows is a physical technique that can help diminish the psycho-physiological fear of failure. Before you decide to apply this technique, make sure the counselee has no history of knee injuries and is not overweight to the point that would place undue stress upon bent knees. To execute the technique you put a soft pillow on the floor and ask the counselee to stand in front of it.

Therapist: "Now we're going to physically symbolize your fear of failure by having you bend your knees over this pillow until your legs develop fatigue and you are forced by gravity to fall. The first time through I want you to resist falling as long as possible, and then give in to gravity when you have no strength left."

Counselee: (Assumes a half-crouched position with knees bent over the pillow). "Is this right?"

Therapist: (Looks to make sure that the knees are bent enough to exert pressure on the thigh muscles, but not so much that the person will collapse). "Yes, that's fine. Just hold this posture for as long as you can. Try as hard as possible not to fall." (The counselee begins straining in an effort to stay above the pillow). "That's right, convince yourself that there's no way you're going to give in to the stress, that you're committed to perfectly controlling this situation by not falling."

Counselee: (Frowns, looking down anxiously at the pillow, straining every muscle to stand half-erect). "This is getting hard. I don't think I can stay up here much longer."

Therapist: "What are you feeling?"

Counselee: "I'm feeling very uncomfortable...afraid I'm going to fall...afraid of failing to stand up!"

Therapist: "Okay, give it all you've got, and then let go to gravity and fall to your knees."

Counselee: (Strains a few more seconds, legs trembling, and then falls to the pillow).

Therapist: "Good. Now what are you aware of?"

Counselee: "Well, I held out as long as I could, but it wasn't good enough. I failed to keep standing."

Therapist: "Can you have compassion for yourself right now, since you were up against gravity, one of the mightiest forces in the universe?"

Counselee: (Smiles). "I suppose so, but I don't want to make excuses."

Therapist: "Well said." (Kneels down to establish eye contact with the counselee). "This exercise helps to show how the compulsive pattern drives you beyond endurance, to numb yourself against pain and stress, and to keep plodding on, no matter what the consequences."

Counselee: "I always thought of it as just doing my duty—you know, doing everything possible not to fail."

Therapist: "What happened when you failed just now?"

Counselee: "Well, actually I felt relieved once I landed on the pillow."

Therapist: "So your compulsive pattern told you it would be terrible and awful to fall, but after you gave it your best shot and then surrendered to gravity, it wasn't so bad. Is that right?"

Counselee: "If only life was this simple."

Therapist: "Perhaps it is. I'd like you to stand up again, only this time, stay in the stress position until you need to rest, and then surrender your body to the pillow, so that you can relax and regain your strength."

Counselee: (Assumes the stress position. Facial muscles, neck, and shoulders are more relaxed). "Okay, I'm starting to feel the weakness in my legs. Now I'm starting to tremble."

Therapist: "Fine. What do you want to tell yourself?"

Counselee: "I want to say that I'll stand up a few more seconds..." (Falls to knees on the pillow). "And that it's not a big deal to give in to gravity."

Therapist: "Are you feeling all the fear of failure that you did the first time?"

Counselee: "No. In fact I feel peaceful. It's like I can give something my best shot, and then relax when I need to break off from it."

Therapist: "Now try it once more, this time relaxing and enjoying yourself while holding the stress position, and then falling to the pillow."

Counselee: (Does so, seeming to feel more comfortable whether in strength, weakness, or recovery). "That was a lot easier. I didn't go through all the mental gymnastics about staying strong. I just held out until I needed to fall."

Therapist: "Let's take our seats again." (Removes the pillow). "How might you relate this to what you're learning about your Self Compass?"

Counselee: "Well, this is obviously about accepting both my Strength and Weakness compass points, and not panicking over whether I'm perfect or not. I guess it means to me that I'm only human. Sometimes I can control things. And sometimes I can't. And I can be more relaxed inside myself either way."

Therapist: "If you printed this insight as a motto on your T-shirt and wore it to work tomorrow, what would it say?"

Counselee: "Ha, that's a good one. I think I'd like it to read: 'Perfectionists of the world unite, and fall!'"

Spirit

The spiritual essence of compulsivity lies in distrust of the present moment and a need to control the immediate future. Just as the compulsive psyche remains segmented between conscious and unconscious, between Strength and Weakness, and between thinking and feeling, the dimension of time remains fragmented into a past that one regrets, a present that one distrusts, and a future that one dreads.

The remedy that makes a whole out of these fragments comes more from the spiritual realm of existence than from the purely psychological.

Research shows that actualizing individuals develop a different experience of time, using most of their awareness for thinking, feeling, and sensing what is going on in the present moment, and a smaller percentage in thinking about the past or preparing for the future (Shostrom, 1976).

By contrast, the compulsive Controller expends more energy in thinking about the past (regrets, resentments, guilt) or anticipating the future. "What should I do?" "How must I do it?" "How can I guarantee that my choices are correct?" This leaves only a small portion of awareness available for living in the present moment.

Compulsive counselees need a daily method for living with more "wholeheartedness" (Horney, 1945/1994); "trust in the organism" (Rogers, 1961); "spontaneity and creativity" (Moreno, 1972); "trust in the now" (Perls, 1973); "present-centeredness" (Shostrom, 1979), and "trust in the spiritual core" (Montgomery & Montgomery, 2007, 2008).

Trust, the antidote to compulsive control, needs to percolate in-and-through the being of the compulsive, thought by thought, feeling by feeling, muscle group by muscle group, right down into the spiritual core, the wellspring of trust versus fear. This is not accomplished through mental belief alone, which is too flimsy to withstand the fear-inducing voice of the compulsive pattern. Spiritual serenity engages the whole of human nature and provides power from a source greater than compulsivity to form a new foundation for living.

Here the therapist suggests the use of prayer, meditative practice, or relaxation imagery as a way of increasing the counselee's trust in the spiritual core and in God as a ready help in the time of need.

14
Borderline Challenger Pattern

From a compass theory perspective, the borderline is a flip-flop pattern. That is, the pattern favors one half of the Self Compass at the expense of the other, yet unpredictably flip-flops to its polar opposite. Borderline-patterned persons primarily exaggerate the Strength and Assertion compass points as "top dogs," yet make regular swings into the lower compass points of Love and Weakness. They feel boldly entitled in social situations, cajoling people to fill the emptiness inside them. When others fail to do so, they shift into blame and attack mode without warning, aggressively challenging others to meet their insatiable dependency needs.

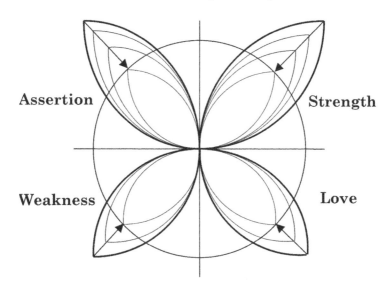

Assertion

Strength

Weakness

Love

The Pattern's Interior

The borderline pattern's self-system fluctuates drastically as emotional explosions are interspersed with the boundless need for reassurance. When caught in the grip of anxiety (Weakness compass point) or longing for nurturance (Love compass point), the person seeks assurance in the manner of the avoidant Worrier or dependent Pleaser patterns. This sends others an SOS signal that elicits a desire to rescue the borderline-patterned person from depression or loneliness. But since the borderline demands assurance that is absolute and comforting that is perfect, these demands are quickly frustrated.

Then self-righteous judgment erupts. Furiously accusing others of neglect, disregard, and untrustworthiness, the behavior now more closely resembles that of the paranoid Arguer and narcissistic Boaster patterns.

Extreme affective volatility, erratic shifts between aggression and neediness, and a lack of trust in self or others render the borderline's Self Compass unstable and volatile; hence the compass theory term, "borderline Challenger." Such shakiness is accentuated by ever-present and contradictory feelings toward others: dependent anger and anxious superiority (Millon & Davis, 1996, p. 658). In other words, "the lives of individuals with borderline personality features resemble a daily roller coaster ride" (Tolpin et al., 2004).

Origins

The borderline personality pattern is formed in a family dynamic where frequent boundary incursions and crises make it difficult for the child to establish a reliable identity. Rather, the child experiences confluence with the parent, in which thoughts and feelings are all tangled into knots. It seems impossible to establish where one's identity begins and another's ends. This amorphous merging prevents the child from successfully developing either attachment or individuation.

Lacking sufficient self-boundaries, the child is stuck in an undifferentiated limbo. Communications are taken personally and reacted against, rather than responded to or understood.

The child interprets these garbled communications as his or her fault or the fault of others. Parents may act out through incessant arguing, drunken fury, physical combativeness, suicide attempts, or incest. Ongoing sexual abuse is the best predictor of the severity of borderline symptoms (Silk et al., 1995). Other empirically validated risk factors include loss, physical or emotional abuse, parental substance abuse or criminality, and severe neglect (Zanarini et al., 1997).

Whatever the particulars, the child learns to become center stage in this chaos, discovering how to create a similar chaos in others. While adult borderlines often search for a romantic relationship to "make everything okay," studies indicate that these pairings are fraught with conflict because they replicate childhood and adolescent difficulties in forming healthy attachment (Dutton, 2002; Hill et al., 2008).

Family-of-origin members usually perceive attempts toward autonomy and individuality as betrayal, and punish the child accordingly. With no Self Compass for balance, the child remains dependent upon family members while feeling rage against them for the invasion of one's personhood. Inner pain that erupts explosively seems perfectly normal. The whole scenario may be framed by a family secret that says, "This is a crazy family, but don't you dare tell anyone that this is a crazy family."

Clinical Literature

Schneider (1950) first employed the term "labile" to accentuate the volatile nature of the borderline pattern. Indeed, this term is more descriptive than "borderline," capturing the pattern's predictable inconsistency (Millon & Davis, 1996).

Stern (1938) characterized this pattern as a "borderline group of neuroses" exhibiting contradictory traits: narcissistic grandiosity combined with feelings of inferiority, and psychic rigidity combined with inordinate hypersensitivity. Stern coined the term "psychic bleeding" to convey the anxious desperation that drives this unstable pattern.

Schmidberg viewed the borderline personality as "stable in his instability, whatever ups and downs he has, and often keeps constant his pattern of peculiarity" (1959, pp. 398-416). More recently, Kernberg (1975) has described the pattern as a "mutual dissociation of contradictory ego states."

Mind

The primary cognitive distortion of the borderline Challenger pattern centers on the chronic use of mutually exclusive categories.

Borderline self-talk sounds like this:

⊕ Either you love me or you hate me.

⊕ I have every right to lash out when you don't show enough love.

⊕ To leave my presence when I need you is abandonment.

⊕ Make my emptiness go away or I'll punish you.

⊕ People need to pay attention to me because I'm very important.

⊕ I can't stand to depend on people because they always disappoint me.

⊕ You don't love me as much as I love you.

⊕ Give me what I want or I'll hate you.

- Don't leave me alone because I need you all the time.

- You should accept my explosions if you love me.

Borderline Challengers lean on the structure of the environment to maintain their cognitive bearings, and hence regress to primitive ego states whenever the environment changes. For instance, when a person they rely upon has needs for privacy, or decides on a course of action that seems to exclude them, borderlines can panic and take desperate measures to counter the show of independence. Moments later, however, they forget their intimidation and threats, and sincerely proclaim themselves as the other person's best friend.

Normal individuals tolerate cognitive dissonance through the integration of polar opposites. They can hold in mind both that a partner cares for them and that the partner needs alone times to function as an independent person.

Actualizing partners blend opposing polarities by offering more sophisticated communications, like caring assertion, or humble requests. Borderlines bypass developing a toleration of opposites, and instead think in stark "either/or" terms that call for ultimatums and showdowns, followed by emotional tirades or collapse.

Borderlines are particularly vulnerable to intrusive thoughts and images, including flashbacks and nightmares. When these occur, they tend to dump the toxic residue of these disturbing experiences straight into a current relationship. But it's not long before they forget what they've just done, and expect an immediate return to a more congenial atmosphere.

Naturally, this relationship-shattering style creates approach-avoidance conflicts within the borderline's partner or friends, causing them to seriously consider abandoning the borderline Challenger. The borderline, then, picks up on these cues and challenges with a vengeance the partner's thoughts about leaving the relationship.

Heart

The emotions and moods of the borderline pattern vary intensely. Extended periods of dejection and disillusionment are interspersed with brief excursions into euphoria. Characteristics of the pattern include elevated hopes, impulsive anger, and self-destructive acts. Contrary to the borderline's perception, these mood swings are more often prompted by internal rigidities than external events.

The borderline-patterned person has not resolved the growth issue of separation anxiety. One borderline counselee wanted to staple her hand to the therapist's chair rather than leave the session. Lacking a sturdy attachment bond from childhood, borderlines can experience panic or rage when another person has to go somewhere or is not instantly available to meet their needs.

There is torment in solitude, a sense of emptiness and boredom. A constant edginess yields relationships rife with fears of desertion. One demands that others fill one's inner vacuum, clinging with angry desperation like a child wrapping arms around a mother's leg. When others shift attention to their own needs, the borderline Challenger blows up with fearful fury.

They are on a perpetual quest for an idealized fusion with another person that will solve all their problems and bring complete and continuous contentment. The therapist can address this topic under the heading of the "fusion illusion" by commending the counselee's desire for love, while discussing how intimacy requires the acceptance of individual differences, the giving of space to one's partner, and a respect for free will choices. In other words, borderlines need to find peace within their spiritual core as a prelude to developing a healthy companionship.

Body

Research suggests that biology plays a major role in the borderline personality pattern. The amygdala, for example, which normally helps to modulate vigilance and emotional states, is overly active in persons diagnosed with borderline personality disorder. Donegan (2003) found that borderline patients showed significantly greater left amygdala activation to the facial expressions of emotion compared to normal control subjects. He suggested that amygdala hyperreactivity contributes to hypervigilance, emotional dysregulation, and disturbed interpersonal relations.

Difficulties in brain function may contribute to impulsive behaviors that include orbitofrontal cortex dysfunction (Berlin, et al., 2005), and low 5-HT synthesis capacity in corticostriatal pathways (Leyton et al., 2001).

The main targets for pharmacotherapy of borderline personality disorder include affective regulation, impulsive-behavioral control, and cognitive-perceptual stability. A few controlled studies have been performed using olanzapine that show improvements in impulsivity, anger, and hostility. A large number of different drugs are being evaluated in the treatment of patients with borderline personality disorder with encouraging results, but many questions still remain (Bellino, et al., 2008).

Spirit

DSM describes one of the criteria for borderline personality disorder as "chronic feelings of emptiness." Recent research reveals that for borderline counselees, emptiness is closely related to feeling hopeless, lonely, and isolated, and predicts depression with suicidal ideation. Emptiness reflects pathologically low positive affect and significant psychiatric distress (Klonsky, 2008). An example of compass intervention follows, in which a borderline wife and her husband ultimately express spiritual growth as a couple.

Compass Intervention Using Couples Therapy

When Paul and Carmen came to their first couple's session, I could feel a continental divide between them. I guided them into self-disclosure about their relational history. Paul sat with arms and legs folded and a poker face with eyes staring straight ahead. Carmen oscillated between bewailing the loneliness she had felt in five years of marriage, followed by hornet's nest attacks on Paul that seemed to heat up the whole office.

I surmised that though Paul had wrapped himself in a cocoon of schizoid detachment, Carmen was waging war to tear away the cocoon. I concentrated on relaxing my body during the attacks, asking strategic questions during interludes, signaling that I understood both Paul's steely silences and Carmen's vacillation between despairing self-pity and scathing accusations.

Toward the end of the session I shifted gears to develop a summary and agreed-upon treatment goals.

Dan: "You two are very intelligent individuals who felt love for each other when you dated and married. But since then it seems you've become locked in a combative stalemate by personality patterns that existed long before you married. If you choose me as your therapist, I will seek to make each of you aware of how you are contributing to communication breakdown, and at the same time explore strategies for building effective communication."

Carmen: "Can you promise to make Paul change?"

Dan: "I can promise to show you both what stands in the way of change."

Dan: (I turned to Paul). "Paul, do you sit in silence with all your friends, or mainly just with Carmen?"

Paul: "Well, most people say I'm friendly. It is true that I don't see much need for talking. But with Carmen anything I say is wrong. So I've pretty much clammed up."

Dan: "Have you developed this silent treatment as a way of punishing her?"

Paul: (Shrugged). "It's more like I want to protect myself from her attacks."

Carmen: "That is absolutely false! I never attack him, Dr. Montgomery. (Glared at Paul). You promised to love me when we got married but you spend so much time by yourself that I might just as well not exist!"

Paul: "It's the only way to have peace of mind."

Carmen: "You're deliberately driving me crazy!"

Dan: (Looked at both of them). "So is this exchange an example of what happens every day?"

Paul: (Shrugged).

Carmen: "Every damned day. And I just can't take it any more."

Dan: "Can we agree on a therapeutic goal of building personality awareness that promotes better communication?"

Paul: "If Carmen wants. She dragged me here."

Carmen: "I did not, you son-of-a-bitch. You said we should go to counseling a year ago."

Paul: "That was before I gave up."

Carmen: (Grabbed her purse as though to hit Paul). "I'm not going to sit here and let you bad mouth me!"

Dan: "So Paul, you feel like there's no hope and don't really want to come back. Is that right?"

Paul: "That's right, but I'll come one more time."

Dan: "And Carmen, you are at your wits end and see therapy as the only hope. Is that right?"

Carmen: "That's right. It's either come here or get an attorney. But I don't want a divorce. (Teared up). I really love Paul."

I wound up the session by giving them a psychodiagnostic assessment battery to complete at home and mail in for computer scoring. The results revealed that Paul was in the 80% range on the schizoid personality disorder and 70% on the avoidant disorder with mild depression. Carmen was in the 90% range for the borderline personality disorder, with significant elevation of anxiety and histrionic trends.

Over the first two months of therapy I did a lot of refereeing, calling communication fouls on both sides, and pointing out what healthier communication styles would look like. Paul took in my input with thoughtful passivity. Carmen often took issue as though she considered any feedback about her communication style a direct insult.

Since Paul's were the lower scores in terms of clinically significant pathology, I gave him more personal and direct feedback about the patterns he had evolved and the ways that these patterns torpedoed any prospects for marital intimacy. Here is an example:

Dan: "Paul, I think it's really healthy that you love your woodworking hobby, but I wonder if you foresaw that the amount of time you spend in the garage would make your wife a psychological widow."

Paul: "My dad did the same thing and my mom never complained."

Dan: "And did you see them develop warm communication? Hugs? Heart-to-heart talks? That kind of thing?"

Paul: "They seemed happy enough, but no, I never saw them show much feeling for each other."

Dan: "Did they define their marriage with pastimes and separate interests?"

Paul: "I suppose. Dad worked and spent all his spare time in the garage. She worked part-time and spent the rest of her day cooking and watching after us kids."

Carmen: "That's exactly what you want from me, Paul. You want to take me down from the shelf and use me for sex and then put me back on the shelf like some power tool!"

Dan: (Made referee hand-signal for 'time-out'). "Carmen, you just levied a broadside against Paul while he was talking to me. That kind of communication is self-defeating, because it will make him gun-shy and afraid to tell me much else."

Carmen: "I'm sorry. Sometimes I feel threatened and say things before I think."

Dan: "That's a superb observation. Now if you can take a deep breath and relax your shoulders to handle your anxiety, I'll continue with Paul. There's an advantage to you in doing this, because Paul is coming clean about a lot of things that you've been accusing him of. And he's doing it of his own free will."

Carmen: (Made a zipping motion over her lips). "Okay."

In this manner I helped Paul to own his longstanding pattern of keeping feelings to himself. He came to see that he had introjected this self-contained solitariness from his father, and that the pattern was an enemy of the love he had originally felt for Carmen. Paul also drew hope from the Self Compass. He decided to become more expressive of love, more open to experiencing vulnerability without spacing out, and more assertive in helping Carmen. By the third month of therapy, Paul and I could regularly refer to his "old avoidant pattern" without him feeling hurt and withdrawing. In the meantime, Carmen expressed nothing short of amazement that the man she married could actually think clearly, express emotions on occasion, and become quite animated as long as she didn't flip out on him.

However, she began to notice her own difficulty in controlling the sudden changes in her behavior that would catapult her from love and need into anger and attack. That's when I knew it was time to break the news to her about her personal pathology.

Dan: "Carmen, you have done very well in learning to let Paul express his thoughts without jumping in to finish them for him. I know it's taking a lot of patience on your part, because he does talk slowly. But we've both seen how much he cares about communication with you, and how he is making progress in responding to some of your emotional needs."

Carmen: "Yes, he is. But I still blow up at him. We were on the golf course Tuesday. When I couldn't get my swing right, I starting bitching. He asked if he could help me. I bit his head off."

Dan: "What were you telling yourself about his offer?"

Carmen: "That he was being a smart aleck by criticizing my stroke."

Dan: "Out of curiosity, is there someone historically who has done this to you—built themselves up by cutting you down?"

Carmen: (Looked stunned). "My older sister. She has spent her lifetime pointing out what's wrong with me and why she's smarter, prettier, and wealthier than me!"

Dan: "So this perception that relationships are a competition in which you do or die, goes clear back into your childhood."

Carmen: "Oh yeah. She got it from my father. He always favored her because she was such a go-getter like him. They both made fun of me. Once we were driving back from a family picnic and a skunk crossed the road in front of us. She shouted, "There goes a Carmen!" She and Dad busted a gut laughing. I felt like a total nothing!"

Dan: "This is an incredibly important memory and I want to thank your unconscious for recalling it. It's like you were ganged up on and your self-esteem beaten senseless by a moronic dad and sister who had great laughs at your expense."

Carmen: (A tear trickled down her cheek. She nodded, looking down at the carpet). "They were always doing things like that. But my sister never stopped."

Dan: (Turned to Paul). "How do you feel in picturing this scene?"

Paul: "I want to punch her dad right in the kisser. I never really knew him, except that he acted like God around their house. But she's absolutely right about her sister. I tell Carmen not to stay on the phone with her, because she always gets hurt in the end."

Dan: "Carmen, how do you feel knowing that Paul loves you so much he felt like socking your father for hurting you?"

Carmen: (Smiled). "Dad's dead now. But it felt good to hear." She reached across the sofa and touched his hand.

With twenty minutes left in the session, and knowing there would never be a perfect time to relay Carmen's clinical diagnosis to her, I decided that now was as good a time as any.

Dan: "Carmen, I want to congratulate you for the warmth you just showed to Paul. And I want to say I feel keenly for the torment you endured growing up."

Carmen: (Nodded).

Dan: "Now there is an important tie-in to your puzzlement about why you suddenly exploded at Paul on the golf course...about why you can shift so rapidly from love to anger, or from feeling secure to feeling like you're a nobody. Would you like to hear about it today or wait until next week?"

Carmen: (Sat up in her seat and focused her eyes on me). "Go ahead."

Dan: "Well, I apologize for not passing this information on to you sooner, but I know that diagnoses about personality structure can feel very threatening—even insulting. And I made a judgment call that we needed to establish a solid track record in therapy that would help you hear the nature of your personality difficulties."

Carmen: "So you're saying all our problems are my fault!"

Dan: "I am saying that the structure of your personality makes its own unique contribution to communication problems, and that you can make significant progress once you understand how it works."

Carmen: "I'm not thrilled, but go ahead."

Dan: "The assessment battery has revealed a borderline pattern in your personality. This explains why you are often riding a roller coaster between love and anger."

Carmen: (Eyes flashed). "Borderline...borderline! That's the worst thing you could say about me! Everybody knows that borderline people are crazy loons who belong in mental institutions. How can you be so cruel to call me that!"

Dan: "I understand your feeling of outrage, but I want to suggest that this is the borderline pattern at work. Would you like to know more?"

Carmen: "Well, I...I...." (She turned to Paul with hands extended). "You don't think I'm a borderline do you?"

Paul: (He clasped her hands in his and spoke softly). "Honey, I don't know what the borderline stuff is all about, but what Dr. Dan just said fits you perfectly."

We ended the session on a calmer note, with Carmen shaken but reassured that coming to grips with her personality pattern could lead to positive developments previously blocked in their couple's communication.

Indeed, over the next three months of therapy they each made unmistakable gains. Now that we could talk openly about her abrupt shifts from feeling close to Paul to blowing her stack at him, Paul opened up considerably, not just about Carmen's behavior, but about his own long-term history of keeping emotions locked inside.

Paul was genuinely troubled about how easy it was to live in his own world, oblivious to Carmen's or anyone else's feelings and needs. In a sobering moment he realized that he was programmed to live and die a lonely man, even though married to a woman who loved him. More than that, he became disgusted with himself for remaining so emotionally stunted and immature for the better part of a lifetime. I framed this to him as coming to terms with his Weakness compass point, and learning to accept that the past was dead but the future was filled with promise for a more actualizing life.

Here is where Carmen's Love compass point and her former borderline directness about expression began to work in a positive direction. "I'm here for you, baby," she'd say, putting an arm around his shoulder. "I love you and you're really changing."

Working with the Borderline's Human Nature

To further assist Carmen, I worked with her whole human nature during sessions. When she'd get hot under the collar, I would have her focus on relaxing her body and becoming aware of her self-talk. When she would suddenly shift topics, I would have her focus on the last feeling she was in touch with so she could develop emotional closure. When her body would tense I would invite her to hold hands with Paul as a form of physical comfort. When she expressed futility about ever getting over her borderline tendencies, I would tell her that with God's help, all things are possible.

When her communication began to jam up, I didn't hesitate to pause and say, "Carmen, can you take a moment to breathe deeply a couple of times, and surrender a bit to your spiritual core? Then we'll see what comes up from your depths." Or I'd make a referee's timeout sign and say, "You're starting to work yourself into a frenzy, but I wonder if you might think about the one point you're making, so we can address it." When she occasionally lashed out at me, I might say, "I respect the anger you're feeling. Would you like us to shift the attention to Paul for a while?"

Slowly and noticeably Carmen began to exercise insight into her own Human Nature Compass. She would stop the session by saying, "Whoops, you lost me. My mind is starting to blur." Or she'd turn to Paul, saying, "What you just said sounds inflammatory. Can you repeat it in different words?" It's as though she was learning to trust the rhythms of her Mind, Heart, Body, and Spirit, and monitor these checks and balances that were bringing her a new level of stability and self-control.

By six months of therapeutic work, we had a recovering borderline Challenger developing an inner center of gravity that held, and a recovering schizoid Loner developing interpersonal skills and thriving on the steadier dose of love that Carmen was providing. Carmen would still take something personally and get testy. However, her growing insight into this pattern and Paul's lack of intimidation made the episodes more manageable.

Now Paul was helping her develop inner security by being more emotionally connected, making sincere apologies for his part in any miscommunication, and gently reminding her when her pattern was acting out.

Carmen, in accessing healthy Weakness, would apologize more quickly and vow to keep making progress in giving him space to live. They both worked on refining the Assertion compass point, Carmen in developing more diplomatic assertion, and Paul in standing up for himself if she went too far.

Truly, he had made the old "silent treatment" a thing of the past.

We didn't just talk about their relationship. New topics came up every week or two. We analyzed and worked through Carmen's discomfiting relationship with one of Paul's friends. Paul learned not to side with this fellow as he did in the past, but to support his wife in holding her own against his friend's obnoxious behavior. Carmen also made steady progress dealing with her sister by feeling less vulnerable to hurt, and developing more of a live-and-let-live philosophy.

When the fading but still active borderline flip-flopping would occur during a session, I would thank them both for giving us a fresh juicy example of marital dysfunction, and move forward with the lab work of dissecting it into component parts, exploring alternate choices and perceptions that might break the behavioral chain, and suggesting homework for practicing self-awareness about the LAWS of mutually effective communication. This led to the development of hardier forms of self-worth (Strength) and quicker apologies (Weakness) when fouls of communication occurred.

In the eighth month of our couples work Paul and Carmen began to act on my recommendations offered earlier in therapy to include their individual spirituality as part of a balanced Self Compass. Since Paul had been a lapsed Methodist and Carmen a lapsed Baptist, both decided to join a spiritual fellowship in a non-denominational church. Their attendance at Sunday services and a Wednesday night couples group strengthened a sense of God's presence within their life as a couple. Each reported a new openness to pray for help instead of trying to make changes by willpower alone. As a consequence, I noticed that a peace and willingness to admit mistakes while taking responsibility to try new behaviors flowed more easily into our sessions.

The next few months focused on consolidating their gains and troubleshooting occasional difficulties. There were still arguments about finances or miscommunications about sex, but on the whole they lived more like a couple in love than perplexed partners in a crazy-making relationship. By mutual consent they graduated from therapy at the end of the year. After we all exchanged hugs for the bond we had developed, I released them to one another's care, and to God's.

In summary, therapist and counselees alike can take heart in the knowledge that the borderline personality disorder is a treatable condition (Clarkin et al., 2007). Gabbard notes that "any thoughtful, systematic approach to borderline personality disorder, based on our knowledge of the disorder, is potentially helpful, whatever its theoretical underpinnings or technical approach" (2007).

15
THE HUMAN NATURE COMPASS

Now that we have explored the most prevalent personality patterns, let's examine how Compass Therapy views human nature and why it employs the multilevel framework of Mind (cognition) and Heart (emotion), Body (biology) and Spirit (values) in treatment strategies.

Historically, counseling theories have tended to emphasize one of these elements as predominant for understanding human nature and promoting behavioral change. These approaches include:

⊕ *Mind*: Cognitive Therapy, Transactional Analysis, Narrative Therapy, & Reality Therapy.

⊕ *Heart*: Client-Centered Therapy & Primal Therapy.

⊕ *Body*: Bioenergetics, Biofeedback, Clinical Hypnotherapy, & EMDR.

⊕ *Spirit*: Jungian Therapy, Existential Therapy, Logotherapy, & Transpersonal Therapy.

Today, contemporary theorists are postulating models of human nature that incorporate several of these elements, like the bio-psycho-social model (Millon et al., 2004; Lazarus, 2006; Corey, 2008).

Compass Therapy consolidates these parameters by applying the compass paradigm to human nature, resulting in a model that gives equal value to each dimension, while demonstrating their dynamic interrelatedness.

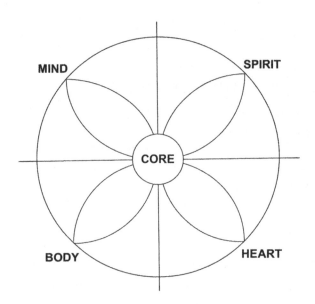

Human Nature Compass

Compass theory holds that each of these dimensions is equally important to the formation of a holistic human nature. The Mind is expressed in a rhythmic polarity with the Heart, and the Body in complementary harmony with the Spirit (Montgomery & Montgomery, 2008).

Other theories of human nature create a dualism by overemphasizing one dimension at the expense of its polar opposite. This leads to preferential treatment in therapy that overlooks the significance of one or more of these four dimensions. However, when placed within the compass framework, each dimension is both represented and balanced by the others. Only when a therapist gives each dimension its due can a counselee's whole being undergo healing and transformation.

Here are definitions for these four dimensions of human nature:

Mind stands for a person's cognition, speech, and subliminal self-talk. The mental dimension of human nature possesses the ability to deduce information, think through problems, analyze or synthesize data, foresee logical consequences of certain choices, construct a practical philosophy of life, reflect on life instead of merely reacting to it, interpret the meaning of feelings, and revise assumptions in light of new evidence that changes one's mind. You always want to engage a counselee's mind so that they can comprehend what is going on in therapy, and convert their learning into long-term memory that exercises a sustained influence over perception.

Heart refers to emotions, feelings, and intuitions. Posterity chooses the symbol of the heart because emotions flow through the inner body cavity as discernable movements of smooth muscle tissue. These e-motions literally create sensations surrounding the heart, bowels, stomach, and solar plexus. Often when an emotion is particularly intense, a person will reflexively place a hand over the heart.

Emotions not only require sensing, they also need interpreting, which occurs in a back-and-forth dialogue between the limbic system of the mid-brain and the neocortex of the frontal lobe. Identification of feelings is deduced from scanning environmental cues, archiving associative memories, and assessing the intensity of arousal.

Therapy teaches counselees that it is human to have feelings, and that by learning to discriminate among their emotions (like love, anger, anxiety, need, joy, or sorrow), they can know how they are reacting within situations, as well as learn how to express themselves to others in diplomatically effective ways. This is no easy undertaking, since every counselee brings a stack of past and current feelings that need sorting through and processing, so they can live more responsively in the present moment.

Body stands for the corporeal existence of a human being, sharing all the features of mammalian anatomy and physiology, plus the sophisticated and complex gray matter of the brain. There are billions of cells in the brain alone, linking it to the tiniest microscopic cells and capillaries of the little toe, not to mention everywhere else. The body provides the person's interface with the world, and without proper nutrition, exercise, and relaxation, the body contributes to psychological distortions. Further, twenty-first century research is shedding more light on a host of significant molecules like enzymes, RNA, DNA, serotonin, adrenaline, epinephrine, and catecholamine compounds that exert a profound impact on personality and the quality of life.

Adding certain psychopharmacological substrates missing from a person's genetic code can help remediate disabling states such as generalized anxiety and panic attacks, depression and dysphoria, bipolar disorder and cyclothymia, schizophrenia and paranoia, aggression and attention-deficit disorder, and certain features of particular personality patterns.

I remember in my post-doctoral supervision days counseling a young woman who suffered from panic attacks. I'm not sure I was that much help to her because after the first session I had my first panic attack. I went to my supervisor, Dr. Everett Shostrom, whose office was down the hall, and fortunately found his door open.

"My counselee just had a meltdown right in front of me," I said, practically gasping. "She was shaking and quivering all over, and said she didn't think she could even drive home."

"Did you finish the session okay?" His calmness somehow reassured me.

"I'm still alive. But I think I should refer her to you."

"If you approach counseling like that you could bail out of your whole practice within a week." He handed me the card of a psychiatrist in our same building. "Here, Dan. This doctor is good about handling psychotherapy referrals for adjunct medical therapy. If an anti-anxiety med is appropriate, he'll prescribe it while at the same time supporting your work as her primary therapist."

I followed his suggestion. The counselee had more equanimity the next time I saw her, and by the time she finished therapy with me six months later, she was off the meds as well as the panic attacks.

Spirit encompasses the qualities of Homo sapiens that differentiate us from other forms of life: compassion and humility; altruism in the face of war, persecution, or natural disaster; kindness toward strangers; and the gift of both loving and feeling loved by God. For actualizing persons, the spiritual dimension contributes to finding meaning, purpose, and social integration in the course of life.

While spirituality was deliberately excluded from the scientific approach to human nature conceived during the Enlightenment, religious and spiritual values persistently find relevance in billions of lives and significantly contribute to health and wellbeing. A growing body of contemporary psychological research demonstrates positive links between religious or spiritual faith and health outcomes (Miller and Thoresen, 2003; Sessanna et al., 2007; Plante, 2009).

Sketching the Human Nature Compass

A therapist can work together with the counselee to sketch out the counselee's use of human nature by filling in a blank Human Nature Compass using the counselee's own impressions.

For instance, a compulsive counselee may exaggerate the Mind to mentally control reality, at the expense of the Heart, Body, and Spirit (Graphic A). A histrionic counselee might exaggerate the Heart and Body to convey medodrama, at the expense of Mind and Spirit (Graphic B).

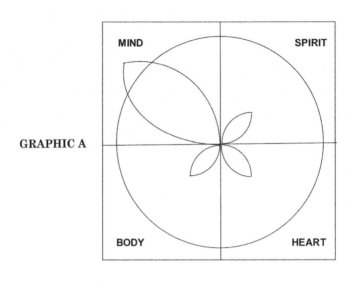

GRAPHIC A

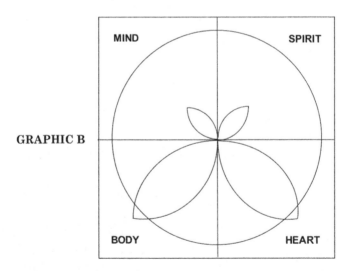

GRAPHIC B

An antisocial counselee may exaggerate Mind and Body language to deceive, at the expense of Heart and Spirit

(Graphic C). A schizoid counselee might truncate all four dimensions to avoid life in general (Graphic D).

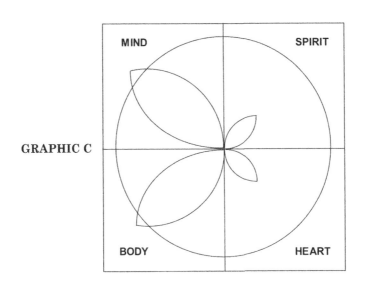

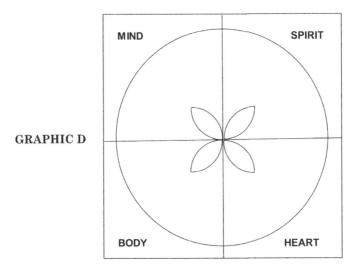

The value of this exercise lies in the counselee's active participation in understanding their own human nature, and at the same time expanding their frontiers for using more of their holistic potential.

Utilizing The Therapist's Human Nature Compass

Here's a way to incorporate your own Human Nature Compass as a therapist during an actual session. You begin by relaxing your whole being, then develop a hovering consciousness concerning the counselee's disclosures (Freud, 1938).

Now your whole being is open to receive data transmitted by your counselee's human nature. You see the slightest movement, whether a microsecond of tearing up or a kneading of fingers. You resonate with nuances of feeling, whether from a tremor in the counselee's voice or a gesture that reveals intensity—even the tentativeness of a shy feeling scampering across the room like a mouse headed for a hiding place. You let your mind form mental impressions that follow the counselee's drift of topics, while scanning your archival memory files for anything that deserves the clarification of a second look, or the elaboration of conceptual development. And in your relaxed openness, down in your spiritual core, you listen for the still small voice of God assisting you to develop maximal responsiveness to this counselee's unfolding needs.

By engaging a counselee's Human Nature Compass, your interventions utilize a "multilevel framework" that enjoys a high correlation with actualizing growth (Allport, 1937; Cacioppo et al., 2000; Sulmasy, 2002; Montgomery & Montgomery, 2008).

16
FINALE: BALANCING THE ACTUALIZING EQUATION

Personality is inextricably bound with relationships. The Actualizing Equation illustrates this interpenetration and helps counselees grasp how actualizing growth connects self-identity with community through a bond of reciprocal communication that compass theory calls existential intimacy. In this equation all three components are equally important and intertwined like three cords in a strong rope. The dynamic basis for this way of living is found in many religions and expressed clearly by Christ's commandment to love God and others as you love yourself.

IDENTITY ←→ INTIMACY ←→ COMMUNITY

The Actualizing Equation

Identity, Intimacy, and Community

As a person progresses through life, self-identity develops a transcendent quality that is greater than the sum of its parts. Though initially formed through genetic capability, parental imprinting, childhood learning, and ethnic influences, adulthood offers a second chance to consciously shape one's identity through contemplation of meaning, interpersonal connections, and an evolving philosophy of life.

The wellspring of this self-actualizing process is the person's spiritual core, represented by the phrase, "I am." The maturing of identity incorporates the discovery of one's interests, talents, and desires; the differentiation of one's self from parents and family; the development of enough autonomy to make choices, learn from consequences, and ponder the great questions of life: "Why am I here?" "How shall I live?" and "Where am I going?"

Environmental, personal, and interpersonal factors can impede or usurp identity formation. Some of these include a debilitating illness, drug addiction, war, poverty, organic brain dysfunction, abuse, victimization through rape or assault, lack of education, or financial ups and downs. When basic needs are not met, there is little motivation for psychological and spiritual development, and precious life energy is shunted into a posture of defensive survival. Even so, evi-dence shows that persons can pass through incredible adver-sity and find their way to fuller identity that is intimately connected to humanity.

A therapist stands with-and-for people in a relationship designed to offset debilitative forces and shore up the counselee's disrupted identity. Research shows that it is not the school of therapy that accomplishes this, but the counselee-therapist bond itself: "The essence of therapy is embodied in the therapist" (Wampold, 2001, p. 202). In other words, the therapeutic bond becomes a microcosm of the Actualizing Equation in which identity, intimacy, and community are renewed and firmed up enough for the counselee to successfully rejoin the macrocosm of the human race.

By guiding the counselee through appropriate techniques and learning experiences that heal intrapsychic and interpersonal wounds, the therapeutic relationship gradually becomes a well-honed template for successful relationships in the counselee's indigenous community.

The therapist and counselee become dialogue partners, two separate "I ams" who co-create existential intimacy within a community of hope. This dyadic community can offer better parenting than the counselee has likely known, in that there is not the generational separation and other baggage that hampers existential intimacy between parents and children, but rather a gentle teaching process in which the therapist-mentor can understand the counselee's deepest concerns, answer penetrating questions, and encourage the counselee to express assertion and love, strength and weakness, without fear of rivalry or reprisal.

The counselee has a rare opportunity to learn how to develop the kind of existential intimacy that can successfully connect personal identity with a network of emotionally significant others: spouse, children, work associates, friends, groups, faith community, and God.

The phrase "existential intimacy" has a specific meaning in Compass Therapy, referring to a relationship balanced by mutuality that is sustained and developed through free will choices. In Christian psychology this intimacy has biblical roots in the way the Trinity relates to one another and to individual human beings. The Father loves the Son and Spirit, yet possesses personal identity that transcends the Son and Spirit. The Son loves the Father and Spirit, yet possesses personal identity that includes his fully actualized human nature, and a personhood that is individuated from the Father and Spirit. The Spirit loves the Father and Son, yet possesses personal identity that transcends the Father and the Son (Montgomery & Montgomery, 2008, 2009).

When the Bible says that God seeks to "know" people, the word conveys the intimate level of mental, emotional, sensual, and spiritual union that a husband and wife know in marriage. God's invitation for all persons to know the

251

embrace of trinitarian intimacy requires free will choices in which individuals learn to trust God in their spiritual core.

Compass theory emphasizes that persons can know God and one another through reciprocal relationships, rather than constrained by manipulative trends and personality patterns. When psychology and spirituality inform one another, they become active partners in understanding holistic human nature and healing the pain and fear which invade the human condition.

In summarizing the material covered in this book, I want to show how personality patterns so often seen in therapy have their own particular way of distorting the Actualizing Equation. By seeing which components of the equation are disabled by these patterns, you see what steps to take in repairing, activating, and connecting these components. This is how psychopathology is neutralized and transformed into actualizing growth.

Dependent Pleasers and Histrionic Storytellers

The Love stuck patterns of the dependent Pleaser and the histrionic Storyteller are addicted to seeking approval and acceptance from others. Yet the nature of these patterns eclipses individual identity, arrests the development of individuation over the lifespan, and replaces authentic intimacy with caricatures of dependent pleasing or histrionic melodrama. What is left is the appearance of community without the substance thereof.

IDENTITY ⟶ INTIMACY ⟶ COMMUNITY

For all their focus on performing for others and toadying for support and reassurance, these patterns cannot truly befriend anyone. Notice how the one-way direction of these arrows moves away from identity and toward community.

Love-stuck counselees give themselves away indiscriminately to others, often trusting people naively and depleting themselves of energy and resources because they focus so much on other people that they forget to take good care of themselves.

They unwittingly break the Golden Rule by trying so hard to love others and/or God that they take no measures to develop self-love, self-renewal, and self-direction. Over the long haul this leads to the secret depression and resentment that haunt so many dependents and histrionics.

In this light, you can commend dependents and histrionics in therapy for their outstanding focus on community. Yet you help them realize that genuine intimacy with others requires a more substantial and autonomous development of self-identity.

In terms of the LAWS, you help them develop more of their Assertion and Strength Compass points so that they replace separation anxiety and identity diffusion with mature self-presence and self-worth.

Now they become able to engage others without losing track of themselves, and find significance whether others agree with them or not. A new serenity gradually displaces the old desperation.

Paranoid Arguers and Antisocial Rule-breakers

In compass theory the Assertion compass point lies opposite the Love compass point. The theory predicts that Assertion-stuck patterns manifest aggression at the expense of intimacy and community. The exploitation of antisocial Rule-breakers and the edgy suspicion of paranoid Arguers make loving bonds with others impossible. Nor can Rule-breakers and Arguers love themselves or God. This leaves them with a survival of the fittest version of the universe where their independent functioning is the final arbiter of all meaning. Paradoxically, though, by dehumanizing others and striving to function through a solely separate identity, they dehumanize themselves, creating the symptoms of callousness, contempt, and cynicism that characterize these aggressive patterns.

IDENTITY◄— IN~~TIMA~~CY◄— COM~~MUN~~ITY

Notice that the arrows move only one way, all pointing toward the identity of the aggressive person. This shows how Assertion-stuck individuals pull energy from their families, spouses, work associates, and other social relationships, draining others of their resources and building themselves up at other's expense.

Counselees with antisocial or paranoid patterns usually hit low bottoms that involve either law enforcement or broken lives and families before they become willing to seek counseling, let alone consider the possibility that their "Me-first" philosophy of life is limited and self-defeating. Yet aggressive counselees can become especially thankful for the healing of inner wounds and the experience of more trust in engaging others, precisely because they have lived without love for so long.

Avoidant Worriers and Schizoid Loners

Fixation on the Weakness compass point does massive damage to the interconnected components of the Actualizing Equation by sucking the life energy out of all of them.

Notice how there are no arrows to connect Weakness-stuck counselees either to themselves or community. There is no intimacy. Only aloneness. The structure for what could have become a living community filled with mutually involved persons has deteriorated into a ghost town instead.

Sometimes counselees stuck in the patterns of avoidant Worrier and schizoid Loner must foresee the bleak future that lies ahead to shake them out of complacency. One avoidant counselee got to the point at seventy years of age that he could no longer drive across town. "I see these stop signs, and each one seems to say, 'Stop and see how disconnected you are from everything.' I suddenly felt so alone that I didn't even have the motivation to keep driving."

By understanding these dynamics, and knowing how to reverse them, therapists can slowly build a living dialogue that may well represent the counselee's first successful exchanges of thoughts, feelings, and life energies with another person. Like a turtle who feels the warmth of the sun on its shell and begins to inch forward, so avoidant and schizoid counselees can begin to discover the benefits of intimacy and community through the therapeutic bond, and in so doing experience a first heartwarming taste of human identity.

Narcissistic Boasters and Compulsive Controllers

Stuck with too much Strength, narcissistic Boasters and compulsive Controllers relate to community on a one-way street that establishes power over others through a superior sense of identity that paradoxically wipes out their prospects for psychological and spiritual intimacy.

Though Boasters are ultra-convinced that they are God's gift to the human race, they nevertheless make boring conversationalists. While they may be knowledgeable in certain domains of life, their self-referential oration interrupts others' self-disclosure with a constant need to toot their own horn. So they remain in the dark about the inner worlds of those around them. This includes spouses, children, and friends. It's not that they know nothing about these people, but rather that they don't care about them except as they are needed to affirm their own glory. There may come a day when the narcissist looks in the mirror and sees a shallow self-absorbed person staring back. Hopefully, this conviction can awaken the willingness to become more involved with people for their own sakes.

Compulsive Controllers, too, create a one-way street toward power over others, except they are more deferent to anyone in the pecking order who has power over them. This means that while they serve community very effectively, they do so as dutiful soldiers. The impersonal style of their object relations makes them emotionally flat when engaging others, including spouses and children. This ruins the prospects for intimacy, which calls for warmth, excitement, and playfulness. Compulsives are so tightly bound up they can't respond positively to surprise, adventure, and joy—all key ingredients of existential intimacy with others and with God.

By learning to take themselves less seriously and develop a modicum of humble concern for those around them, both narcissistic Boasters and compulsive Controllers can form bonds of intimacy with others that bring them true identity and community.

Borderline Challengers

For good reason the borderline personality pattern has a reputation for being the most difficult to treat. In some cases the pattern extracts its pound of flesh from the therapist. One of the reasons for this seeming intractability of the pattern has to do with the Actualizing Equation.

As you can see from the graphic, the arrows between identity, intimacy, and community remain intact, ready to carry thoughts and feelings back and forth between the person and others. Yet the Xs strike out identity, intimacy, and community, indicating that what is carried back and forth is chaos, not communication. No wonder the counselee vacillates from feeling like the center of the universe to feeling completely annihilated.

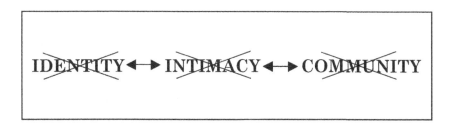

There is no spiritual core that holds the identity intact, no interior "I am" from which the counselee can think: "I don't need to approach others in a love-me-or-leave-me mentality. I don't need to assume every moment that love and hate are the principle forces of the cosmos, or that my existence depends upon another person's response to me."

The beginning of growth involves accepting that one is indeed a borderline Challenger, and that one's own behavior is the true cause of such on-again, off-again, relationships.

As William James (1890/1950) observed, life doesn't change by manipulating outer events or other persons, but by altering one's inner attitudes. By making a few crucial interior changes, the architecture of the self undergoes a reconstitution. In therapy this may occur very gradually over a long period of time, but sometimes with the Actualizing Equation graphic explained to them, borderlines can make more rapid progress.

A therapist might say, "Look. You are hard-wired to care deeply about others, and you are very close to solving the equation of loving others as you love yourself. What we need to do is help you develop more realistic interpersonal expectations, coupled with a more relaxed self-presence. You can really make progress in solidifying your identity so that you experience more stable outcomes with intimacy and community."

Compass Therapy suggests that working toward a health psychology is as important as diagnosing and treating psychopathology. Counselees can understand and transform their personality rigidities within an interpersonal context that helps them develop identity, intimacy, and community.

IDENTITY◄──► INTIMACY◄──► COMMUNITY

Taken together, the growth tools of the Self Compass, the Human Nature Compass, and the Actualizing Equation empower counselees to integrate personal power and social affiliation (Adler, 1931), develop individuation throughout the lifespan (Jung, 1968), build identity and intimacy into relationships (Erikson, 1959), foster peak experiences of loving and belonging (Maslow, 1971), cultivate basic trust (Horney, 1991), heal alienation and estrangement (Yalom, 1980), express a full range of emotions (Shostrom, 1979), bear spiritual fruit in personal, family, and communal life (van Kaam & Muto, 2006), and make progress in being and becoming their unique self in God (Montgomery & Montgomery, 2008).

In closing let me say I appreciate your commitment to the field of counseling. I wish I could hear about some of your experiences and take note of the positive outcomes you've facilitated. I consider us companions in our therapeutic calling and pray that God's healing love indwell and strengthen us in its fulfillment. Welcome back anytime.

BIBLIOGRAPHY

Abraham, K. (1927). Contributions to the theory of the anal character. In *Selected papers on psychoanalysis*. London: Hogarth.

Abraham, K. (1968). Notes on the psychoanalytic investigation and treatment of manic-depressive insanity and allied conditions. In *Selected papers of Karl Abraham*. London: Hogarth. (Original work published 1911).

Adler, A. (1965). *Understanding human nature*. New York: Premier. (Original work published in 1927).

Akhtar, S., & Thompson, A. J. (1982). Overview: Narcissistic personality pattern. *American Journal of Psychiatry, 139*, 12-20.

Alexander, F. (1961). *The scope of psychoanalysis: selected papers of Franz Alexander, 1921-1961*. New York: Basic Books.

Allport, G. W. (1937). *Personality: a psychological interpretation*. New York: Holt, Rinehart, and Winston.

Allport, G. W. (1937). The functional autonomy of motives. *American Journal of Psychology, 50*, 141-156.

American Psychiatric Association. (1994). *Diagnostic and statistical manual of mental disorders* (4th ed.). Washington, D. C: American Psychiatric Association.

Anandarajah, G. (2008). The 3 H and BMSEST models for spirituality in multicultural whole-person medicine. *Journal of American Family Medicine, 6*, 448-458.

Anchin, J. C. (1987). Functional analysis and the social-interactional perspective: Toward an integration in the behavior change enterprise. *Journal of Integrative and Eclectic Psychotherapy, 6,* 387-399.

Andrews, J. D. (1991). *The act of self in psychotherapy: an integration of therapeutic styles.* New York: Gardner.

Aron, E. (2010). *Psychotherapy and the highly sensitive person.* London: Routledge.

Assagioli, R. (2000). *Psychosynthesis: A collection of basic writings.* Amherst, MA: Synthesis Center.

Aizawa, N. (2002). Grandiose traits and hypersensitivity of the narcissistic personality. *Japanese Journal of Educational Psychology, 50,* 215-224.

Bahlmann, M., Preuss, U. W., & Soyka, M. (2002). Chronological relationship between antisocial personality disorder and alcohol dependence. *Journal of European Addiction Research, 8,* 195-200.

Barnow, S., Ulrich, I., Grabe, H. J., Freyberger, H. J. & Spitzer, C. (2007). The influence of parental drinking behaviour and antisocial personality disorder on adolescent behavioural problems: Results of the Greifswalder family study. *Journal of Alcohol and Alcoholism, 42,* 623-628.

Bauer, L. O. (2001). Antisocial personality disorder and cocaine dependence: Their effects on behavioral and electroencephalographic measures of time estimation. *Journal of Drug and Alcohol Dependence, 63,* 87-95.

Baumeister, R. F., Campbell, J. D., Krueger, J. I., & Vohs, K. D. (2007). Does high self-esteem cause better performance, interpersonal success, happiness, or healthier lifestyles? *Psychological Science in the Public Interest, 4,* 1-44.

Beck, A., & Freeman, A. (1990). *Cognitive therapy of personality disorders.* New York: Guilford Press.

Beck, A., Freeman, A., & Davis, D. (2007). *Cognitive therapy of personality disorders* (2nd ed.). New York: Guilford Press.

Bellino, S., Paradiso, E., & Bogetto, F. (2008). Efficacy and tolerability of pharmacotherapies for borderline personality disorder. *CNS Drugs, 22,* 671-692.

Benjamin, L. S. (1987). An interpersonal approach. *Journal of Personality Disorders, 1,* 334-339.

Benjamin, L. S. (1996). *Interpersonal diagnosis and treatment of personality disorders.* New York: Guilford Press.

Benjamin, L. S. (2003). *Interpersonal diagnosis and treatment of personality disorders* (2nd ed.). New York: Guilford Press.

Benjamin, L. S. (2006). *Interpersonal reconstructive therapy: an integrative personality-based treatment for complex cases.* New York: Guilford Press.

Bergin, A. E., & Garfield, S. L. (Eds.) (1994). *Handbook of psychotherapy and behavior change* (3rd ed.). New York: Wiley.

Berlin, H. A., Rolls, E. T., & Iversen, S. D. (2005). Borderline personality disorder, impulsivity, and the orbitofrontal cortex. *American Journal of Psychiatry, 162,* 2360-2373.

Berman, S. M. W., & McCann, J. T. (1995). Defense mechanisms and personality disorders: An empirical test of Millon's theory. *Journal of Personality Assessment, 64,* 132-144.

Berne, E. (1985). *Games people play.* New York: Ballantine Books.

Berne, E. (2004). *What do you say after you say hello.* New York: Bantam.

Bienenfeld, D., & Yager, J. (2007). Issues of spirituality and religion in psychotherapy supervision. *The Israeli Journal of Psychiatry and Related Sciences, 44,* 178-186.

Bienvenu, O. J., & Brandes, M. (2005). The interface of personality traits and anxiety disorders. *Journal of Primary Psychiatry, 12,* 35-39.

Blair, R. J. R. (2005). Applying a cognitive neuroscience perspective to the disorder of psychopathy. *Journal of Development and Psychopathology, 17,* 865-891.

Blair, R. J. R., Peschardt, K. S., Budhani, S., Mitchell, D. G. V., & Pine, D. S. (2006). The development of psychopathy. *Journal of Child Psychology and Psychiatry, 47,* 262-275.

Bluck, S., & Gluck, J. (2004). Making things better and learning a lesson: Experiencing wisdom across the lifespan. *Journal of Personality, 72,* 543-572.

Blueler, E. (1924). *Textbook of psychiatry.* New York: Macmillan.

Bleuler, E. (1950). *Dementia praecox.* New York: International Universities Press.

Blum, H. (1982). Paranoia and beating fantasy: psychoanalytic theory of paranoia. *Journal of American Psychoanalytic Association, 29,* 331-361.

Brammer, L. M., Shostrom, E. L., & Abrego, P. J. (1993, 1989, 1982, 1977, 1968, 1960). *Therapeutic psychology.* Englewood Cliffs, New Jersey: Prentice Hall.

Britton, R. (2004). Narcissistic disorders in clinical practice. *Journal of Analytic Psychology, 49,* 477-490.

Buber, M. (1970). *I and thou.* New York: Charles Scribner's Sons.

Bursten, B. (1972). The manipulative personality. *Archives of General Psychiatry, 26,* 318-321.

Cacioppo, J. T., Berntson, G. G., Sheridan, J. F., & McClintock, M. K. (2000). Multilevel integrative analysis of human behavior. *Psychological Bulletin, 126,* 829-843.

Cain, N. M., Pincus, A. L., & Ansell, E. B. (2008). Narcissism at the crossroads: phenotypic description of pathological narcissism across clinical theory, social/personality psychology, and psychiatric diagnosis. *Clinical Psychological Review, 28,* 638-56.

Cale, E. M., & Lilienfeld, S. O. (2006). Psychopathy factors and risk for aggressive behavior: A test of the "threatened egotism" hypothesis. *Law and Human Behavior, 30,* 51-74.

Calsyn, D. A., Fleming, C., Wells, E. A., & Saxon, A. J. (1996). Personality disorder subtypes among opiate addicts in methadone maintenance. *Psychology of Addictive Behaviors, 10,* 3-8.

Cameron, N. (1963). *Personality development and psychopathology.* Boston: Houghton Mifflin.

Cameron, N. (1974). Paranoid conditions and paranoia. In S. Arieti & Ebrody (Eds.), *American Handbook of Psychiatry* (Vol. 3, pp. 676-693). New York: Basic Books.

Campbell, W. K., Rudich, E., & Sedikides, C. (2002). Narcissism, self-esteem, and the positivity of self-views: Two portraits of self-love. *Personality and Social Psychology Bulletin, 28,* 358-368.

Carmody, J., Reed, G., Kristeller, J., & Merriam, P. (2008). Mindfulness, spirituality, and health-related symptoms. *Journal of Psychosomatic Research, 64,* 393-403.

Carson, R. C. (1969). *Interaction concepts of personality.* Chicago: Aldine.

Carson, R. C. (1991). The social interactionist viewpoint. In M. Hersen, A Kazdin, & A. Bellack (Eds.), *The clinical psychology handbook* (pp. 185-199). NY: Pergamon.

Caspi, A., & Roberts, B. W. (2001). Personality development across the life course: The argument for change and continuity. *Journal of Psychological Inquiry, 12,* 49-66.

Clark, L. A. (2005). Temperament as a unifying basis for personality and psychopathology. *Journal of Abnormal Psychology, 114,* 505-521.

Clarkin, J. F., Levy, K. N., Lenzenweger, M. F., & Kernberg, O. F. (2007). Evaluating three treatments for borderline personality disorder: A multiwave study. *American Journal of Psychiatry, 164,* 922-928.

Cleckley, H. (1964). *The mask of sanity* (2nd ed.). St. Louis, MO: Mosby.

Cogswell, A., & Alloy, L. B. (2006). The relation of neediness and Axis II pathology. *Journal of Personality Disorders, 20,* 16-21.

Cohen, R. A., Paul, R. H., Stroud, L., Gunstad, J., Hitsman, B. L., McCaffery. J., Sweet, L., Niaura, R., MacFarlane,

A., Bryant, R. A., & Gordon, E. (2006). Early life stress and adult emotional experience: An international perspective. *International Journal of Psychiatry in Medicine, 36,* 35-52.

Collins, L. M., Blanchard J. J., & Biondo, K. M. (2005). Behavioral signs of schizoidia and schizotypy in social anhedonics. *Journal of Schizophrenia Research, 78,* 309-322.

Conte, H. R., & Plutchik, R. (1981). A circumplex model for interpersonal personality traits. *Journal of Personality and Social Psychology, 40,* 701-711.

Coolidge, E. L., DenBoer, J. W., & Segal, D. L. (2004). Personality and neuropsychological correlates of bullying behavior. *Personality and Individual Differences, 36,* 1559-1569.

Cooper, A. M., & Sacks, M. (1991). Sadism and masochism in character patterns and resistance: Panel report. *Journal of American Psychoanalytic Association, 39,* 215-226.

Corey, G. (2008). *The art of integrative counseling.* Boston: Brooks Cole.

Corrigan, P. W. (1998). The impact of stigma on severe mental illness. *Cognitive and Behavioral Practice, 5,* 201-222.

Corrigan, P. W., & Miller, D. (2004). Shame, blame, and contamination: A review of the impact of mental illness stigma on family members. *Journal of Mental Health, 13,* 537-548.

Corsini, R., Ed. (1981, 2001). *Handbook on innovative therapy (2nd ed.): Ch. 1, Actualizing Therapy.* New York: John Wiley and Sons.

Crawford, T. N., Cohen, P., & Brook, J. S. (2001). Dramatic-erratic personality disorder symptoms: Pt. I. Continuity from early adolescence into adulthood. *Journal of Personality Disorders, 15,* 319-335.

Crocker, J., Brook, A. T., Niiya, Y., & Villacorta, M. (2006). The pursuit of self-esteem: Contingencies of self-worth & self-regulation. *Journal of Personality, 74,* 1749-1771.

Crossley, J. P., & Salter, D. P. (2005). A question of finding harmony: A grounded theory study of clinical psychologists' experience of addressing spiritual beliefs in therapy. *Journal of Psychology and Psychotherapy: Theory, Research, and Practice, 78,* 295-313.

Dadds, M. R., Fraser, J., Frost, A., & Hawes, D. J. (2005). Disentangling the underlying dimensions of psychopathy and conduct problems in childhood: A community study. *Journal of Consulting and Clinical Psychology, 73,* 400-410.

Davies, J. C. (1991). Maslow and theory of political development: Getting to fundamentals. *Political Psychology, 12,* 289-420.

Dimaggio, G., Catania, D., Salvatore, G., Carcione, A., & Nicolo, G. (2006). Psychotherapy of paranoid personality disorder from the perspective of dialogical self theory. *Counseling Psychology Quarterly, 19,* 69-87.

Dimic, S., Tosevski, D. L., & Janovic, J. G. (2004). The relationship between personality dimensions and posttraumatic stress disorder. *Psychiatry Today, 36,* 39-50.

Donegan, N., (2003). Amygdala hyperreactivity in borderline personality disorder: Implications for emotional dysregulation. *Biological Psychiatry, 54,* 1284-1293.

Dru, A. (Ed.) (1959). *The journals of Kierkegaard.* New York: Harper & Row.

Dutton, D. G., (2002). Personality dynamics of intimate abusiveness. *Journal of Psychiatric Practice, 8,* 216-28.

Easser, R., & Lesser, S. (1965). Hysterical personality: a re-evaluation. *Psychoanalytic Quarterly 34,* 390-402.

Eckert, P. A., Abeles, N., & Graham, R. N. (1988). Symptom severity, psychotherapy process, and outcome. *Professional Psychology, 19,* 560-564.

Egana, S. J., Pieka, J. P., Dyckb, M. J., & Reesa, C. S. (2007). The role of dichotomous thinking and rigidity in perfectionism. *Journal of Behaviour Research and Therapy, 45,* 1813-1822.

Eissler, K. R. (1949). *Searchlights on delinquency: Essays in honor of August Aichhorn.* New York: International Universities Press.

Ellis, A. (1962/1994). *Reason and emotion in psychotherapy.* New York: Carol Publishing Group.

Ellis, A., & Harper, R. (1997). *A new guide to rational living.* Englewood Cliffs, NJ: Prentice Hall.

Emrick, C. D., Tonigan, J. S., Montgomery, H., & Little, L. (1993). Alcoholics Anonymous: What is currently known? In B. S. McCrady & W. R. Miller (Eds.), *Research on Alcoholics Anonymous: Opportunities and alternatives* (pp. 41-76). New Brunswick, NJ: Rutgers Center of Alcohol Studies.

Erikson, E. H. (1959). *Identity and the life cycle.* New York: International Universities Press.

Erikson, E. H. (1993). *Childhood and society.* New York: W. W. Norton. (Original work published in 1950).

Exline, J. J., Bushman, B. J., Baumeister, R. F., Campbell, W. K., & Finkel, E. J. (2004). Too proud to let go: Narcissistic entitlement as a barrier to forgiveness. *Journal of Personality and Social Psychology, 87,* 894-912.

Exline, J. J., & Geyer, A. L. (2004). Perceptions of humility: A preliminary study. *Self and Identity, 3,* 95-114.

Fairbairn, W. (1940). Schizoid factors in the personality. In W. Fairbairn (Ed.), *Psychoanalytic studies of the personality.* London: Tavistock.

Farmer, R. F., Nash, H. M., & Dance, D. (2004). Mood patterns and variations associated with personality disorder pathology. *Comprehensive Psychiatry, 45,* 289-303.

Fehr, B., & Broughton, R. (2001). Gender and personality differences in conceptions of love: An interpersonal theory analysis. *Personal Relationships, 8,*115-136.

Fenichel, O. (1945). *The psychoanalytic theory of neurosis.* New York: Norton.

Feuchtersleben, E. (1847). *Lehrbuch der arztlichen seelenkunde.* Vienna: Gerold. In T. Millon, T. & R. Davis,

(1996). *Disorders of personality, DSM IV and beyond.* New York: Wiley.

Flanagan, E. H., & Blashfield, R. K. (2005). Gender bias in the diagnosis of personality disorders: The roles of base rates and social stereotypes. *Journal of Personality Disorders, 17,* 431-446.

Fogelson, D. L., Nuechterlein, K. H., Asarnow, R. A., Payne, D. L., Subotnik, K. L., Jacobson, K. C., Neale, M. C., & Kendler, K. S. (2007). Avoidant personality disorder is a separable schizophrenia-spectrum personality disorder even when controlling for the presence of paranoid and schizotypal personality disorders: The UCLA family study. *Schizophrenia Research, 91,* 192–199.

Fossati, A., Feeney, J., Donati, D., Donini, M., Novella, L., Bagnato, M., et al. (2003). Personality disorders and adult attachment dimensions in a mixed psychiatric sample. *Journal of Nervous and Mental Diseases, 191,* 30-37.

Frank, P. (2002). *Einstein: His life and times.* Cambridge: MA: Da Capo Press.

Frankl, V. E. (2006). *Man's search for meaning.* Boston: Beacon Press.

Freedman, M. B. (1985). Symposium: Interpersonal circumplex models (1948-1983). *Journal of Personality Assessment, 49,* 622-625.

Freedman, M. B., Leary, T. F., Ossario, A. G., & Coffey, H. S. (1951). The interpersonal dimensions of personality. *Journal of Personality, 20,* 143-161.

Freud, A. (1936). *Ego and the mechanisms of defense.* Madison, CT: International Universities Press.

Freud, S. (1925). Character and anal eroticism. In *Collected papers,* Vol. 2. London: Hogarth.

Freud, S. (1933). *The interpretation of dreams.* New York: Norton.

Freud, S. (1938). *The basic writings of Sigmund Freud.* New York: Modern Library.

Freud, S. (1950). Libidinal types. In *Collected papers*, Vol. 5. London: Hogarth. (Original work published in 1931).

Freud, S. (1959). *Turnings in the way of psychoanalytic therapy.* In J. Rivier (Ed.) *Collected papers*, Vol. 2. New York: Basic Books, 393-402.

Freud, S. (1989). *An outline of psycho-analysis.* New York: W. W. Norton.

Fromm, E. (1947). *Man for himself.* Greenwich, CT: Fawcett Books.

Gabbard, G.O. (2007). Do all roads lead to Rome? New findings on borderline personality disorder. *American Journal of Psychiatry, 164,* 853-855.

Giesbrecht, T., Merckelbach, H., Kater, M., & Sluis, A. F. (2007). Why dissociation and schizotypy overlap: the joint influence of fantasy proneness, cognitive failures, and childhood trauma. *Journal of Nervous and Mental Disease, 195,* 812-818.

Glasser, W. (1965). *Reality therapy.* New York: Harper & Row.

Glasser, W. (2001). *Counseling with choice theory.* New York: Harper.

Gold, J. M. (2009). *Counseling and spirituality: Integrating spiritual and clinical orientations.* New York: Prentice-Hall.

Gooding, D. C., Tallent, K. A., & Matts, C. W. (2005). Clinical status of at-risk individuals five years later: Further validation of the psychometric high-risk strategy. *Journal of Abnormal Psychology, 114,* 170–175.

Gooding, D. C., Tallent, K. A., & Matts, C. W. (2007). Rates of avoidant, schizotypal, schizoid and paranoid personality disorders in psychometric high-risk groups at five-year follow-up. *Journal of Schizophrenia Research, 94,* 373-374.

Gosling, S. D., John, O. P., Craik, K. H., & Robins, R. W. (1998). Do people know how they behave? Self-reported act frequencies compared with online codings by observers. *Journal of Personality and Social Psychology, 74,* 1337-1349.

Grant, B. E., Hasin, D. S., et al. (2005). Co-occurence of 12-month mood and anxiety disorders and personality disorders in the U. S.: Results from the national epidemiologic survey on alcohol and related conditions. *Journal of Psychiatric Research, 39,* 1-9.

Greencavage, L. M. (1990). What are the commonalities among the therapeutic factors? *Professional Psychology, 21,* 372-378.

Griesinger, W. (1867). *Mental pathology and therapeutics.* London: New Syndenham Society.

Griesinger, W. (1868). A little recognized psychopathic state. *Archiv fuer Psychiatric and Neurologie, 1,* 626-631. In T. Millon, S. Grossman, C. Millon, S. Meagher, & R. Ramnath, *Personality Disorder in Modern Life (2nd ed.).* New York: Wiley.

Grilo, C. M., Sanislow, C. A. at el. (2005). Two-year prospective naturalistic study of remission from major depressive disorder as a function of personality disorder comorbidity. *Journal of Consulting and Clinical Psychology, 73,* 78-85.

Gude, T., Hoffart, A., Hedley, L., & Ro, O. (2004). The dimensionality of dependent personality disorder. *Journal of Personality Disorders, 18,* 604-610.

Gurtman, M. B. (2009). Exploring personality with the interpersonal circumplex. *Social & Personality Psychology Compass, 3,* 601-619.

Guttman, L. (1966). Order analysis of correlation matrixes. In R. B. Cattell (Ed.), *Handbook of Multivariate Experimental Psychology.* Chicago: Rand McNally.

Habel, U., Koehn, E., Salloum, J. B., Devos, H., & Schneider, F. (2002). Emotional processing in the psychopathic personality. *Journal of Aggressive Behavior, 28,* 394-400.

Haller, D. L., & Miles, D. R. (2004). Personality disturbances in drug-dependent women: Relationship to childhood abuse. *American Journal of Drug and Alcohol Abuse, 30,* 269-286.

Halmi, K. A. (2005). Obsessive-compulsive personality disorder and eating disorders. *Eating Disorders: Journal of Treatment and Prevention, 13,* 85-92.

Haloway, R. M, Heimberg, R. G., & Coles, M. E. (2006). A comparison of intolerance of uncertainty in analogue obsessive-compulsive disorder and generalized anxiety disorder. *Journal of Anxiety Disorders, 20,* 158-174.

Hans, S. L., et al. (2004). Offspring of parents with schizophrenia: Mental disorders during childhood and adolescence. *Schizophrenia Bulletin, 30,* 303-315.

Harper, D. J. (1996). Deconstructing "paranoia": Towards a discursive understanding of apparently unwarranted suspicion. *Journal of Theory and Psychology, 6,* 423-448.

Harper, R. G. (2004). Paranoid personality. In R. G. Harper (Ed.), *Personality-guided therapy in behavioral medicine* (pp. 65-90). Washington, D. C.: American Psychological Association.

Haznedar, M.M., Buchsbaum, M.S., Hazlett, E.A., Shihabuddin, L., New, A., & Siever, L. J. (2004). Cingulate gyrus volume and metabolism in the schizophrenia spectrum. *Schizophrenia Research, 71,* 249-262.

Hesselbrock, V. M., Meyer, R. E., & Keener, J. J. (1985). Psychopathology and hospitalized alcoholics. *Archives of General Psychiatry, 42,* 1050-1055.

Heymans, G., & Wiersma, E. (1906-1909). Beitrage zur speziellen psychologie auf grundeiner massenuntersuchung. *Zeitsehrift Fuer Psychologie, 42, 46, 49, 51.* In T. Millon & R. Davis. (1996). *Disorders of personality, DSM IV and beyond.* New York: Wiley.

Hill, J., Pilkonis, P., Morse, J., Feske, U., Reynolds, S., Hope, H., Charest, C., & Broyden, N. (2008). Social domain dysfunction and disorganization in borderline personality disorder. *Psychological Medicine, 38,*135-46.

Hirose, S. (2001). Effective treatment of aggression and impulsivity in antisocial personality disorder with risperidone. *Psychiatry and Clinical Neurosciences, 55,* 161-162.

Hoch, A. (1910). Constitutional factors in the dementia praecox group. *Review of Neurology and Psychiatry, 8:* 463-475.

Holaway, R. M., Heimberg, R. G., & Coles, M. E. (2006). A comparison of intolerance of uncertainty in analogue obsessive-compulsive disorder and generalized anxiety disorder. *Journal of Anxiety Disorders, 20,* 158-174.

Holmes, E. P., & River, L. P. (1998). Individual strategies for coping with the stigma of severe mental illness. *Cognitive and Behavioral Practice, 5,* 231-239.

Horney, K. (1939). *New ways in psychoanalysis.* New York: W. W. Norton.

Horney, K. (1991). *Neurosis and human growth: The struggle for self-realization.* New York: W. W. Norton. (Original work published in 1950).

Horney, K. (1993). *Self-analysis.* New York: W. W. Norton.

Horney, K. (1994). *Our inner conflicts: A constructive theory of neurosis.* New York: W. W. Norton. (Original work published in 1945).

Horowitz, L. M., Wilson, K. R., Turan, B., Zolotsev, P., Constantino, M. J., & Henderson, L. (2006). How interpersonal motives clarify the meaning of interpersonal behavior: A revised circumplex model. *Personality and Social Psychology Review, 10,* 67-86.

Huprich, S. K. (2005). Differentiating avoidant and depressive personality disorders. *Journal of Personality Disorders, 19.* 659-673.

James, W. (1950). *The principles of psychology.* New York: Dover. (Original work published in 1890).

Jaspers, K. (1948). *General psychopathology.* London: Oxford.

Johnson, J. J., Cohen, P., Smailes, E. M., Skodol, A. E., Brown, J., & Oldham, J. M. (2001). Childhood verbal abuse and risk for personality disorders during adolescence and early adulthood. *Comprehensive Psychiatry, 42,* 16-23.

Johnson, J. J., Smailes, E. M., Cohen, P., Brown, J., & Bernstein, D. P. (2000). Associations between four types of childhood neglect and personality disorder symptoms during adolescence and early adulthood: Findings of a community-based longitudinal study. *Journal of Personality Disorders, 14,* 171-187.

Joseph, S. (1997). *Personality disorders: Symptom-focused drug therapy.* New York: Hayworth Press.

Jovev, M., & Jackson, H. J. (2004). Early maladaptive schemas in personality disordered individuals. *Journal of Personality Disorders, 18,* 467-478.

Jung, C. G. (1921). *Psychological types.* Zurich: Rasher Verlag.

Jung, C. G. (1968). *Modern man in search of a soul.* New York: Harcourt, Brace, & World.

Jung, C. G. (1984). *Man and his symbols.* New York: Dell.

Jung, C. G. (1989). *Memories, dreams, and reflections.* New York: Vintage.

Kagan, J. (1994). *Galen's prophecy.* New York: Basic Books.

Kernberg, O. (1975). *Borderline conditions and pathological narcissism.* New York: Jason Aronson.

Kernberg, O. (1984). *Severe personality disorders: Psychotherapeutic strategies.* New Haven, CT: Yale Univ. Press.

Kiesler, D. J. (1983). The 1982 interpersonal circle: A taxonomy for complementarity in human transactions. *Psychological Review, 90,* 185-214.

Kiesler, D. J. (1992). Interpersonal circle inventories: Pantheoretical applications to psychotherapy research and practice. *Journal of Psychotherapy Integration, 2,* 77-99.

Kiesler, D. J. (1996). *Contemporary interpersonal theory and research: Personality, psychopathology, and psychotherapy.* New York: Wiley.

Kiesler, D. J., & Auerbach, S. M. (2004). Integrating measurement of control and affiliation in studies of physician–patient interaction: The interpersonal circumplex. *Social Science & Medicine, 57,* 1707-1722.

Kinnel, G. (2006). *Strong is your hold.* Boston: Houghton Mifflin.

Klonsky, E. D., (2008). What is emptiness? Clarifying the 7th criterion for borderline personality disorder. *Journal of Personality Disorders, 22,* 418-26.

Klonsky, E. D., Oltmanns, T. F., Turkheimer, E., & Fiedler, E. R. (2000). Recollections of conflict with parents and family support in the personality disorders. *Journal of Personality Disorders, 14,* 327-338.

Koenig, H. G. (2004). Religion, spirituality and medicine: Research findings and implications for clinical practice. *Southern Medical Journal 97,* 1194-1200.

Kotler, J. S., & McMahon, R. J. (2005). Child psychopathy: Theories, measurement, and relations with the development and persistence of conflict problems. *Clinical Child and Family Psychology Review, 8,* 291-325.

Knapp, R. K. (1990). *POI handbook (2nd ed.): Handbook for the Personal Orientation Inventory.* San Diego, CA: Edits.

Kraepelin, E. (1919). *Dementia praecox and paraphrenia.* Edinburgh: Livingstone.

Kraepelin, E. (1921). *Manic-depressive insanity and paranoia.* Edinburgh: Livingstone.

Kretschmer, E. (1925). *Physique and character.* New York: Harcourt, Brace & Company.

Kretschmer, E. (1926). *Hysteria.* New York: Nervous and Mental Disease Publishers.

Krueger, J., et al. (2003). Research fails to support link between high self-esteem, positive behavior. *George St. Journal,* May.

Krueger, R. F., Hicks, B. M., Patrick, C. J., Carlson, S. R., Iacono, W. G., & McGue. M. (2002). Etiologic connections among substance dependence, antisocial behavior, and personality: Modeling the externalizing spectrum. *Journal of Abnormal Psychology, 111,* 411-424.

Kusher, M. G., & Sher, K. J. (1991). The relation of treatment fearfulness and psychological service utilization. *Professional Psychology, 22,* 196-203.

Lahey, V. B., Loeber, R., Burke, J. D., & Applegate, B. (2005). Predicting future antisocial personality disorder in males from a clinical assessment in childhood. *Journal of Counseling and Clinical Psychology, 73,* 389-399.

Laing, R. D. (1960). *The divided self.* Chicago: Quadrangle.

LaForge, R., (1985). The early development of the Freedman-Leary-Coffey interpersonal system. *Journal of Personality Assessment, 49,* 613-621.

LaForge, R., Leary, T. F., Naboisek, H., Coffey, H. S., & Freedman, M. B. (1954). The interpersonal dimension of personality: II. An objective study of repression. *Journal of Personality, 23,* 129-153.

LaForge, R., & Suczek, R. F. (1955). The interpersonal dimension of personality: III. An interpersonal checklist. *Journal of Personality, 24,* 94-112.

Lambert, M. J., & Bergin, A. E. (1994). The effectiveness of psychotherapy. In A. E. Bergin & S. L. Bergin (Eds.), *Handbook of psychotherapy and behavior change* (4th ed., pp. 143-189). New York: Wiley.

Lazarus, A. (2006). *Brief but comprehensive therapy: The multimodal way.* New York: Springer.

Leary, M. R., Tate, E. B., Allen, A. B., Adams, C. E., & Hancock, J. (2007). Self-compassion and reactions to unpleasant self-relevant events: The implications of treating oneself kindly. *Journal of Personality and Social Psychology, 97,* 887-904.

Leary, T. (1955). The theory and measurement of interpersonal communication. *Psychiatry, 18,* 147-161.

Leary, T. (1957). *Interpersonal diagnosis of personality: A functional theory and methodology for personality evaluation.* New York: The Ronald Press.

Leary, T., & Harvey, J. S. (1956). A methodology for measuring personality changes in psychotherapy. *Journal of Clinical Psychology, 12,* 123-132.

Lee, H. (1999). An exploratory study on the cause of paranoia: The self-concept and reasoning bias. *Korean Journal of Clinical Psychology, 18,* 1-15.

Levy, S. T. (1996). *Principles of interpretation: Mastering clear and concise interventions in psychotherapy.* Northvale, NJ: Jason Aronson.

Link, B. G. (1987). Understanding labeling effects in mental disorders: Assessing the effects of expectations of rejection. *American Sociological Review, 52,* 96-112.

Link, B. G., & Phelan, J. C. (2001). Conceptualizing stigma. *Annual Review of Sociology, 27,* 363-385.

Locke, K. D. (2000). Circumplex scales of interpersonal values: Reliability, validity, and applicability to interpersonal problems and personality disorders. *Journal of Personality Assessment, 75,* 249-267.

Locke, K. D., & Sadler, P. (2007). Self-efficacy, values, and complementarity in dyadic interactions: Integrating interpersonal and social-cognitive theory. *Personality and Social Psychology Bulletin, 33,* 94-109.

Loeber, R., Burke, J. D., & Lahey, B. B. (2002). What are adolescent antecedents to antisocial personality disorder? *Criminal Behaviour and Mental Health, 12,* 24-36.

Lorr, M. (1996). The interpersonal circle as a heuristic model for interpersonal research. *Journal of Personality Assessment, 66,* 234-239.

Lowen, A. (2006). *The language of the body.* Alachua, Fl: Bioenergetics Press.

Maddi, S. R. (2004). Hardiness: An operationalization of existential courage. *Journal of Humanistic Psychology, 44,* 279-298.

Maddi, S. R. (2006). Hardiness: The courage to grow from stresses. *The Journal of Positive Psychology, 1,* 2006, 160-168.

Maddi, S. R., Harvey, R., Khoshaba, D. M., Lu, J., Persico, M., & Brow, M. (2006). The personality construct of hardiness III: Relationships with repression, innovativeness, authoritarianism, and performance. *Journal of Personality, 74*, 575-598.

Magai, C., & Haviland-Jones, J. (2010). *The hidden dimension of emotions: Lifespan transformations of personality.* West Nyack, NY: Cambridge Univ. Press.

Marchesi, C., Cantoni, A., Fonto, S., Giannelli, M. R., & Maggini, C. (2005). The effect of pharmacotherapy on personality disorders in panic disorder: A one-year naturalistic study. *Journal of Affective Disorders, 89*, 189-194.

Martens, W. H. J. (2005). Multidimensional model of trauma and correlated antisocial personality disorder. *Journal of Loss and Trauma, 10*, 115-129.

Martens, W. H. J. (2010). Schizoid personality disorder linked to unbearable loneliness. *The European Journal of Psychiatry, March.*

Maslow, A. H. (1971). *The further reaches of human nature.* New York: Viking.

Maslow, A. H. (1998). *Toward a psychology of being (3rd ed.).* New York: Wiley. (Original work published in 1962).

Maslow, A. H. (2000). *The Maslow business reader.* New York: Wiley.

Massion, A. O., et al. (2001). Personality disorders and time to remission in generalized anxiety, social phobia and panic disorder. *Archives of General Psychiatry, 59*, 434-440.

May, R. (2007). *Love and will.* New York: W. W. Norton. (Original work published in 1969).

May, R. (1989). *Art of counseling.* New York: Gardner Press. (Original work published in 1939).

McCullough, M. E., Fincham, F. D., & Tsang, J. (2003). Forgiveness, forbearance, and time: The temporal unfolding of transgression-related interpersonal motivations. *Journal of Personality and Social Psychology, 84*, 540-557.

McDougall, W. (1932). *Introduction to social psychology.* New York: Scribners.

McHoskey, J. W. (2001). Machiavellianism and personality dysfunction. *Personality and Individual Differences, 31,* 791-798.

McMahon, R. C., & Richards, S. K. (1996). Profile patterns, consistency and change in the Millon clinical multiaxial inventory-II in cocaine abusers. *Journal of Clinical Psychology, 52,* 75-79.

McWilliams, N. (1994). *Psychoanalytic diagnosis.* New York: Guilford Press.

Meissner, W. W. (1991). *What is effective in psychoanalytic therapy: The move from interpretation to relation.* Northvale, NJ: Jason Aronson.

Meissner, W. W., Stone, M. H., Meloy, J. R., & Gunderson, J. G. (1996). Personality disorders. In G. O. Gabbard & S. D. Atkinson (Eds.), *Synopsis of treatments of psychiatric disorders* (2nd ed., pp. 947-1010). Washington, D. C.: American Psychiatric Association.

Menninger, K. (1930). *The human mind.* New York: Alfred Knopf.

Messer, S. B. (1992). A critical examination of belief structures in integrative and eclectic psychotherapy. In J. C. Norcross & M. R. Goldfried (Eds.), *Handbook of Psychotherapy Integration* (pp. 130-165). NY: Basic Books.

Meyers, D. G. (1995). *Psychology* (4th ed.). New York: Worth Publishers.

Miller, J., Campbell, W., & Pilkonis, P. (2008). Narcissistic personality disorder: Relations with distress and functional impairment. *Journal of Comprehensive Psychiatry, 48,* 170-177.

Miller, W. R., & Rollnick, S. (2002). *Motivational interviewing: Preparing people to change.* NY: Guilford Press.

Miller, W. R., & Thoreson, C. E. (2003). Spirituality, religion, and health: An emerging research field. *American Psychologist, 58,* 24-35.

Millon, T. (1999). *Personality-guided therapy*. New York: Wiley.

Millon, T., & Bloom, C. (2008). *The Millon inventories: A practitioner's guide to personalized clinical assessment*. New York: Guilford Press.

Millon, T., & Davis, R. (1996). *Disorders of personality: DSM-IV and beyond*. New York: Wiley.

Millon, T., & Davis, R. (2000). *Personality disorders in modern life*. New York: Wiley.

Millon, T., & Everly, G. (1985). *Personality and its disorders: A biosocial learning approach*. New York: Wiley.

Millon, T., & Grossman, S. (2007a). *Moderating severe personality disorders*. New York: Wiley.

Millon, T., & Grossman, S. (2007b). *Overcoming resistant personality disorders*. New York: Wiley.

Millon, T., Millon, C., Meagher, S., et al. (2004). *Personality disorders in modern life*. New York: Wiley.

Mitchell, D. G. V., Avny, S. B., & Blair, R. J. R. (2006). Divergent patterns of aggressive and neurocognitive characteristics in acquired vs. developmental psychopathy. *Neurocase, 12*, 164-178.

Montgomery, D. (1971). The search for authentic human existence: an existential approach to Christianity. Master's thesis, Goddard College.

Montgomery, D. (1975). Personality fulfillment in religious life. Doctoral dissertation. University of New Mexico.

Montgomery, D. (1996a). *Beauty in the stone: How God sculpts you into the image of Christ*. Nashville, TN: Thomas Nelson.

Montgomery, D. (1996b). *Practical counseling tools for pastoral workers*. Boston: Pauline Books and Media.

Montgomery, D. (2006). *Christian counseling that really works*, Morrisville, NC: Lulu Press Inc.

Montgomery, D., & Montgomery, K. (2007). *The self compass: Charting your personality in Christ*. Morrisville, NC: Lulu Press Inc.

Montgomery, D., & Montgomery, K. (2008). *Compass psychotheology: Where psychology and theology really meet.* Morrisville, NC: Lulu Press Inc.

Montgomery, D., & Montgomery, K. (2009). *Christian personality theory: A self compass for humanity.* Morrisville, NC: Lulu Press Inc.

Moreno, J. (1972). *Psychodrama, Vol. 1* (4th ed.). Beacon, New York: Beacon House Press.

Morse, J. O., Robins, C. J., et al. (2002). Sociotropy, autonomy, and personality disorder criteria in psychiatric patients. *Journal of Personality Disorders, 16*, 549-560.

Moss, D. (2002). The circle of the soul: The role of spirituality in health care. *Journal of Applied Psychophysiology and Biofeedback, 27*, 283-297.

Mudrack, P. E. (2004). Job involvement, obsessive-compulsive personality traits, and workaholic behavioral tendencies. *Journal of Organizational Change Management, 17*, 490-508.

Mulder, R. (1996). Antisocial personality disorder: Current drug treatment recommendations. *CNS Drugs, 5*, 257-263.

Myers, M. G., Stewart, D. G., & Brown, S. A. (1998). Progression from conduct disorder to antisocial personality disorder following treatment for adolescent substance abuse. *American Journal of Psychiatry, 155*, 479-485.

Nicolo, G., Carcione, A., Semerari A., & Dimaggio G., (2007). Reaching the covert, fragile side of patients: The case of narcissistic personality disorder. *Journal of Clinical Psychology, 63,*141-52.

Noonan, J. R. (1999). Competency to stand trial and the paranoid spectrum. *American Journal of Forensic Psychology, 17*, 5-27.

Oldham, J. M., Skodol, A. E., & Bender, D. S. (2009). *Essentials of personality disorders.* American Psychiatric Pub.

Orlinsky, D. E., Grawe, K., & Parks, B. K. (1994). Process and outcome in psychotherapy. In A. E. Bergin & S. L.

Garfield (Eds.). *Handbook of psychotherapy and behavior change* (4th ed.). New York: Wiley.

Overholser, J. C., Stockmeier, C., Dilley, G., & Freiheit, S. (2002). Personality disorders in suicide attempters and completers: Preliminary findings. *Archives of Suicide Research, 6,* 123-133.

Pargament, K. I., Koenig, H. G., Tarakeshwar, N., & Hahn, J. (2004). Religious coping methods as predictors of psychological, physical and spiritual outcomes among medically ill elderly patients: A two-year longitudinal study. *Journal of Health Psychology, 9,* 713-730.

Patterson, C. H. (1984). Empathy, warmth, and genuineness in psychotherapy: A review of reviews. *Journal of Psychotherapy, 21,* 431-438.

Patterson, G. (1976). The aggressive child: Victim and architect of a coercive system. In L. A. Hamerlynck and L. C. Handy (Eds.), *Behavior modification and families.* New York: Brunner/Mazel, 267-311.

Patton, M. J., & Meara, N. M. (1996). Kohut and counseling: Applications of self psychology. *Journal of Psychodynamic Counseling, 2,* 328-355.

Perls, F. (1973). *The Gestalt approach & eyewitness to therapy.* Palo Alto, CA: Science and Behavior Books.

Perls, F. (1989). *Gestalt therapy verbatim.* Gouldsboro, ME: Gestalt Journal Press.

Perls, F. (1992). *Ego, hunger, and aggression: A revision of Freud's theory and method.* Gouldsboro, Maine: Gestalt Journal Press.

Pincus, A. L. (1994). The interpersonal circumplex and the interpersonal theory: Perspectives of personality and its pathology. In S. Strack & M. Lorr (Eds.), *Differentiating normal and abnormal personality* (pp. 114-136). New York: Springer.

Pincus, A. L., & Wilson, K. R. (2001). Interpersonal variability in dependent personality. *Journal of Personality, 69,* 223-251.

Plante, T. G. (2009). *Spiritual practices in psychotherapy.* Washington, D.C.: American Psychological Association.

Plante, T. G. (2010). *Contemplative practices in action.* Santa Barbara, CA: Praeger-Greenwood.

Plante, T. G., & Sherman, A. C. (2001). *Faith and health: Psychological perspectives.* New York: Guilford Press.

Plutchik, R., & Conte, H. R. (1997). *Circumplex models of personality and emotions.* Washington, D.C.: American Psychological Association.

Pollack, J. (1987). Obsessive compulsive personality: Theoretical and clinical perspective and recent research findings. *Journal of Personality Disorders, 2,* 248-262.

Porcerelli, J. H., Cogan, R., & Hibbard, S. (2004). Personality characteristics of partner violent men: A Q-sort approach. *Journal of Personality Disorders, 18,* 151-162.

Pretzel, J., & Hampl, S. (2009) Cognitive behavioral treatment of obsessive-compulsive personality disorder. *Clinical Psychology & Psychotherapy, June.*

Pritchard, J. C. (1835). *A treatise on insanity.* London: Sherwood, Gilbert and Piper.

Rado, S. (1959). Obsessive behavior. In S. Ariett (Ed.) *American handbook of psychiatry, 1.* NY: Basic Books.

Raine, A., Ishikawa, S. S., Arce, E., Lencz, T., Knuth, K. H, Bihrle, S., et al. (2004). Hippocampal structural asymmetry in unsuccessful psychopaths. *Journal of Biological Psychiatry, 55,* 185-191.

Raja, M. (2006). The diagnosis of Asperger's syndrome. *Directions in Psychiatry, 26,* 89-104.

Ramsey, A., Watson, P. J., Biderman, M. D., & Reeves, A. L. (1996). Self-reported narcissism and perceived parental permissiveness and authoritarianism. *Journal of Genetic Psychology, 157,* 227-238.

Reich, W. (1980). *Character analysis.* New York: Farrar, Straus and Giroux. (Original published in 1933).

Reid, W. H. (2005). Delusional disorder and the law. *Journal of Psychiatric Practice, 11,* 126-130.

Reyes-Ortiz, C. A., Berges, I. M., Raji, M. A., Koenig, H. G., Kuo, Y., & Markides, K. S. (2008). Church attendance mediates the association between depressive symptoms and cognitive functioning among older Mexican Americans. *The Journals of Gerontology Series A: Biological Sciences and Medical Sciences, 63,* 480-486.

Riesman, D. (1950). *The lonely crowd.* Garden City, NY: Doubleday.

Riesman, D., Glazer, N., & Denney, R. (2001). *The lonely crowd, revised edition: A study of the changing American character.* New Haven, CT: Yale University Press.

Riesenberg-Malcolm, R. (1996). How can we know the dancer from the dance?: Hyperbole in hysteria. *International Journal of Psycho-Analysis, 77,* 679-688.

Roberts, B. W., Walton, K. E., & Viechtbauer, W. (2006). Patterns of mean-level change in personality traits across the life course: A meta-analysis of longitudinal studies. *Psychological Bulletin, 132,* 1-25

Rogers, C. (1965). *Client-centered therapy: Its current practice, implications, and theory.* Boston: Houghton-Mifflin.

Rogers, C. (1970). *On encounter groups.* New York: Harper-Collins.

Rogers, C. (1995). *On becoming a person.* New York: Mariner Books.

Russ, E., Shedler, J., Bradley, R., & Westen, D. (2008). Refining the construct of narcissistic personality disorder: Diagnostic criteria and subtypes. *American Journal of Psychiatry, 15,* 370-376.

Safran, J. D.. & Segal, Z. V. (1990). *Cognitive therapy: An interpersonal process perspective.* New York: Basic Books.

Salekin, R. T., Leistico, A. R., et al. (2005). Adolescent psychopathy and personality theory: The interpersonal circumplex—Expanding evidence of a nomological net. *Journal of Abnormal Child Psychology, 33,* 445-460.

Saltzman, L. (1985). *Treatment of the obsessive personality.* New York: Aronson.

Sansone, R. A., Levitt, J. L., & Sansone, L. A. (2005). The prevalence of personality disorders among those with eating disorders. *Eating Disorders: Journal of Treatment and Prevention, 13,* 7-21.

Satir, V. (1983). *Conjoint family therapy.* Palo Alto, CA: Science and Behavior Books.

Saulsman, L. M., & Page, A. C. (2004). Five-factor model & personality disorder empirical literature: A meta-analytic review. *Clinical Psychology Review, 23,* 1055-1085.

Schaefer, E. (1965). Configurational analysis of children's reports of parent behavior. *Journal of Consulting Psychology, 29,* 552-557.

Schmidberg, M. (1959). The borderline patient. In S. Arieti, Ed., *American handbook of psychiatry,* Vol. 1. New York: Basic Books, 398-416.

Schneider, K. (1950). *Psychopathic personalities* (9th ed.). London: Cassell. (Original work published in 1923).

Schneider, A. M., & Tarshis, B. (1975). *An introduction to physiological psychology.* New York: Random House.

Schwartz, R. C. (2001). Psychotherapeutic diagnosis and treatment of histrionic personality disorder: Reply. *Annals of the American Psychotherapy Association, 4,* 4.

Scott, S. (2006). The medicalization of shyness: From social misfits to social fitness. *Sociology of Health and Illness, 28,* 133-153.

Seedat, S., & Stein, M. B. (2004). Double-blind, placebo-controlled assessment of combined clonazepam with paroxetine compared with paroxetine monotherapy for generalized social anxiety disorder. *Journal of Clinical Psychiatry, 65,* 244-248.

Seeman, T. E., et al. (2003). Religiousity/spirituality and health: A critical review of the evidence for biological pathways. *American Psychologist, 58,* 53-63.

Sessanna, L., Finnell, D., & Jezewski, M. A. (2007). Spirituality in nursing and health-related literature. *Journal of Holistic Nursing, 25,* 252-262.

Shapiro, D. (1965). *Neurotic styles.* New York: Basic Books.

Sharoots, J. F. (2003). Life-course dynamics: A research program in progress from the Netherlands. *European Psychologist, 8,* 192-199.

Shay, J. J. (1996). Psychotherapy with the reluctant male. *Psychotherapy, 33,* 503-513.

Shaw, A., Joseph, S., & Linley, P. A. (2005). Religion, spirituality, and posttraumatic growth: A systematic review. *Journal of Mental Health, Religion, and Culture, 8,* 1-11.

Shea, M. T., et al. (2004). Associations in the course of personality disorders and Axis I disorders over time. *Journal of Abnormal Psychology, 113,* 499-508.

Sheldon, W. H., & Stevens, S. S. (1942). *The varieties of temperament: A psychology of constitutional differences.* New York: Harper.

Shostrom, E. L. (1963). *Personal orientation inventory.* San Diego: Edits/Educational and Industrial Testing Service.

Shostrom, E. L. (1964). A test for the measurement of self-actualization. *Educational and Psychological Measurement, 24,* 207-218.

Shostrom, E. L. (1970). *Pair attraction inventory.* San Diego: Edits/Educational and Industrial Testing Service.

Shostrom, E. L. (1972). The measurement of growth in psychotherapy. *Psychotherapy: Theory, Research, and Practice, 9,* 194-199.

Shostrom, E. L. (1976). *Actualizing therapy: Foundations for a scientific ethic.* San Diego: Edits.

Shostrom, E. L., & Knapp, R. (1966). The relationship of a measure of self-actualization (POI) to a measure of pathology (MMPI) and to therapeutic growth, *American Journal of Psychotherapy, 20,* 193-202.

Shostrom, E. L., Knapp, R. R. & Knapp, L. (1976). Validation of the Personal Orientation Dimensions: an inventory for the dimensions of actualizing. *Educational and Psychological Measurement, 36,* 491-494.

Shostrom, E. L., & Montgomery, D. (1978). *Healing love: How God works within the personality.* Nashville, TN: Abingdon.

Shostrom, E. L., & Montgomery, D. (1986). *God in your personality.* Nashville, TN: Abingdon.

Shostrom, E. L., & Montgomery, D. (1990). *The manipulators.* Nashville, TN: Abingdon.

Shostrom, E. L., & Riley, C. (1968). Parametric analysis of psychotherapy. *Journal of Consulting and Clinical Psychology, 32,* 628-632.

Showers, C. J., & Zeigler-Hill, V. (2008). Compartmentalization and integration: The evaluative organization of contextualized selves. *Journal of Personality, 75,* 1181-1204.

Silk, K., Lee, S., Hill, E., & Lohr, N. (1995). Borderline personality symptoms and severity of sexual abuse. *American Journal of Psychiatry, 152,* 1059-1064.

Sinha, B. K. et al. (2006). Hostility & personality disorder. *Imagination, Cognition & Personality, 25,* 45-57.

Skodol, A. E., Grilo, C. M., Pagano, M. E., Bender, D. S., Gunderson, J. G., Shea, M. T., et al. (2005). Effects of personality disorders on functioning and wellbeing in major depressive disorder. *Journal of Psychiatric Practice, 11,* 363-368.

Speer, P. W., Jackson, C. B., & Peterson, N. (2001). Relationship between social cohesion & empowerment. *Health Education & Behavior, 28,* 716-732.

Stajkovic, A. D. (2006). Development of a core confidence-higher order construct. *Journal of Applied Psychology, 91,* 1208-1224.

Stein D. J. et al. (1996). Impulsivity and serotonergic function in compulsive personality disorder. *Journal of Neuropsychiatry Clinical Neuroscience, 8:* 393–8.

Steketee, G., & Frost, R. (2003). Compulsive hoarding: Current status of the research. *Clinical Psychology Review, 23,* 905-927.

Stern, A. (1938). Psychoanalytic investigation of and therapy in the borderline group of neuroses. *Psychoanalytic Quarterly 7*, 467-489.

Stinson, F. S., Dawson, D. A., et al. (2008). Prevalence, correlates, disability, and comorbidity of DSM-IV narcissistic personality disorder: Results from the wave 2 national epidemiologic survey on alcohol and related conditions. *Journal of Clinical Psychiatry, 69*,1033-45.

Stone, M. H. (1993). *Abnormalities of personality: Within and beyond the realm of treatment.* NY: Norton, 361.

Stormberg, D., Ronningstam, E., Gunderson, J., & Tohen, M. (1998). Pathological narcissism in bipolar disorder patients. *Journal of Personality Disorders, 12*, 179-185.

Strupp, H. (1989). Psychotherapy: Can the practitioner learn from the researcher? *American Psychologist, 44*, 718.

Stubbs, J. P., & Bozarth, J. D. (1994). The Dodo bird revisited: Qualitative study of psychotherapy efficacy. *Applied and Preventive Applied Psychology, 3*, 109-120.

Stumpf, S. E. (2003). *Socrates to Sartre and beyond, 7th ed.* New York: McGraw-Hill, 466.

Sullivan, H. S. (1947). *Conceptions of modern psychiatry.* New York: W. W. Norton.

Sullivan, H. S. (1953). *The interpersonal theory of psychiatry.* New York: W. W. Norton.

Sullivan, H. S. (1954). *The psychiatric interview.* New York: W. W. Norton.

Sullivan, H. S. (1956). *Clinical studies in psychiatry.* New York: W. W. Norton.

Sulmasy, D. P. (2002). A biopsychosocial-spiritual model for care of patients at the end of life. *Gerontologist, 42,* 34-39.

Tangney, I. P. (2000). Humility: Theoretical perspectives, empirical findings and directions for future research. *Journal of Social and Clinical Psychology, 19,* 70-82.

Tartakoff, H. (1966). The normal personality in our culture and the Nobel Prize complex. In R. M. Loewenstein, L. M. Newman, and M. Schur (Eds.), *Psychoanalysis: A gen-*

eral psychology. New York: International Universities Press.

Tcheremissine, O.V., & Lieving, L. M. (2006). Pharmacological aspects of the treatment of conduct disorder in children and adolescents. *CNS Drugs, 20,* 549-565.

Tolpin, L. H., Gunthert, K. C., Cohen, L. H., & O'Neill, S. C. (2004). The psychodynamics of borderline personality disorder: A view from developmental psychopathology. *Journal of Personality, 72,* 135.

Tonigan, J. S., Connors, G. J., & Miller, W. R. (1996). Alcoholics Anonymous Involvement Scale (AAI): Reliability and norms. *Psychology of Addictive Behaviors, 10,* 75-80.

Torgersen, S., Kringlen, E., & Cramer, V. (2001). The prevalence of personality disorders in a community sample. *Archives of General Psychiatry, 58,* 590-596.

Tournier, P. (1963). *The strong and the weak.* Philadelphia: Westminster, 27.

Tracey, T. J. G. (2005). Interpersonal rigidity & complementarity. *Journal of Research in Personality, 39,* 592-614.

Tracya, J. L., Chenga, J.T. et al. (2009). Authentic and hubristic pride: The affective core of self-esteem and narcissism. *Self and Identity, 8,* 196-213.

Triebwasser, J., & Siever, L. J. (2006). Pharmacology of personality disorders. *Psychiatric Times, July,* 1-2.

Turkheimer, E. (2000). Three laws of behavior genetics and what they mean. *Current Directions in Psychological Science, 9,* 160-164.

Twenge, J. M., & Campbell, W. K. (2009). *The narcissism epidemic: Living in the age of entitlement.* New York: Simon & Schuster.

Tyrer, P., Morgan, J., & Cicchetti, D. (2004). The Dependent Personality Questionnaire (DPQ): A screening instrument for dependent personality. *International Journal of Social Psychiatry, 50,* 10-17.

Van Kaam, A., & Muto, S. (2006). *Am I living a spiritual life?* Manchester, NH: Sophia Institute Press.

Vasey, M. W., Kotov, R., Frick, P. J., & Loney, B. R. (2005). The latent structure of psychopathy in youth; A taxometric investigation. *Journal of Abnormal Child Psychology, 33*, 411-429.

Vien, A., & Beech, A. R. (2006). Psychopathy: Theory, measurement, and treatment. *Trauma, Violence, and Abuse, 7,* 155-174.

Villemarette-Pittman, N. R., Stanford, M. S., Greve, K. W., et al. (2004). Obsessive-compulsive personality disorder and behavioral disinhibition. *Journal of Psychology: Interdisciplinary and Applied, 138,* 5-22.

Vloet, T. D., Herpertz-Dahlmann, B., & Herpertz, S. (2006). Predictors of antisocial behavior: Peripheral psychophysiological findings in children and adults with conduct disorder. *Nervenarzt, 77,* 782-790.

Vollebergh, W. A. M., Iedema, J., Bijl, R. V., de Graaf, R., Smit, F., & Ormel, J. (2001). The structure and stability of common mental disorders. *Archives of General Psychiatry, 58,* 597-603.

Wachtel, P. (1993). *Therapeutic communication: Knowing what to say when.* New York: Guilford Press.

Wagner, C. C., Kiesler, D. J., & Schmidt, J. A. (1995). Assessing the interpersonal transaction cycle: Convergence of action and reaction interpersonal circumplex measures. *Journal of Personality and Social Psychology, 69,* 938-949.

Wampold, B. E. (2001). *The great psychotherapy debate: Models, methods and findings.* Mahwah, NJ: Lawrence Erlbaum.

Warner, M. D., Morey, L. C., Finch, J. F., Gunderson, J. G., Skodol, A. E., Sanislow, C. A., et al. (2004). The longitudinal relationship of personality traits and disorders. *Journal of Abnormal Psychology, 113,* 217-227.

Watson, D. (2005). Rethinking the mood and anxiety disorders: A symptom-based hierarchical model for *DSM-V. Journal of Abnormal Psychology, 114,* 522-536.

West, M., et al. (1995). Interpersonal disorder in schizoid and avoidant personality disorders: An attachment perspective. *Canadian Journal of Psychiatry, 40,* 411.

Weiner, I. B. (2009). *Principles of psychotherapy, 3rd ed.* New York: Wiley.

Wiggins, J. S. (1979). A psychological taxonomy of trait descriptive terms: The interpersonal domain. *Journal of Personality and Social Psychology, 37,* 395-412.

Wiggins, J. S. (1982). Circumplex models of interpersonal behavior in clinical psychology. In P. C. Kendall & J. N. Butcher (Eds.), *Handbook of research methods in clinical psychology.* New York: Wiley.

Wiggins, J. S., & Broughton, R. (1985). The interpersonal circle: A structural model for the integration of personality research. In R. Hogan & W. H. Jones (Eds.), *Perspectives in personality* (Vol. 1). Greenwich, CT: JAI Press.

Wiggins, J. S. (1995). *Interpersonal adjective scales professional manual.* Odessa, FL: Psychological Assessment Resources.

Witte, T. H., Callahan, K. L., & Perez-Lopez, M. (2002). Narcissism and anger: an exploration of underlying correlates. *Psychological Reports, 90,* 871-875.

Wolpe, J. (1969). *The practice of behavior therapy.* New York: Pergamon Press.

Worthington E. L. et al. (2011). Religion and spirituality. *Journal of Clinical Psychology, 67,* Issue 2, 204-214.

Zanarini, M. C., Williams, A., et al. (1997). Reported pathological childhood experiences and the development of borderline personality disorder. *American Journal of Psychiatry, 154,* 1101-1106.

Zimmerman, M., Rothschild, L., & Chelminski, I. (2005). Prevalence of personality disorders in psychiatric outpatients. *American Journal of Psychiatry, 162,* 1911-1918.

Yalom, I. (1980). *Existential psychotherapy.* New York: Basic Books.

Young, W. E. (1990). *Cognitive therapy for personality disorders: A schema-focused approach.* Sarasota, FL: Professional Resource Exchange.

Zur, O. (2007). *Boundaries in psychotherapy: Ethical and clinical considerations.* Washington, D. C.: American Psychological Association.

INDEX

circulargram, 11
circumplex model, 11, 266, 269, 273, 282, 290
Cognitive Therapy, 65
collaborative implantation, 115-118
Compass Model, 3, 5, 6, 12, 25, 36, 40, 41, 68, 208
compass intervention, 30, 46, 56, 57, 109, 161, 187, 227, 228
compass theory, 3, 6, 11, 18, 35, 41, 74, 80, 95, 101, 113, 120, 154, 183, 204, 214, 221, 222, 242, 249, 252, 253
conditional alignment, 115-118
confluence, 201, 202, 222
continuum, 5, 11, 98, 119
continuum of personality, 5
core fear, 9, 19, 28, 29, 30, 32, 73, 140
counselee participation, 21
couples therapy, 228-239
cyclothymia, 244
diagnosis-to-treatment, 3, 23
diplomatic warm-up, 50-53
eating disorders, iv, 214, 271, 284
ego-dystonic, 29, 138
ego-syntonic, 29, 44
Ellis, Albert, 29, 66, 268
emotional rapport, 50-51
epinephrine, 244
Erikson, Erik, 259, 268
existential intimacy, 249, 251, 257
existential transference, 72-73
Fenichel, Otto, 65, 269
Five-Factor Model of personality, 13, 284
flexibility, 4, 13, 18, 210, 212
flip-flop pattern, 221
Frankl, Victor, 9, 269
free agency, 6, 9
Freud, Sigmund, 44, 65, 100, 142, 182, 183, 205, 248, 270, 282
Fromm, Erich, 65, 203, 270
fusion illusion, 226
Glasser, William, 125, 270
God, 3, 4, 7, 8, 14, 15, 16, 25, 72, 73, 74, 101, 133, 152, 161, 199, 219, 234, 236, 238, 239, 245, 248, 249, 251, 256, 257, 259, 280, 286
goodism, 201

holistic human nature, 242, 252

Holy Spirit, 4, 5, 8, 16,

Horney, Karen, 5, 9, 26, 29, 30, 31, 65, 74, 101, 154, 183, 209, 219, 259, 273

Human Nature Compass, viii, 237, 241-248, 259

identity, intimacy, and community, vii, 3, 4, 249-259

inflexibility, 32, 47

integration of polar opposites, 225

interpersonal theory, 5, 6, 10, 11, 12, 16, 47, 49, 75, 125, 163, 186, 207, 258, 262, 263, 266, 269, 273, 274, 275, 276, 277, 278, 282, 284, 288, 289, 290

interpersonal circle, 11, 274, 277, 290

interpersonal climate, 19

interpersonal communication, 133, 276

introjection, 201, 204

joining technique, 146-147

Jung, Carl, 9-11, 83, 120, 135, 158, 241, 259, 274

Kernberg, Otto, 121, 224, 265, 274

Kiesler, Donald, 5, 11, 13, 14, 29, 124, 184, 274

Kraepelin, Emil, 101, 158, 275

Kretschmer, Emil, 83, 140, 153, 161, 275

LAWS (of personality and relationships), 12, 17, 28, 40, 41, 45, 54, 77, 87, 137, 155, 163, 198, 238, 253

Lowen, Alexander, 70, 190, 277

Love/Assertion polarity, 11, 20

mandala, 11

manipulation, 4, 18, 28, 29, 40, 62, 75, 133, 202

manipulative trends, 25-30
    aggressive, 25, 30
    controlling, 25, 31
    dependent, 25, 30
    withdrawn, 25, 31

Maslow, Abraham, 9, 120, 208, 259, 267, 268

May, Rollo, 16, 155, 278

Millon, Theodore, 5, 11, 34, 35, 80, 84, 124, 154, 190, 201, 205, 206, 222, 223, 241, 271, 272, 278, 279

Moreno, Jacob, 219, 280

Motivational Interviewing, 138, 279

multilevel framework, 241, 248

object relations, 256

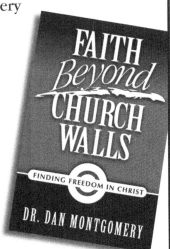

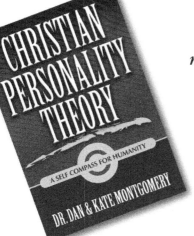

Made in the USA
Coppell, TX
13 June 2021